Battle Cries

Battle Cries

Black Women and
Intimate Partner Abuse

Hillary Potter

NEW YORK UNIVERSITY PRESS

New York and London

NEW YORK UNIVERSITY PRESS
New York and London
www.nyupress.org

Library of Congress Cataloging-in-Publication Data
Potter, Hillary, 1969–
Battle cries : Black women and intimate partner abuse /
Hillary Potter.
p.cm.
Includes bibliographical references and index.
ISBN-13: 978-0-8147-6729-0 (cl : alk. paper)
ISBN-10: 0-8147-6729-X (cl : alk. paper)
ISBN-13: 978-0-8147-6730-6 (pb : alk. paper)
ISBN-10: 0-8147-6730-3 (pb : alk. paper)
1. Family violence—United States—Case studies. 2. African American
women—Abuse of—Case studies. 3. Abused women—United
States—Case studies. I. Title.
HV6626.2.P68   2008
362.82'9208996073—dc22   2008023332

c 10 9 8 7 6 5 4 3 2 1
p 10 9 8 7 6 5 4 3 2 1

I dedicate this book to my adoring and devoted parents, Laurette A. Hildebrandt Potter and W. Fred Potter.

I also dedicate this book to the many resilient women who have come into my life—including those with whom I share a blood bond, those who are in my circle of friends, and those who shared their stories with me to make this book possible.

Contents

Acknowledgments

Many individuals are to be acknowledged for aiding me in initiating and completing this book. To start, I am greatly indebted to the 40 phenomenal women who candidly and unselfishly shared their life stories with me. Their input provided me with an immense amount of noteworthy information that developed into a personally meaningful journey.

Of course, the study imparted in this book would not have been possible without my mentor, committee chair, guru, and, most important, friend, Dr. Joanne Belknap. It was by pure coincidence that I first met Dr. Belknap in her graduate course on violence against women, which I took prior to applying for the Ph.D. program in sociology at the University of Colorado at Boulder. It was during this course that I chose to author a paper on intimate partner violence against Black women, a decision that was optimistically supported by Dr. Belknap. Little did I know that that paper and my serendipitous encounter with Dr. Belknap would grow into a treasured research project and a cherished relationship. I am also grateful to Dr. Michael Radelet, who provided valuable feedback and encouragement for this investigative undertaking. The mentoring and support by Drs. Belknap and Radelet led me back to Boulder soon after I completed my doctoral studies and moved on to the next post in my career. It was their tenacity and belief in me as a dedicated scholar that aided me in securing a faculty position in my doctorate-granting program and institution. My years on faculty thus far have been rewarding and rewarded because of the faithful backing of Drs. Belknap and Radelet.

The transition to writing a first book would not have come to be without Ilene Kalish, my editor at NYU Press, and the anonymous reviewers of earlier manuscripts of this work. The suggestions by Ms. Kalish and the reviewers unmistakably strengthened the presentation of my study. Specifically, Ms. Kalish helped me transform my earlier drafts into a piece of work that remains loyal both to academic standards *and* to the voices and experiences of the women interviewed. Indeed, it was Ms. Kalish who renamed my theoretical concept of "multiplicative resistance," a quite cumbersome designation, into the more suitable term "dynamic resistance." Ms. Kalish has gone beyond what I believed an editor was and did. She is owed much praise for her belief in my abilities as an academic and for her enthusiasm for my project.

My deepest appreciation goes to my family, which is certainly my foundation of support. My parents are first and foremost responsible for the accomplishments I have achieved in my life. I am thankful for the strength, resilience, forthrightness, and unwavering adoration exhibited and bestowed by my mother, Laurette Potter. To my father, Fred Potter, I am grateful for his exemplary work ethic, vigor, and tacit, but undeniable, love and support. To be sure, the reverent, stable, and equitable 50 years of marriage between my parents have not been lost on me. Also, my brother, Jason Potter, has unquestionably always "been there" for me. If not for my big brother, who relentlessly reminded me to relax, laugh, and not be so terribly serious about all things all the time, I would certainly not have sustained myself through this harrowing project. Undoubtedly, the same can be extended to my big sisters, Nina "Boots" Potter and Cheryl Potter, and to my beautiful and bright nieces and nephews, Lauren, Cheyne, Lindsay, Caelan, Magenta, Myah and Maya. Their vivaciousness and encouragement continually nourish me in my daily subsistence and professional undertakings. Finally, my many dear friends—with a special shout-out going to Allison Cotton—have been particularly obliging and supportive during my pursuits to achieve my goals and dreams. The support of my homegirls—especially Alan Gibbons, Sonja Coleman-Harris, Dimitria Cook, and Stephanie Perez—has not wavered as I have repeatedly gone "missing in action" over the years.

It is to all these bonds—old and new—that I am greatly indebted.

1

Introduction

The Call

I use myself as an example. I was dealing with the issues of being Black, a descendant of Black people that have been enslaved, being a person displaced from their country, dealing with incest of my dad, dealing with rape, with depression and suicide. How the hell are you supposed to get out from under? And you're Black, too? And I think I had more variables than some Black women. For some people it's easy to say maybe I deserved it, maybe I did wrong by fighting back, maybe I was too strong. . . . Or if you're dealing with the issues, you're also trying to raise kids, and the kids become the priority instead of you. You don't even take a chance to heal because you're too busy taking care of everybody else. And that's what you're supposed to do, somebody says. I think for Black women it's harder. They deal with imaginary expectations as well as real expectations.

—Lola, age 42

Popular rhetoric often portrays Black[1] women as being strong, independent, and resilient. Although these are seemingly positive qualities to possess, they also have the potential to stereotype Black women in ways that can restrict their seeking help or needed support. The motivational speaker Debrena Jackson Gandy describes this as the Strong Black Woman Syndrome. The syndrome is steeped in the historically powerful images of the Mammy or the Matriarch who "was the nurturer, 'the omnipotent caregiver,' the always-listening ear, the 'everlasting arm.' . . . She was the Rock of Gibraltar, the Strong Black Woman who constantly gave out love, attention, and affection but who didn't ask for it, appear to need it, or require it in return."[2] This image of the Strong Black Woman is a misleading notion that permeates the lives of many present-day Black women. Indeed, many Black women have strength, resiliency, and other tenacious and laudable qualities (as do countless other women); however, to continue to accept this stereotype of Black women, without question, overlooks the real challenges of their life struggles and needs for assistance. This is particularly troubling when considering intimate partner abuse[3] in the lives of Black women. Often, Black women enduring intimate partner abuse forgo their right to be free of endangerment and harm by internalizing this identity of the Strong Black Woman.[4] Consequently, the welfare of even the most resilient woman can be compromised as a result of intimate partner abuse.[5]

Although survey research and arrest records indicate that the number of battered Black women is relatively large,[6] battered Black women as a group are often obscured and ignored because of their race, gender, class, and victim statuses. Black women who endure abuse by their intimate partners are often invisible to the general public (conceivably because of the racialized and gendered priorities of news media outlets) or are further victimized by institutions that are intended to assist battered women. When official entities have intervened, ostensibly on behalf of these women, they have frequently relied on biased beliefs and often caused more harm than good.

Intimate partner abuse against Black women has also been ignored or discounted within the communities from which these women originate. Blacks in the United States have many focal points in their struggle for equality, including inadequate access to suitable housing, health care, and education; underemployment and poverty; substance abuse and high rates of HIV/AIDS; and excessive police contact, criminal prosecution, and imprisonment—all of which tend to be the result of historical and contemporary race and class discrimination. However, violence against women is not often deemed a high priority within the Black community. Even though intimate partner abuse has been addressed by several Black feminist scholars and novelists (such as Patricia Hill Collins, Angela Y. Davis, bell hooks, Toni Morrison, Beth Richie, and Alice Walker),[7] Black leaders have seemingly ignored this epidemic.[8] In discussing the lack of interest within the Black community, Marcia Smith argued, in a 1997 article in *The Nation*, that "Putting domestic violence on the front burner would allow the community to rally *all* the troops for the tough battles ahead. Failure to do so not only abandons the women who must live with violence every day, but undermines families, communities, and political solidarity."[9]

Given that women of color do not always experience racism in the same ways that their male counterparts do and that the experience of sexism against women of color is not always the same as the experience of White women, prevailing theories and practices with regard to violence against women (as a homogeneous group) are limited.[10] I argue that explicitly considering accounts of intimate partner abuse against Black women affords a more comprehensive view of all women's experiences. Accordingly, in this book, my investigation augments the relatively small amount of research conducted solely on intimate partner abuse against Black women.[11] A notable exception is Beth E. Richie's *Compelled to Crime: The Gender Entrapment of Battered Black Women*, a seminal work on violence against women. Her exploration of battered Black women's paths to committing criminal acts as a result of their victimization provides a pioneering contribution to the existing research on intimate partner abuse. *Battle Cries* builds on Richie's fine work, as the study described in this book considers a nonincarcerated and more diverse sample of battered Black women. Given the broader group of Black women in my study, my examination can expand on Richie's work in terms of how culture and the social structure shape the experiences of and responses by Black women to intimate partner abuse and the effectiveness of the support networks in place to assist with this distressing phenomenon.

Development of Feminist Advocacy Against Intimate Partner Abuse

An increased awareness of the problem of intimate partner abuse against women has developed only during the past few decades. Until the 1970s, concern, advocacy, and protection for battered women among the general public and criminal justice officials were glaringly sparse.[12] Historians had sporadically recorded attempts of various individuals to raise public concern for these victims. However, until the 1970s, these endeavors were largely unsuccessful. During this decade, there was an accelerating trend toward the criminalization of batterers and an increase in the assistance afforded battered women. Feminist organizations began to highlight intimate partner abuse against women as a social problem needing to be remedied,[13] and books written by battered women and their advocates began to appear with fervor.[14] In 1973, the United States saw one of its first shelters to assist wives battered by their alcoholic husbands at the

Rainbow Retreat in Phoenix, Arizona,[15] and since this time, shelters have rapidly appeared across the country.[16] In addition to establishing places to harbor battered women and their children away from their male batterers, police and court intervention agents began to address woman battering more seriously with the enactment and increased enforcement of laws and sanctions relating to intimate partner abuse.[17] In 1994, President Bill Clinton signed into law the landmark Violence Against Women Act to combat violence against women by providing assistance to workers in the criminal justice system (for example, training for police officers and court workers), support for battered women's shelters and a national telephone "hotline," and funding for research on violence against women. The Act was renewed by Congress in 2000 and provided financial support in excess of $3 billion for five years. The second reauthorization of the Act was passed by both the U.S. Senate and the House of Representatives and was signed into law by President George W. Bush in January 2006.

Along with the diligent labor of feminist activists, the battered women's movement was further assisted in its development and awareness efforts by the news media's attention to the movement.[18] Through the mid-1970s, some popular magazines considered domestic violence to be an act of rioting and terrorism, but by the end of the decade, the term became equivalent with "wife abuse"[19] and other forms of family-related interpersonal violence.[20] Indeed, one research project showed that between 1987 and 1997, media representations of intimate partner abuse as a serious issue were instrumental in decreasing the public's tolerance of "wife abuse."[21]

Although various definitions are offered to characterize intimate partner abuse, for the purposes of this book, I have used a broad definition that includes "physical assault, threats, emotional abuse, verbal abuse, harassment, and humiliation by current or former intimate partners."[22] This broad definition is used because women who have been victims of both physical and emotional abuse are often cited as stating that the emotional abuse is more damaging and lasting. Because battering is often accompanied by other forms of abuse, the physical abuse described by women in this book was not quantified. That is, a woman who had experienced a single, isolated physically abusive event was still eligible to share her story with me, as that single event may have been preceded or followed by other forms of maltreatment. As stated by the Black feminist scholar bell hooks, intimate partner abuse "is an important area for feminist research precisely because many cases of extreme physical abuse begin with an isolated incident of hitting."[23] Additionally, given that the women's narrations of their *life* histories are the basis of this study and that obtaining these stories was necessary to observe how Black women respond to abuse on the basis of their lived experiences, my definition is not limited by time parameters.

Because of what we know about intimate partner abuse, gender, and the use of a feminist standpoint, throughout this book I mostly use gender-specific pronouns when referring to the victims and the perpetrators. Female pronouns are used in describing victims of intimate partner abuse, and male pronouns are used for the abusers. This is not to diminish the abuse that takes place against individuals in same-gender relationships or abuse against men by their female intimate partners. Indeed, many of the concepts delineated throughout this book are likely applicable to Black women in abusive lesbian relationships and to other victims of intimate partner abuse. However, as the study undertaken focused on Black women in abusive heterosexual relationships, the way in which victims and batterers are identified is gendered.

Even with increased attention to the issue, abuse among intimate partners as a social problem is still not receiving the level of attention it deserves from criminal justice agents[24] and health professionals.[25] For instance, there is fairly recent evidence showing that police officers still respond leniently to male batterers.[26] That is, men who abuse their female intimate partners are arrested less often than other violent offenders. In addition, battered women's shelters continue to suffer from poor financial support and the inability to house every woman and child who need and request sanctuary from their abusers.[27] As indicated by a survey conducted by the Center for the Advancement of Women in 2001, a sizable number of women believe that intimate partner abuse warrants continued attention. In fact, the report shows that 92 percent of the women surveyed believed that intimate partner abuse and sexual assault should be the very top priority for the women's movement. Reducing violence against women was trailed by the following priorities: receiving equal pay for equal work (90%), improving child care (85%), reducing drug and alcohol addiction among women (72%), and keeping abortion legal (41%).[28] This finding underlines the belief that much more work is needed to improve the lives of battered women and to better address the unwarranted behavior of batterers.

It is unmistakable that with the identification of intimate partner abuse as a social problem more than three decades ago came an unprecedented amount of research and activism surrounding the plight of battered women. In both the research and the responses to intimate partner abuse, however, cultural, racial, and ethnic distinctions among women victims of intimate partner abuse have not been afforded equal levels of consideration.[29] Much of the research and many of the policies see all battered women as victims with similar life experiences,[30] neglecting the fact that Black women and other women of color typically have life experiences distinct from those of White women.

The research in the 1970s was conducted with predominately White samples and failed to take into account how the surveys and findings might be problematic in reference to victims and offenders of color. Criticism has been directed at the research instruments used to determine the intricacies of intimate partner abuse because the measurements were not tested on women of color, nor did they take into account cultural differences among women who endure intimate partner abuse.[31] As such, research on intimate partner abuse is not complete without attention to the cultural arenas in which Black women participate. Regrettably, more recent investigations continue to follow this precedent. Research designed to study battered White women may not adequately explain how Black women experience and respond to intimate partner abuse. Basing investigations on theories that do not defer to the unique experiences of Black women does them a disservice because they must confront daily both racism and sexism within U.S. society.

Collective members of *Incite! Women of Color Against Violence* argue that organizations established to assist women victims of physical and sexual abuse are now beholden to government funding and bureaucracy because of their move toward professionalization. This results in a focus on institutionalized responses to violence against women that often prompts the punishment or restriction of the rights of women victims, particularly women of color.[32] For instance, there has been an increase in arrests of women victims of intimate partner abuse, and, as demonstrated by the stories of the women in my study, stereotypical images (such as that of the "angry Black woman") reinforce this practice. This is supported by bell hooks, who concludes, "Black male violence against black females is the most acceptable form of acting out. Since the racist sexist white world sees black women as angry bitches who must be kept in check, it turns away from relational violence in black life."[33] Feminist criminologists have regularly advocated that, in addressing women's victimization and offending in studying crime and the workings of the criminal justice system, it is not feasible to simply "add women and stir."[34] Because multicultural interventions and programming that are based on middle-class White women do not typically meet the needs of women of color,[35] a similar adage can be applied to address the admonitions of women activists of color in the antiviolence movement: We cannot simply "add women *of color* and stir." To effectively attend to issues of violence against Black women and other women of color, we must heed the approach advanced by *Incite!* activists and scholars:

> That is, what if we do not make any assumptions about what a domestic violence program should look like, but instead ask: What would it take to end violence against women of color? What would this movement look like? What if we do not presume that this movement would share any of the features we take for granted in the current domestic violence movement? . . . [W]hen we shift the center to women of color, the importance of addressing state violence becomes evident. This perspective then benefits not only women of color, but all peoples, because it is becoming increasingly clear that the criminal justice system is not effectively ending violence for anyone.[36]

The theoretical framework that I use here is called "Black feminist criminology" and has roots in existing feminist ideology. Black feminist criminology expands on feminist criminology and is grounded firmly in Black feminist and critical race feminist theories. In conforming to these feminist theories, Black feminist criminology necessarily places the Black woman and her intersecting identities at the center of any analysis, as opposed to considering her identity as nonessential. Black feminist criminology specifically considers issues of crime, deviance, violence, and the workings of the criminal justice system in the lives of people of color. An explicit description of Black feminist criminology and the way in which it is a better framework for understanding how Black women experience intimate partner abuse is supplied in the following chapter.

The Extent of Intimate Partner Abuse by Race and Gender

Several sources document variation in the rate of intimate partner abuse by race. In general, as a group, it has been estimated that Blacks typically experience more intimate partner abuse than do other racial or ethnic groups.[37] Shannan Catalano's analysis of the National Crime Victimization Survey (NCVS) revealed that women encountered partner violence at lower rates in 2004 than in 1993. According to the NCVS, 9.8 per 1,000 women were victims of intimate partner assaults in 1993, whereas 3.8 per

1,000 women experienced such assaults in 2004.[38] While U.S. women in general have recently experienced lower rates of intimate partner abuse, women of color continued to experience some of the highest rates among all women victimized by their intimate partners. Both the NCVS and the National Violence Against Women Survey[39] revealed that Native American women and Black women report the largest proportion of intimate partner abuse. From 1993 through 2004, the average annual rate of intimate partner violence that did not end in death (nonfatal) was 18.2 for every 1,000 Native American women and 8.2 per 1,000 Black women. The rate was 6.3 for White women and 1.5 for Asian women. Although my presentation in this book focuses on Black women and the call for more attention to intimate partner abuse against Black women, the large number of battered Native American women also warrants our serious attention.

In addition to race, there are several other so-called risk factors for being or becoming a victim of intimate partner abuse. These include earning low incomes, being divorced or separated, living in rental housing, and living in urban areas.[40] However, Michael L. Benson and his co-authors criticized certain investigations,[41] asserting that these studies did not consider that Blacks and Whites reside in different types of neighborhoods, which affects the levels of intimate partner abuse.[42] Evan Stark and Anne Filtcraft report that unemployment, substance abuse, physical disabilities, unwanted pregnancies, AIDS, suicide, homicide, and the living conditions (including homelessness) of some Black women can be attributed to intimate partner abuse.[43] Such findings indicate the importance of the need for intensive research on intimate partner abuse experienced by Black women because of multiple marginalization factors. Essentially, the findings suggest that the stress of being the object of disobliging racial discrimination and residing in distressed neighborhoods negatively impacts Blacks by adding to other life stressors and causing strain and conflict within intimate relationships.

Toward Understanding and Confronting Intimate Partner Abuse Against Black Women

Considering the rates of intimate partner abuse against Black women and seen against the relatively large amount of intimate partner abuse research carried out on White women, little research has been conducted specifically on battered Black women. Studies that include Black women in their samples often do no more than state this occurrence, and, particularly in statistical studies, minimal (if any) effort is made to address the experiences and concerns of Black women. Thus, the outcomes from the carefully planned and executed study detailed in this book provide a means of furthering the understanding of intimate partner abuse generally and the experiences of battered Black women specifically. Throughout this book, I address the major themes in the lives of battered Black women, the theoretical contribution of the current study, policy implications, and recommendations for ways we can respond to the issue so that we can continue to confront intimate partner abuse based on the accounts of *all* of the women affected by it.

In my study, the way of determining how Black women contend with intimate partner abuse is established from intensive interviews with 40 remarkable individuals who desired to share their stories of abuse, resistance, and triumph. I briefly describe the approach I employed to investigate heterosexual intimate partner abuse against Black women in Chapter 2. An extensive description of the research method and the women's social backgrounds and demographics can be found in the Appendices.

The life histories gathered for this exploration, including the stories of the often perilous childhoods of many of the women conveyed in Chapter 4, provide a unique and significant window through which to view intimate partner abuse. My analysis establishes similarities and variations in the women's experiences based on age, socioeconomic or wealth status, and education level of the women. While the women suffered from behaviors that are typically meted out by most batterers, regardless of race and ethnicity, in Chapter 5 I discuss the common abuses the women endured and their perceptions of their abusive male mates in order to provide an ample view into their lives.

Near the start of the process of gathering the women's stories, a significant pattern emerged that was similar to the outlook depicted in Lola's[44] narrative at the opening of this chapter. Lola's illustration of her existence as a Black woman in the United States eloquently describes the scope of this book: the acknowledgment of each woman's multifaceted identity along with her individual experiences with intimate partner abuse. The conceptual model I developed from looking into the women's lives, which I have called "dynamic resistance," is evident throughout Lola's passage and is discussed in Chapter 3, along with the women's identification with the Strong Black Woman image. Dynamic resistance considers the numerous forms of domination and discrimination that confront battered Black women because of their abusive circumstances and their interwoven identities due to race, gender, and other social, cultural, and individual circumstances. The women's self-perception as Strong Black Women, and not as victims, is considered to account for their efforts to resist abuse and other life distress. Included in this resistance is the propensity for the women to verbally and physically retaliate against their abusers, an important finding that is the focus of Chapter 6.

My assessment also led to the identification of presumably beneficial social and policy implications, which are implied throughout the book and summarized in the concluding chapter. The effectiveness of the various resources used by the women in my study—including family, friends, religion, spirituality, and social and public services—is examined in Chapter 7. The outcome of this work introduces and draws attention to ways to improve the well-being of battered Black women by providing important information for these women and their family and friends, as well as assisting the workers and volunteers in community organizations, the professionals in mental and physical health fields, the police who respond to intimate partner abuse calls, and the judges and attorneys who process these cases.

Taken as a whole, four overarching conclusions are emphasized in *Battle Cries*. First, the women's physical abuse by and resistance against their batterers was often referred by the women as *battling* (or similar terms). There was a substantial rejection of the victim label, and referring to the abuse in these terms provided the women with a form of agency. Even though there was some level of satisfaction in fighting back, the denunciation of their victimization along with the stereotypical portrayals of "true victims" of intimate partner abuse (for example, defenseless White women) reduced the assistance afforded the women. Consequently, the second conclusion is that the cries of battered Black women often go unheard. Third, the co-occurrence of abuse and disregard of the turmoil resulting from the abuse are a call for action to work toward alleviating the often silent suffering of battered Black women, in part by understanding the devalued position of Black women in U.S. society. These efforts are unquestionably a battle—a prolonged struggle that will take concerted and devoted efforts by various factions, including the Black, activist, academic, and legal communities. Last, the term "battle cry" is usually taken to mean a cry used to rally soldiers into battle, but it has also been used to incite individuals and groups into action for a cause. Accordingly, the accounts, concepts, and implications imparted in this book will serve to rally those who contest the unremitting and overlooked abuse against Black women into an active and advocating stance.

2

Black Feminist Criminology and the Power of Narrative

"I Just Wanted to Tell My Story"

Billie is a 42-year-old who has remained in the same western U.S. city and lived in low-income status her entire life. Although she has completed some formal vocational training, she left high school in her final year and throughout her life has maintained sporadic employment. Billie experienced abuse from a number of family members during her upbringing, including her mother, a brother, an aunt, and her grandmother. During adulthood, she has encountered four abusive heterosexual intimate relationships, including that with her current common-law husband, Odell, whose main form of abuse is mental and verbal. Billie began abusing alcohol and other drugs in her twenties, and, though she was able to overcome her addiction to crack cocaine, she continues to struggle with her abuse of alcohol. In fact, a day after I set my interview appointment with Billie and a week prior to the actual interview, she telephoned me in great despair and in desperate need of assistance. She phoned while at her home, where she said Odell and her teenage son were verbally abusing her. I could hear the men yelling at Billie, and her son eventually picked up the phone to inform me that "everything's all right. She's OK." After the phone was handed back to Billie, I found it difficult to understand her, as she slurred many of her words, making incomprehensible statements. I surmised that she was likely under the influence of alcohol or other drugs, but, and more important at that moment, I determined that there was indeed some form of significant discord occurring in the home and against Billie. I asked Billie if she felt her physical well-being was in imminent danger,[1] and she contended that it was not but that I was the only person she knew to call. This declaration by Billie supports other research on Black women that has suggested that they are unaware of or do not feel comfortable in seeking assistance from professionally established sources of support.² It was both poignant and revealing that I, a researcher to whom Billie had spoken on the phone on only one occasion, was her resource for dealing with her victimization.

I confirmed the happenings in the home at that time with Billie's adult daughter, Nia, to whom I had spoken the day before when Billie called to set an appointment to participate in the study.³ After Billie again returned to the phone to speak with me, she insisted that she needed to talk to someone. Although it was well beyond the scope of my research (and certainly not approved by the Human Research Committee of my university) to conduct any form of counseling with the women interviewed, I made the decision to simply conduct my interview with Billie that day and provide her with referrals to social service agencies. Billie and I agreed to have Nia drive her to a convenience store near their home, where I would meet them. However, the two did not show, and I was subsequently unable to reach Billie by phone for several days. I had no last name for Billie at that time, no complete address, and only a wireless phone number, so I was unable to even contact police to conduct a welfare check on the home and could only hope that nothing grave resulted from the verbal altercation.

Fortunately, the day before Billie's originally scheduled interview with me, she contacted me to confirm the appointment. I verified that Billie was safe, but she did not offer any explanation for the incident or for why she did not meet me at the convenience store. Only once we met did I learn of Billie's extensive history of drug use and her continued struggles with alcohol addiction. Essentially, even though family and intimate partner abuse were undoubtedly occurring when she called me the week before, Billie had been heavily intoxicated with alcohol. She did not wish for me to provide her with any social services resources to assist her with the familial abuse or her alcohol and drug addictions. Billie expressed that she was proud that she had not drunk since the day of her frantic call to me a week before, and we both wished out loud for her continued strength in combating both her alcohol abuse and the emotional abuse sometimes carried out by Odell and her son. To judge from my time with Billie, perhaps her admonition that she needed "to talk to someone" can be considered in the symbolic sense: She needed to tell her story to someone who would pass it on to others with the hope that transgressions against Black women and the life chances they have been afforded will be placed at the forefront of issues throughout the Black community.

Medea was another woman from whom I gained much insight. Medea is a 54-year-old who was raised in the southeast United States in upper-middle-class surroundings and who has since fluctuated between class levels but never dropped below the middle class. Her educational and professional pursuits have taken her throughout the United States and out of the country. She earned both bachelor's and master's degrees and currently works in a high-level administrative position with an agency that addresses intimate partner abuse. Like Billie, Medea also suffered abuse during her formative years, though not to the same physical extent as Billie. The abuse suffered by Medea was largely emotional and involved various forms of neglect by her guardians. Medea also shared that she was regularly harassed by classmates about her aspirations to focus on education and not on boyfriends, which was a form of "acting White." She recalled, "Being smart was not acceptable, at least being smart in the way I was smart. Because that was viewed in the Black community as a White thing. White people have the privilege to be smart. White women could do things. But I couldn't. There was a boundary there, and I kept crossing that boundary."

At the time of our conversation, Medea had been without intimate relationships and had been celibate for many years, believing that because of the string of abusive partners in her life she is better off being alone: "I gradually came to a point where I decided, I've really got to learn to love myself. And I can't do that with anybody else." Medea's current employment allowed her to take an active and more far-reaching role in fighting violence against women by helping other women in situations similar to hers. Still, Medea stressed that the intimate partner abuse of Black women remains hidden and ignored within many advocacy circles.

Although their lives are different in terms of educational, employment, and class standings, both Billie and Medea have made efforts throughout their lives to resist the abuse and violence perpetrated against them. Both women realized the constraints they faced as Black women within general society, the Black community, their families, and their intimate relationships. These factors were unearthed during the time I spent with them and with each of the other 38 women who volunteered to participate in this study and in my analysis of their stories. Like Billie, the bulk of the women wished only to share their life stories of adversity and triumph, which, in and of itself, was a form of continued healing from the hardships in their lives. They wished to call attention to what they and other Black women they knew endured from the men they loved. It was the exploratory and qualitative method of social science research that enabled me to stay true to the women's motivations for reaching out to me and revealing some of the most painful experiences of their lives. That is, this research method is intended as an open-minded, open-ended, and detailed recounting and examination of personal narratives. While before initiating the project I developed a list of questions that I would ask the women, the list was used only as a guide, and the interviews resulted in more of a conversational style of inquiry (as is typically done in ethnographic research).

Exploratory and qualitative methods of inquiry into social life do not require that one begin with a theory or premise before entering the field to conduct research. However, individual researchers, including those who are of the ethnographic or qualitative bent, generally still have a point of view. Often, particularly for feminist scholars and scholars of color, this is based on a philosophy developed from personal experiences or activist pursuits. Arguably, it proves quite difficult to enter a research setting without having some preconceived ideas. What is left open to exploration, however, is the opportunity to truly learn from one's informants. As such, while an interpretive scholar may penetrate a site with some theoretical foundation, she or he may be introduced to unexpected findings. This was true in my case. Although I had not yet connected a name to my overarching theoretical perspective, I entered the research through the lens of Black feminist, critical race feminist, and feminist criminology ways of thinking. In time, I labeled this perspective on crime and violence "Black feminist criminology."[4]

Black Feminist Criminology

Just as there are many types of feminisms and feminists, it undoubtedly follows that no single feminist criminology can exist.[5] Feminist criminology has aided in a notably improved understanding of gender variations in criminal activity and victimization and of the criminal justice system's dealings with female and male offenders and victims. Feminist criminology has significantly expanded the foci within the field of criminology beyond simply exploring female criminal offending and female offenders to also examining violent acts against girls and women.[6] Although gender is certainly important and crucial to considering women's (and men's) involvement in crime either as victims or as offenders, for Black women, and arguably for all women, other inequities must be considered principal, not peripheral, to such an analysis. This includes key factors such as race and/or ethnicity, sexuality, and economic status into any examination. Kathleen Daly argues that considering how gender, race, and class distinctions intersect is absolutely necessary in criminology.[7] Because traditional feminist criminology is built on mainstream feminism, which historically has seen issues of race as secondary to those of gender,[8] Black feminist theory and critical race feminist theory are also necessary to explain fully the source of and reactions to crime among Blacks and, especially, Black women's positions in society, in their communities, and in their familial and intimate relationships. This proposition does not serve to devalue the remarkable work that has resulted from the establishment of feminist criminology or the concepts put forth and examined under this rubric. Instead, Black feminist criminology extends beyond traditional feminist criminology to view Black women (and, conceivably, other women of color) from their multiple marginalized and dominated positions in society, culture, community, and families. Although the example provided in this book to tender a Black feminist criminological theory focuses on one form of victimization of Black women, it has been well documented in feminist criminology analyses that there is often a clear correlation between women's victimization and any ultimate criminal behavior by the women.[9] As such, using intimate partner abuse perpetrated against Black women as an illustration provides us with an example that may be applied beyond Black women's experiences with victimization into other encounters with crime and the criminal justice system.

Black feminist criminology addresses concerns in the lives of Black women that I categorize into four themes: (1) social structural oppression, (2) the Black community and culture, (3) intimate and familial relations, and (4) the Black woman as an individual. As outlined earlier, the first three themes are components of interconnected social forces, whereas the fourth theme considers the interconnected identities of the Black woman as affected by the societal influences. The tenets of Black feminist criminology are an outgrowth of Black feminist theory and critical race feminist theory. In general, Black feminist theory is the theoretical perspective that places the lived experiences of Black women, including any forms of resistance to their situations, at the focal point of the analysis. This theory considers Black women as individuals encompassing numerous and interwoven identities. The crux of this theory is that Black women are frequently oppressed within both the Black community (by Black men) and society at large because of their subordinated statuses within each of these spheres. Although the sexist oppression in the Black community presents itself in a different form from that in the larger society and may not appear as obvious, it undeniably exists. Critical race feminist theory is similar to Black feminist theory in that it also considers women of color as individuals with multiple intersecting identities that do not eclipse each other. Specifically, however, critical race feminist theory has been used to consider the devalued position of women of color in greater society as their status relates to questions of the law.

Unlike many White women who enjoyed the "feminist lifestyle" because it provided them the opportunity to meet and bond with other women, Black women have always had a sense of sisterhood.[10] Although it is often assumed that Black women did not participate in the development of feminist ideology and the practice of gender equality, it is evident that Black women have indeed been involved in liberation efforts. By reading the works of women who considered themselves to be Black feminists or were identified as such by others, one becomes aware that Black women have a lengthy and valiant history in the liberation movement.[11] Their struggles can be traced back to the 1600s, when African women who were captured and enslaved in the so-called New World endured multiple forms of oppression by their slave masters.[12] Many of these women made attempts to defend themselves against the inhumane treatment. Recent survey research demonstrates that Black women, even more than White women, are discontented with women's situation in society and want to see changes in the social world that benefit women. In a Gallup poll conducted in June 2002, 48 percent of Black women affirmed that they were dissatisfied with the treatment of women within society; only 26 percent of White women responded similarly.[13]

Mainstream feminist theory places gender as the primary consideration in women's liberation efforts.[14] Black women have expressed difficulty in identifying with mainstream feminist theory because of its focus on this single aspect of womanhood and because historically the lives and concerns of White middle-class women were placed at the forefront of the liberation efforts.[15] Black women regularly convey that they deal not only with issues of gender inequality but also with racial inequality. It is in this regard that Kimberlé W. Crenshaw argues that women of color are relegated to an invisible class in which they are pulled in two conflicting directions: the need to choose between being loyal to feminist ideas or being loyal to their racial or ethnic community.[16] Patricia Hill Collins, author of *Black Feminist Thought: Knowledge, Consciousness, and the*

Politics of Empowerment, distinguished Black women's experiences from those of other groups of women and also considered Black women's lives as individuals:

> On the one hand, all African-American women face similar challenges that result from living in a society that historically and routinely derogates women of African descent. Despite the fact that U.S. Black women face common challenges, this neither means that individual African-American women have all had the same experiences nor that we agree on the significance of our varying experiences. Thus, on the other hand, despite the common challenges confronting U.S. Black women as a group, diverse responses to these core themes characterize U.S. Black women's group knowledge or standpoint.[17]

This collective yet individualized aspect of Black women's lives is an important aspect in Black feminism and must be taken into account when considering the lives of Black women.

Used in conjunction with Black feminist theory, critical race feminist theory is a valuable approach for studies of crime and Black women because it provides a specific application to issues of women of color involved in the criminal justice system as victims, offenders, or both. Like many Black feminists, most critical race feminists have not involved themselves in the mainstream feminist movement but admit that they make use of certain themes of mainstream feminism in the social sciences.[18] Developed in the 1990s, critical race feminist theory is based in the tradition of Black feminist theory, critical legal studies, and critical race theory. People of color, White women, and others were initially attracted to critical legal studies because this approach challenged laws related to oppression based on race and gender.[19] Those credited with developing critical race theory reported disillusionment with critical legal studies' exclusion of the personal and intellectual viewpoints of scholars of color and of White women scholars. Accordingly, critical race theory places more focus on the role of racism and a racist and classist society in the construction of realities among people of color. Although the new discipline was seen as a move toward the inclusion of the experiences of all people in the analysis of social interaction and social justice, many women of color continued to feel that gender was not often introduced as a concern within critical race theory discourse, and, consequently, critical race feminist theory was born. According to Adrien K. Wing, critical race feminist theory, like Black feminist theory, is grounded in "antiessentialism" and intersectionality.[20] Antiessentialism asserts that women do not speak with one essential voice.[21]

Although there is increased acceptance of a variety of feminist theories, hooks has continued to question whether contemporary White women understand that their perspectives may not be indicative of all women's realities and that their views may still be racist and classist.[22] In referring to the issues raised regarding Anita Hill's reports of sexual harassment during the U.S. Senate hearings before Clarence Thomas's confirmation to the U.S. Supreme Court, Nellie Y. McKay wrote that White women feminists "forgot that for Black women, issues of gender are always connected to race. . . . Black women cannot choose between their commitment to feminism and the struggle with their men for racial justice."[23] Crenshaw echoed this sentiment by maintaining that modern discussions of feminism and antiracism have disregarded how racism and sexism are interwoven and that, "because of their intersectional identity as both women *and* people of color within discourses that are shaped to respond to one *or* the other, the interests and experiences of women of color are frequently marginalized within both."[24] Collins's theoretical approach can be applied to the way in which investigations into the lives of battered Black women should be conducted, as was evident when she established that Black feminist theory is positioned within the "matrix of domination," as opposed to being dissociated from sociostructural truths.[25]

Numerous Black feminist and critical race feminist scholars have addressed the "intersecting oppressions" of Black women. In the classic 1970 article "Double Jeopardy: To Be Black and Female," Frances Beale, a journalist and civil rights activist, wrote of the burden of the Black woman's disadvantaged status, which is based on gender, race, and class.[26] Vivian V. Gordon's analysis identified these three conditions as Black women's "trilogy of oppression," and she stated that Black women are often confronted with determining which form of oppression is most important.[27] Deborah K. King advocated for the term "multiple jeopardy" to describe Black women's oppression, given that Black women often undergo even more than three forms of subjugation and that these categories of oppression affect Black women simultaneously.[28] Wing, who used the term "multiplicative identity" to capture the identity of women of color, argues that "women of color are not merely White women *plus* color or men of color *plus* gender. Instead, their identities must be multiplied together to create a holistic One when analyzing the nature of the discrimination against them."[29]

Intimate partner abuse has been considered by many Black feminist scholars, even if only in a portion of their work.[30] Although still in its youthful stage, critical race feminist theory has been specifically applied to intimate partner abuse in the lives of women of color.[31] Considering issues of both identity intersectionality and intimate partner abuse, Beth E. Richie argues, "We now have data that supports [*sic*] the existence of racial and ethnic differences in rates but a theoretical orientation and public policy that can't accommodate or make sense of this new understanding."[32] The use of Black feminist theory and critical race feminist theory as foundations in considering the issues with intimate partner abuse against Black women, as well as considering battered Black women's involvement in "criminal behavior," will assist in addressing this limitation and contribute to the development of Black feminist criminology. The labeling of a Black feminist criminology brings attention to the need to simultaneously consider several levels of social interaction that affect an individual's responses to crime and violence.

Black feminist criminology incorporates the tenets of interconnected identities, interconnected social forces, and distinct circumstances to better theorize, conduct research, and inform policy regarding criminal behavior and victimization among Blacks. The interconnected identities to be considered among Black individuals include race and/or ethnicity, gender, sexuality, class status, national origin, and religion. Certainly, this is not a comprehensive list, as this precept allows for other identities to be included according to how an individual self-identifies. In U.S. society's stratified composition, occurrences of inequity are often experienced because of the spectrum of diversity within each identity and the intolerance and ignorance among some members of society. As such, various identities are seen as of less value than others. This devaluation affects how certain individuals maneuver through life, including how they respond to events and opportunities with which they are confronted. Starting from this vantage point can help us begin to improve our explanations for the experiences of battered Black women's entry into abusive relationships, their responses to their abusers, and their use of systemic resources to help them withdraw from the relationships.

These interconnected identities are greatly shaped by larger social forces. Specifically, groups of individuals and society at large produce and perpetuate conflict, competition, and differences in merit among the members of society. It is not battered Black women's identities that exclusively form their perceptions and reactions but the treatment of these identities filtered by (a) the impact of the social structure through (b) the community or culture to (c) familial and intimate exchanges. Nevertheless, this does not necessitate a linear association in every case; instead, it serves to demonstrate that a patriarchal, paternalistic, and racialized social structure affects all other institutions and interactions in society. Black women's reactions to abuse are affected by their "place" in society because of their intersecting identities. Being at the least valued end of the spectrum for both race and gender places these women in a peculiar position not faced by Black men or White women (although Black men and White women are indeed challenged by their relative and respective dominating forces). In a similar manner, other women of color, such as Latinas, Native American women, Asian American women, and immigrant women (of color), can easily be placed alongside Black women in this analysis.

Last, the characterization "battered woman" or "criminal offender" should not be considered an element of the identities of women victims or offenders. Being abused or having committed criminal acts is a situation that women encounter or in which women become implicated, not one that is endemic to their identity. Of course, this is not to diminish the seriousness of the victimization of women or of criminality among women; instead, it is to emphasize that the individuals themselves rarely recognize these parts of their lives as central to their identities. Furthermore, incorporating these distinct circumstances into Black women's identities risks pathologizing Black women victims or offenders by making these events appear normal or expected among Black women.

Themes of Black Feminist Criminology

As mentioned earlier, the four themes considered within Black feminist criminology include social structural oppression, interactions within the Black community, intimate and familial relations, and the Black woman as an individual, all under the premise that these segments are interconnected. Use of this framework allows us to make the connection between woman battering and structural, cultural, and familial restraints. Under the theme of social structural oppression, matters of institutional racism, damaging stereotypical images, sexism, and classism are routinely addressed by Black feminists and critical race feminists and incorporated for analysis. Included in the examination is the limited access to adequate education and employment as consequences of racism, sexism, and classism.

The second theme addressed by Black feminist criminology, the interactions within the Black community, is based on the cultural distinctions of Blacks. The nature of relationships among Blacks is a topic scrupulously discussed by critical race and Black feminists. These discussions often include the impact of historical experiences of Blacks in the United States. Some specific subjects addressed by Black feminists (although this is not an exhaustive list) include issues of Black women's and Black men's roles in the Black community, the occurrence of violence within the Black community, and the role of spirituality and the Black church as a staple institution in the Black community. Such a concentration allows for each of these features to be considered in how it affects Black women's encounters with intimate partner abuse.

The theme of intimate and familial relationships is the third area on which Black feminist criminology concentrates. The family of origin and generational characteristics of the Black family are among the foci here, including the embeddedness in othermothers[33] and family members outside the immediate family unit (the extended family). Last, the theme of Black women as individuals is examined in Black feminist criminology. Although the Black woman is studied as an individual, her life as a Black woman is strongly connected to her location, status, and role in the social structure, the Black community, and interpersonal relationships. Within this category, issues such as mental health, sexual health, and sexuality are addressed. Inclusion of this precept allows a personal yet comprehensive view of battered Black women.

Some criticism of Black feminist criminology can be foreseen. To start, this theoretical contribution may be viewed as being too limiting because the examination expounded here is grounded in Black and critical race feminist theories and focuses on Black women specifically. The claim might be made that this approach does not serve an overarching benefit as we seek ways to respond to and prevent intimate partner abuse. A rejoinder to this potential criticism would rationalize that because Black women are estimated to be victims of abuse at higher rates than White women, it is imperative that we make greater efforts to understand and determine how to address this concern. In addition, because Black women are also overrepresented in areas of the criminal justice system as offenders (number of arrests, incarceration, and so on), a new approach for comprehending this trend should be welcomed. For both victim and offender status among Black women, starting at a place where Black women's historically and contemporarily situated place in society is strongly embraced affords a more comprehensive understanding of a group disproportionately implicated in offending and victimization. Ignoring distinctions in identity and experiences based on that identity serves only to perpetuate indifference toward Black women and their plight.

Black feminist criminology may also be critiqued as pathologizing Black women. By focusing on Black women's distinctive standpoint, it may be seen as viewing Black women's victimization and criminality as something normal and endemic to their personality or genetic traits. Although there is a history within communities of color of not wanting to reveal the injurious behavior taking place between members of these communities—often for fear of upholding criminal stereotypes—it is imperative that more attention be given to the abuses inflicted on women of color. Exposing these concerns via a Black feminist criminology demonstrates that the instances of crime and violence in the Black community occur not because of a so-called acceptance of such behavior and illuminates the compelling effects of structural influences. In turn, this approach helps explain the prevalence of intimate partner abuse, how Black women experience such abuse, and the reactions by the criminal justice system and its representatives.

A third anticipated criticism of Black feminist criminology is that by examining Black women as a group, it assumes that all Black women have the same experiences. Although Black women in U.S. society indeed encounter similar circumstances, there are numerous gradations and variations in their lived experiences. As addressed earlier, both Black feminist theory and Black feminist criminology consider Black women from their collective and individual experiences simultaneously. Stories communicated by battered Black women reveal similarities that will aid efforts to make culturally competent services available to Black women. As with all battered women, the individual circumstances of Black women must always be considered in conjunction with the shared experiences of these women.

The specifying of a theory that seems to consider only Black females actually opens the field to considering gender, race, and class analyses of criminality, crime victimization, and observation of the criminal justice system. Black feminist criminology highlights the need to consider the intersectionality of individual identities in all crime-related concerns. Certain individuals in society are more privileged than others, and social structure influences culture, families, and the individual; thus, it stands to reason that individuals other than Black women and Black men are affected by their positions in society.

As established at the outset, there can be many variations on feminist criminology. There may be variations on Black feminist criminology, as well. Even so, this concept provides a solid starting point for placing Black women victims of intimate partner abuse at the center of analysis. As such, even if another Black feminist criminology theoretical proposition leads in a direction different from that presented here, at least Black women's (and Black men's) interlocking identities will be considered central, as opposed to tangential or not at all, in relative investigations. Although there exists the potential for disapproving reactions to a Black feminist criminology, such an approach to understanding abuse in Black women's intimate relationships is more desirable than disadvantageous.

The Power of Narrative

Black feminist criminology places *Black women* at the focal point of consideration, as opposed to wedging them into theories developed based on the lives of men or White women that may not necessarily represent the experiences of Black women in the United States. Therefore, it was important that my study focus only on Black women, their lives, and the stories of the abuse perpetrated against them. To do this, I set out to conduct in-depth interviews with a diverse group of Black women.

Women who identified themselves as Black or African American, who were at least 18 years of age at the time of the interviews, and who had been or were at the time of the interviews involved in abusive intimate relationships were eligible to participate in this study. I did not restrict the study to heterosexual women and relationships; however, only heterosexual women abused by men replied to the solicitation. I also did not limit the participants to those who had been abused only by Black men. As a result, one woman's only abusers were non-Black men, and an additional three women were in relationships with non-Black abusers in addition to their Black male abusers.

The majority of the women came to me by way of an advertisement of the study in a monthly Denver-based newspaper mainly geared toward a Black audience. Thirty-nine-year-old Zora captured the sentiment of many of the women regarding the placement of the advertisement in the community newspaper: "I was so happy to see an ad regarding African Americans and domestic violence. Just seeing the ad and knowing that that's an issue and hoping that people were taking advantage of the resource. To be able to talk about it and to know that there are other people that are in the same situation or have been."

Between May and November of 2003, I made contact with 95 women who fit the study criteria. While I would have been delighted to speak with each of these women, I was limited by time and funding (each woman received a monetary incentive upon completion of the interview, and a transcriber had to be employed to expedite the completion of the project). Further, theoretical saturation was attained before the fortieth interview; it was highly likely that the additional interviews would have revealed similarities among the women's stories.

A detailed account of the study recruitment and the demographics of the women can be found in the Appendices, but a brief description is outlined here. Ultimately, 40 women were interviewed. The women ranged between the ages of 18 and 69; most were of the Christian faith, and they had a variety of educational backgrounds and levels of wealth. Eight of the women belonged to four mother-daughter sets (mothers and daughters were interviewed independent of each other). All 40 women had experienced at least one physically abusive relationship that also included verbal or mental abuse. At the time of the interviews, three women were in verbally or mentally abusive relationships that they thought had the potential to also become physical.

Among other things, feminist research expects the researcher to identify her or his position in the context of the subject matter.[34] This enables the researcher to identify any personal values that may have an effect on the findings. Sandra Harding writes that many feminist investigators employ the phrase "reflexivity of social science" to describe this new relationship between the researcher and the participant.[35] A particular characteristic of feminist research methods includes variations in the interviewing process. Feminist investigators do not believe that social distance needs to be maintained between the informant and the researcher. Feminist researchers often prefer semistructured or even nonstructured interviewing because it provides a medium for gathering more information from interviewees.[36] In addition, informants' questions are answered, and forming personal relationships with informants occurs and is sometimes expected. The entire interview environment is usually documented, including such factors as whether others were present, how long the interview lasted, and how the investigator established rapport with the informants.[37] As for feminist ethnography and other qualitative research settings, Shulamit Reinharz suggests that the goals of such research involve documenting the lives of women, understanding the experiences of women from *their* points of view, and conceptualizing the women's behaviors as expressions of contemporary social environment.[38]

Leon E. Pettiway makes the case that, in the quest to make criminology a real science, criminologists overemphasize the need to remain neutral in their research. Pettiway argues that this has resulted in criminologists who "fail to consider their own identity in their investigative enterprises."[39] While reflexivity is generally inherent—and maybe required—in qualitative research, Pettiway's arguments rest on the need for reflexivity in all criminological pursuits. Reflexivity in social science research should involve both *being* reflexive and *doing* reflexivity.[40] Specifically, the researcher must understand not only how her beliefs affect the research process but also how to consider how these beliefs affect the way in which the data are analyzed.

Early on in my gathering of the women's narratives, I began to consider the relational aspects between the women as interviewees and myself as the interviewer. One of the first issues of contemplation was comments made by a few of the women upon my meeting them at the designated interview site. In these cases, prior to the start of the interview and during the signing of the informed consent form, the women stated their appreciation of the fact that I am a Black woman. They admitted to having assumed that I am a White woman because, in part, the advertisement for the study listed the University of Colorado at Boulder as the affiliation; this is a predominantly White university in a predominantly White town. One woman stated, "I thought you were some White person from Boulder trying to study us." It was statements like this that led me to believe that the women likely felt less inhibited about disclosing their stories to me, particularly those reports that involved their perceptions of White people and the criminal justice system. Even though I had not experienced intimate partner abuse as they had (and I wholly recognized how this might affect my interpretation of the women's stories), the women seemed to assume that as a Black woman I could understand their views of the world around them. This is supported by Patricia Hill Collins, who argues that "Black women intellectuals best contribute to a Black women's group standpoint by using their experiences as situated knowers."[41] Accordingly, she concludes, "In terms of Black women's relationships with one another, African-American women may find it easier than others to recognize connectedness as a primary way of knowing, simply because we have more opportunities to do so and must rely upon it more heavily than others."[42] In the process of telling their stories, a few of the older women were eager to offer me protective advice about ways to avoid finding myself in abusive relationships with men.

Collins discusses at length the place of Black women scholars in the theory, research, and activism process. She argues that the continued development of Black feminist thought is imperative to the discipline of social theory. This does not preclude those who are not Black women from participating in the advancement of Black feminist thought but instead places Black women's intellectual and activist work on Black women at the forefront of theoretical hypothesizing and investigation.[43] It is from this stance that examinations of the lives and experiences of Black women victims and offenders should be investigated. An analysis of approaching intimate partner abuse against Black women from this position may offer a more comprehensive appraisal of their experiences with and responses to their victimization. Considering the historical experiences of Black women in the United States, which have been couched in multiple forms of domination, the approach advanced here is based on a fresh viewpoint that regards how Black women's lives may position them to encounter intimate partner abuse differently from women of other races and ethnicities (especially White women).

My arguments by no intention undervalue the important and noble work done by original feminist criminology and its adherents. It is the advent, subsistence, and practice of feminist criminology that makes the concept insisted on here obtainable because of feminist criminology's position that, although women and girl victims and offenders have parallel life circumstances, there are variations among them that are based on cultural, racial, and other distinctions. Indeed, mainstream feminist theory and feminist criminology allow for a more suitable assessment of women and criminal victimization than traditional male-centered criminology, but Black feminist criminology necessarily provides for consideration of Black women's multiple and interconnected identities and their position in U.S. society as a central element of any examination.

3

Dynamic Resistance

"I'm a Strong Black Woman!"

Beginning in her formative years, Billie was faced with a multitude of circumstances that she had to regularly resist. These battles not only included the intimate partner abuse she endured during adulthood but involved events during childhood that included combating child abuse by her mother, sexual molestation by her brother, and teasing by other school children because of her low-income class status. As she aged, Billie had to deal with recurrent financial stress, the authority of the criminal justice system, employment discrimination because of her arrest record, her alcohol and cocaine abuse, and physical health problems. She summed up her life by stating, "I've had a rough life. Now I go to church. I'm trying to get it together." During our time together, Billie regularly spoke in a manner that encompassed her entire life, her entire life struggles, and the strength that she and other Black women must possess in order to contend with these difficulties. The general consensus among the women in the study was demonstrated by Billie's declaration: "Black women are strong. They go through everything. From the time I could remember, Black women have been going through hell. White women have been pampered. . . . I think White women, they've got it so easy and Black women don't."

The women I interviewed undoubtedly understood the gender disparities within society, in which all women are in a devalued position compared to that of men.[1] They also overwhelmingly believed that they were at an even greater disadvantage than White women because of their race. Further, although understanding the place in which they, as Black women, are situated in the general social order and in relation to men in their immediate communities, the women consistently conveyed that they had a stronger conviction than White women in resisting the patriarchal hierarchy. The women's observations of their life experiences typically intertwined their gender, race, and class locations. This supports the reality of Black women as individuals with intersecting identities. The women were asked to articulate how they believed they were different from other women and their circumstances different from the circumstances other women face. They compared themselves to battered and nonbattered women, typically using White women as their comparison base. Their self-depictions and descriptions of other Black women overwhelmingly included the use of the term "Strong Black Woman," while White women and battered White women were often described as "weak." In most cases, "Black woman" was synonymous with "strong woman." The women were also acutely aware that in the view of other people one element of their identity might supersede another. For example, in their experiences, race often trumped gender in the views of non-Blacks.[2] Employing a Black feminist criminology and interpretive approach to my study enabled me to genuinely listen to what the women were telling me and to develop a way of knowing how their lives as Black women affected the way they experienced all that comes with intimate partner abuse. Using these methods of Black feminist criminology and story telling led to the conceptual model of *dynamic resistance*. Dynamic resistance is the concept that links the varied and similar experiences and identities of battered Black women to provide improved understanding of their encounters with and reactions to the violent events in their lives and the existing support networks. Dynamic resistance will become even more evident as the reader progresses through the remainder of this book, where the model is clearly linked to the evaluations of the women's formative life experiences (Chapter 4), encounters with battering and perceptions of the batterers (Chapter 5), rejection of victimization and physical efforts at resistance (Chapter 6), and resources used for departure from the abusive relationships (Chapter 7).

Perceptions of Other Battered Women

The women's perspectives on other women and the ways some of them handled intimate partner abuse were based on several sources. First, general interaction with other women of color and White women served as a partial foundation for their opinions. This interaction was with women they encountered in daily associations within their communities. The extent of interaction with White individuals varied greatly among the women. They were raised in and lived in many types of communities across the United States and internationally, ranging from rural, mostly

White towns to highly populated metropolitan neighborhoods that were predominantly Black and Latina/o. Yet none of the women were completely isolated from daily interactions with Whites. Another source for scrutinizing differences and similarities between Black women and White women was the media. Celebrated women in the news media and dramatic television shows were the typical sources. However, the women were aware that White women, as well as Black women, are often presented by the media in a stereotypical manner. Last, several of the women had extensive interaction with battered White women through their experiences with the criminal justice system and with social services agencies, including stays in battered women's shelters, and from employment or voluntary work experiences in which they interacted directly with battered women. The women with these direct encounters provided more extensive statements than the other study participants about battered White women's experiences with and responses to intimate partner abuse.

The comments presented throughout this chapter were provided by a diverse selection of the women. That is, regardless of education level, socioeconomic status, and age or generation, the women tended to see their status as that of Black women in U.S. society, which they contrasted with White women's status. But some of the women, when initially asked about differences between women based on ethnicity or race, denied any differences. Interestingly, though, as they progressed through their answers and thought process, they all identified distinctions.

Paula, a 41-year-old who was raised middle-class and who began attending college a few years prior to my interview with her, demonstrated the greater attempts that Black women must make because of their lack of resources. If strength *was* attributed to White women, it was in the context of their established position in the social structure:

> I think more so, not all, but some White families as being more intact than a lot of Hispanic and Black families. . . . A lot of times [the White families'] moms and dads are working individuals, are teachers, lawyers, doctors; their grandparents probably are, too. The things they are coming from is a stronger base. Having someone to talk to them about, "What's your plan?" Maybe they never get off course and stumble and go into these little diversions and never have to jump some of these hurdles that Hispanic families and some Black people start out with. One mother, a couple aunts over here, maybe a grandmother still alive, and it's a weaker base from the get-go. It's more stressful. So when I'm down at campus, I

think of the women in the classes as the majority of them probably coming from a stronger base from the get-go. . . . A lot of the White kids are
coming from high schools that are preparing them earlier than a lot of
these schools in the public school system. . . . I look at a lot of the [White]
women, especially the younger ones, and they're coming in already prepared. They're coming in from a different place from the get-go.

With regard to differences between *battered* Black and White women,
I identified several themes in the women's perceptions. The consensus
among the women in my study was that White women stayed in the
relationships longer.[3] Angie, a 39-year-old who was in a low-income socioeconomic status from childhood through to the time of our conversation, did not utilize battered women's shelter care or any other service programs for battered women. Angie's deduction on the differences
between battered women by race was based on her general knowledge
about White women and the representations of these women in television programs: "I think White women just stay there like I did. It depends on the person. It's hard to say, Black or White. 'Cause I stayed,
and I didn't think I would. But I think White women stay more and
I think they get messed up more, but that's just maybe 'cause I watch
too much TV." Angie's account provided an insightful perspective into
the often stereotypical images presented in television programming on
the portrayal of Black and White women. Billie's perception was also
based on media representations. She stated that White women will "put
up with a little bit more. They'll go with an abusive guy for 17, 18 years.
Most Black women won't put up with it that long, I don't think." Other
women's observations were more resolute than Angie's and Billie's re-
marks. Cicely's opinion was based on her personal commitment to edu-
cating herself on the social injustices involving Blacks. The 52-year-old
offered the following comparison between battered White women and
battered Black women regarding the length of time these women remain
in abusive relationships: "A Black woman is more likely to leave. A Black
woman will be in a relationship five years. She's more likely to get out of
that one way or another. Where the White woman, she'll stay in there 20
and 30 years before she either kill him or she get killed."

Medea's employment in a position involving work in intimate partner
abuse afforded her regular contact with battered women. Accordingly,
she offered several professional, educated, and personal interpretations.
Although she had interactions with battered women in a professional

capacity, it is notable that her comments resemble those furnished earlier. Like the others, Medea relayed that White women are trapped in abusive relationships longer than Black women and provided her reasoning for this outlook:

> I find White victims are far more passive. They are far more likely to take it for a longer period of time, and they don't identify, they don't internalize that strength that is needed to break away. Of course, that's a generalization. That's not every White victim. But the White women that I encounter just in daily life just incorporate [abuse] into their world and go on, and that amazes me.

Medea's comment that battered White women do not internalize the strength to allow them to free themselves from the relationships as battered Black women do was echoed by Jade, who is a social worker. Because her position involved working with families in need, the 35-year-old Jade had numerous interactions with battered women. She identified an additional, as well as harrowing, aspect of battered Black women that puts them at risk of further intimate partner abuse even if they do not stay in the relationships as long as White women:

> I must say the White women stayed in it. I remember that right away. They stayed with their husbands. They somehow claimed that they worked it out and worked through it. The Black women, no, they *think* they're handling it. . . . They continue getting into unhealthy relationships. . . . Most of them don't stay. But they do keep hopping into other unhealthy relationships.

Jade's perception is supported by the women's experiences as a whole; three-quarters of the women were in two or more abusive relationships. Perhaps Billie's assessment can begin to aid us in understanding this phenomenon. Billie offered her observation about White women in the context of interracial relationships. She discussed how White women in relationships with Black men will tolerate more than Black women with Black men would: "Things that Black women wouldn't put up with, [White women] will." Also, the description of the women's reasoning for their batterers' abusive behaviors (outlined in Chapter 5) can assist in explaining the women's encounters with multiple abusive relationships. Further, it can be speculated that Black women find their way out of these relationships quicker but that they are not closely evaluating their situations once they leave an abuser and thus find themselves in similar relationships.

On the basis of their interactions and familiarity with battered White women, the women perceived that the White women were more reliant on batterers than battered Black women. During her group counseling experience targeted specifically at victims of intimate partner abuse, 48-year-old Olivia, who was raised middle-class, said of the White women in the group: "They became dependent on [the batterers]. They felt women couldn't survive without a man. I could never figure it out." Forty-seven-year-old Harriet's observations derived from her experiences volunteering in a battered women's shelter after getting out of her abusive relationship. Harriet found in her work with White and Black women in the shelter that the women would say, "Nobody would want me, I don't know how to take care of myself." She concluded, "It's called brainwashing, propaganda, whatever you want to call it. I'd think, 'Don't believe it. Get out of there, get out on your own.' . . . Some of [the Black women] were like that, too, but not as much."

Fifty-one-year-old Wendy was raised middle-class and was working-class during her abusive relationship (her husband was in the military) and at the time of her interview. She formed her opinion about the differences between battered White women and battered Black women during her stay in a battered women's shelter:

[The White women] were scared to go out and venture out on their own: "I can't do it. I have to go back to him." They were used to being pampered. Living the good life, but taking the abuse behind closed doors. They were scared to step out and do for themselves [and] give up what they would call the good life, as far as material things. I didn't care about the material things. If I had it, I had it. If I didn't, I'll get it. That's what I was focused on. Me being different from them was they had it all. They didn't want to give up that nice livin' to live in a shelter like this. To live in a one-bedroom apartment, not have nice furniture, have to have used furniture. They wasn't used to that. So they'd rather go back and take the abuse and send their kids through hell than to go out and stand up on their own two feet. When we had group meetings and we'd talk about things like this, that's all I heard from all of them. I was like, "Oh no, honey, you need to get over yourself. You ran away because you didn't like it. You need to stand up on your own two feet. I'm gonna stand up on my own two feet. I'm gonna succeed anyway that I can. I'm gonna succeed.

And I'm gonna show my girls that there's a better life out there than to have to hang on to some man to beat you just so you can have material things. Get over it." That's the way I look at it. That's why [the counselor] took me to the side and said, "You're gonna be a strong woman."

Clearly, the belief that battered White women are more reliant on their batterers than battered Black women is peculiar since all of the women remained in the relationships for a certain time. But this must be considered in the context of how Black women experience intimate partner abuse and their activities during the relationships. Many of the women's discernments are rooted in the configuration of Black families that are frequently female-headed households with nonresident male intimate partners, where Black mothers often also serve the role of "father."[4] Even if the women were raised in two-parent households, they were personally cognizant of the prevalence of this pattern in many Black families through their personal experiences with extended family members and basic knowledge of this occurrence. Overall, the women reasoned that Black women, married or not, could effectively and successfully handle life on their own without the assistance of a male partner.

Akin to the appraisal that battered White women are more dependent on men than battered Black women is the women's perception that Black women make greater attempts at being equal with men than other women do. Regarding the Latina/o community, Olivia talked about her Latina friend and Latina/o culture regarding the roles of women and men:

I found out in their culture, and I never knew this until I hung out with them, that women are upstairs and the men are downstairs. You're not allowed to interact when you're at parties. I been there, I seen it. . . . We always got to be separated. We can't be their equal. If we want to be their equal, there's something wrong with us. Then they want to get violent.

The women in this study clearly recognized that sexism by Black men toward Black women exists, but they often considered themselves to be on equal footing with men. And, in some instances, as demonstrated in Chapter 5, when they felt pity for their Black male mates, the women considered themselves stronger than their batterers because of the women's endurance of the abuse and their daily struggles as Black women in the United States. Accordingly, they believed they, unlike women of other ethnicities and races, were able to at least *attempt* to be equal with men.

In Chapter 6, I assess the women's overwhelming response to abuse from batterers by employing the resistance endeavors of talking back and fighting back. The women expounded on the level at which White and Latina women, in comparison to Black women, verbally and physically challenge their batterers. As rooted in their dealings with and exposure to battered women of other races and ethnicities, the women in this study believed these other women to not be as vocal as Black women in abusive relationships. Harriet's volunteer experience at the shelter led her to the view that "White women were more submissive than the Black women during the times that they were in the abusive relationship. Passive. They were more passive. They won't say nothin', where a Black woman would speak anyway, a White woman wouldn't." Similarly, Olivia stated that "a lot of White women, they don't stand up to their husbands." And she spoke again about the relationship her Latina friends have with their Latino partners: "I've seen [the men] tell [the women] to go to their room. I said, 'Go to your room? You're a grown woman! Why do you have to go to your room? Talk back to your husband!' She says, 'If I don't [do what he says], he'll try and fight me after everybody goes.'"

The women's opinions about battered White women's propensity to retaliate physically against their batterers were similar to their opinions of the tendency to talk back. Forty-three-year-old Jacqueline formed her opinion about the differences between battered White women and battered Black women during her stay in a battered women's shelter. Her main conclusion was simply but keenly stated: "The Black women fight back. The White women don't fight back." Cicely's experience with battered women of different races elicited her prediction that "Black women are more likely to fight back a lot quicker than the White women. A White woman will get beat to the pulp, whereas a Black woman, she might get beat to the pulp, but the man is goin' be beat halfway down, too." This statement is evident in the assessment, presented in Chapter 6, that most of the women made valiant efforts to fight off their batterers. As with talking back, they viewed their efforts to be more *active* than those of battered White women, supporting battered Black women's reluctance to view themselves as "victims."[5] In opposition to this, the recollections about battered White women were told in the context of viewing the White women as "victims" because of the belief that White women do not make major efforts to defend themselves against the abuse.

In sum, in answering what they think the differences are between White and Black women, the women notably framed their answers from an *emotional* strength perspective, which was partly demonstrated in the aforementioned accounts. Throughout the following chapters, the subject of strength of battered Black women is prevalent in the women's life stories and as they describe their association with intimate partner abuse. Hence, when recounting what they knew or thought they knew about the lives of White women, they made many comparisons based on the adapted strength of Black women and the force exuded by Black women who are battered. This is evident in the comments regarding the length of time the women remain in abusive relationships, White women's reliance on their batterers, and Black women's belief in women's parity with men and their personal strategies to combat the abuse. Excerpts from interviews with three women from various upbringings and socioeconomic statuses offer just a sampling of the women's perceptions of White women's *general* strength as distinguished from that of Black women:

> I know that Black women in general have to fight harder.
> I think Black women just have to put up with a lot more shit [than White women].
> I think Black women are stronger. White women get more support, so they just *look* stronger. Their package looks better.

The women's perceptions of White women's personal power are what led to their conclusions presented in the preceding accounts of the reasons White women respond to intimate partner abuse the way they do. Medea's extended experience with intimate partner abuse victims allowed her to establish conclusions about battered White women's level of strength, taking into consideration White women's location in the U.S. societal hierarchy:

> The differences that I've noticed, that are apparent to me, are the White women are really weak. They don't see, they who are the second most privileged class in the world, do not see that they have options. They're like, "Oh, but I can't do that. How can you stand up?" They are also more attached to the material aspects of the situation, because he is a doctor, lawyer, Indian chief, because of the position, because of the money. It seems to me that they take more shit [from batterers] than women of color, or at least than I would. . . . They seem to be more passive somehow. It's odd that you ask that question, 'cause this is something I've thought of a lot. I can't figure it out. I mean, they can take some abuse. I said to one

one day, I said, "Your ass has been kicked from here around the block. How can you tell me you're not strong? If you can take the amount of abuse and be battered to the extent that you have, you've got to be strong. A lesser person would be dead. So how can you then say, "Oh, I'm so weak?" It just doesn't make sense to me. (This was a personal conversation. I'd never say that to a victim at work in a professional setting.) She said, "You know, I never thought of it that way." The White women I've dealt with have a perception that they are weak. It may be because you have a whole civilization catering to you. That may be a part of it. . . . But their perception is that they are weak and powerless. And that's amazing to me. . . . There's a whole world out there doing your bidding and you don't have to identify that strength and use it.

Medea's narrative emphasizes that Black women are forced to summon their inner strength in order to resist various sources and methods of abuse and domination on a regular basis. Many of the women believed, as is obvious in Medea's explanation, that White women do not have to call up their strength to the extent that Black women do because White women are pampered and socialized as such, and because, though they face sexism, they are not confronted by the range of discriminatory and dominating acts that is imposed on Black women.

Further, Medea's comments offered insight into how many of the other women viewed strength in their experiences with intimate partner abuse. The women equated strength with the ability to endure and survive an abusive relationship. In part, this resiliency aided in raising the women's ability to empower themselves to be active in contending with the violence. Nevertheless, viewing the endurance of and retaliation against abuse as only a positive attribute may cause the women to ignore the emotional damage the abuse produced. In all of the life situations where strength is expected to be and often is actually used by Black women, we must take into account the intricacies associated with the concept of the Strong Black Woman and its connection to Black women who have been in abusive relationships.

Complexities of the "Strong Black Woman" Maxim

References to the Strong Black Woman can be found in academic or intellectual reports, fiction writings, poetry, self-help resources, the popular print media, and the entertainment domain, such as television programs.[6]

In particular, there are references to the Strong Black Woman phenomenon in research on intimate partner abuse against Black women.[7] Commentary on Black women taking on the characteristics of the Strong Black Woman is presented from both positive and negative viewpoints. That is, scholars consider how appropriating this image can both help and harm the individual Black woman. Angie identified some of the positive and negative characteristics of the Strong Black Woman. She recognized that many Black women are able to singlehandedly manage a multitude of duties in their lives (the positive aspect) but that taking on these countless responsibilities leads the women to ignore or undervalue their need for emotional, financial, and other forms of assistance (the negative aspect):

> I think that Black women are strong women and they take a lot. I'm including myself. . . . I think they're most likely to be head of the households and they have to run the family, keep things together, hold things together. Sometimes they gotta put theirselves on the back burner and take care of what needs to be taken care of and put theirselves second.

The Black woman as the Strong Black Woman is simultaneously a stereotype and a reality. Although Black women may possess strength, they are at the same time "devoid of power."[8] Black women's tendency to focus on being strong, which includes taking care of others by providing mothering and financial security, does not allow them to be seen or to see themselves as being in need of emotional support or as "victims" of others' misdeeds.[9] In Michele Wallace's controversial 1979 book, *Black Macho and the Myth of the Superwoman*, she provides a detailed and conflicting description of the image of the Strong Black Woman, based on both an historical and a contemporary analysis. Although parts of the description are not supported by present-day research, such as her comparison of Black women's level of wealth and professional employment to those of Black men,[10] the characterization is still useful. The description is extensive but provides a portrayal of the Strong Black Woman for my analysis:

> Sapphire. Mammy. Tragic mulatto wench. Workhorse, can swing an ax, lift a load, pick cotton with any man. A wonderful housekeeper. Excellent with children. Very clean. Very religious. A terrific mother. A great little singer and dancer and a devoted teacher and social worker. She's always had more opportunities than the Black man because she was no threat to the White man so he made it easy for her. But curiously enough, she frequently ends

up on welfare. Nevertheless, she is more educated and makes more money than the Black man. She is more likely to be employed and more likely to be a professional than the Black man. And subsequently she provides the main support for the family. Not beautiful, rather hard looking unless she has White blood, but then very beautiful. The Black ones are exotic though, great in bed, tigers. And very fertile. If she is middle class she tends to be uptight about sex, prudish. She is hard on and unsupportive of Black men, domineering, castrating. She tends to wear the pants around her house. Very strong. Sorrow rolls right off her brow like so much rain. Tough, un-feminine. Opposed to women's rights movements, considers herself already liberated. Nevertheless, unworldly. Definitely not a dreamer, rigid, inflex-ible, uncompassionate, lacking in goals any more imaginative than a basket of fried chicken and a good fuck.[11]

When the women in my study spoke of the Strong Black Woman, they used this term or similar descriptions of Black women without leading questions posed by me. Sometimes they spoke on this issue while answer-ing other indirectly related questions, and other times it was in response to the question "What do you think are the differences between Black women and White women?" While some of the women did not specifi-cally describe themselves or certain other Black women as strong, they still viewed their actions in the context of strength. Such women were seen by those who spoke in this manner as failed Black women because they did not exhibit the Black woman's assumed characteristic of strength. Although other researchers had mentioned the connection between the internalization of the Strong Black Woman character and intimate part-ner abuse, in the spirit of the ethnographic approach of research, where propositions are developed as the researcher is immersed in data collec-tion and analysis,[12] this was an area where I did not expect to make any significant discoveries. But, as the interviews progressed (beginning with the first interview with Paula), I became aware of the overpowering im-portance of the image of the Strong Black Woman and its association with managing intimate partner abuse through the women's numerous refer-ences to the attribute.

Most of the women's initiation into the idea of the Strong Black Woman undeniably began with their observing their mothers and othermothers as they were growing up.[13] The Black criminologist Laura Fishman has described the lessons she learned from her "female black elders" about being a Black woman, rooted in her elders' personal experiences and the messages they received from misreported media images and folktales about the Black experience, crime, and violence:

> The implications of these messages were clear. We young black girls had to learn to protect ourselves against physical hurt, to figure things out in order to maximize our safety within both private and public space. To cushion ourselves against physical mistreatment meant learning to fight to defend ourselves and to win. To cushion ourselves therefore meant that we could not expect any protection from black men or, especially, from the police. I was able to be on my own as a strong, independent black woman who could handle anything life threw at me.[14]

In my study, the observation of their mothers as Strong Black Women was particularly important for most of the women who witnessed their mothers being abused by male mates. The women who witnessed their mothers' victimization and whose mothers fit the Strong Black Woman characterization formed the idea that Strong Black Women are confronted not only with racism, sexism, classism, and the responsibility of running a household and raising children but also with abuse. Violence inflicted on their mothers became yet another form of strain in the Strong Black Woman's life.

The majority of the women provided descriptions of their mothers and othermothers that fit within the qualities of the Strong Black Woman. Even women who did not have healthy relationships with their mothers described their mothers as strong because of their lifelong and recurring struggles to maintain the family emotionally and economically, while coping with sociostructural stressors. Angie addressed this when she spoke of her grandmother's life as a basis for observing the Strong Black Woman: "Looking at my grandmother being the single parent of nine kids and doing what you can to keep food and roof over your family's head. Just strong to me." Fifty-one-year-old Shahida, who was raised in the lower class but became a college-educated professional of middle-class status in adulthood, described her mother as "an Angela Davis-type radical." Wendy also spoke of her reverence for her mother's strength:

> She was wonderful. Sweetest little lady you ever want to meet. Very sweet, very gentle. She talked to you, she was very forward. She never beat around the bush about anything; she'd just come out let you know how she felt, what was going on. She taught you how to take care of business.

You always want to know how to take care of business, you never leave anything undone. She was like that. Very stern. Very strong Black woman. Very strong. I've seen her go through a lot. I've seen her work to the point where she would just crawl through the front door. You know, 'cause she would be so tired, she worked a lot. We had a beautiful home. She always kept her house immaculate.

As indicated, the women also attributed their mothers' strength to the mothers' endurance in abusive relationships. In Chapter 4, I describe how many of these women witnessed their mothers' attempts at verbally and physically repelling the abusive acts perpetuated by their husbands and boyfriends and note that this aided in the women's decisions to fight off their own batterers. Still, as 18-year-old Keisha said about her 38-year-old mother, Leah, with whom I also spoke, the women were often at a loss to explain why their strong mothers would endure the abuse at all. Keisha acknowledged, "I think with her relationship with my dad and Vic, the stalker, I seen this strong woman. This strong woman, she's my mother, and she's just going through ridiculous trials and tribulations over guys."

The strong mothers often helped the women to resist further intimate partner abuse. As I describe in Chapter 7, the women's mothers were a substantial resource for leaving abusive relationships. Thirty-nine-year-old Rebecca elaborated on how her mother and othermothers were a source of strength while she dealt with abuse: "There were a very, very large amount of strong women in my family who helped me get through a lot of what I've been through."

I will expand on the relevance of some of the women receiving special treatment in their families of origin in the following chapter, but there are connections between this status in their families and issues of Strong Black Women that should be introduced here. The women who did not describe their mothers or main mother-figures as Strong Black Women included six of the seven women who received special treatment in their families of origin (four of the seven were not exposed to any major forms of violence in childhood). Harriet's mother died when Harriet was young, leaving her father as her main parent and role model, and the mothers of the other six women would not have been considered to fit the definition of the Strong Black Woman during the women's childhoods. An additional three women who did not describe their mothers as Strong Black Women (a) did not fit within the special-treatment category; (b) were exposed to at least one form of violence during their upbringing; and (c) were raised by both biological parents. One woman's parents were regularly under the influence of drugs and were virtually absent as parents. Within the other two sets of parents, the mothers were particularly docile and modeled the more "traditional" role of mother and wife by being fairly reserved and not major decision makers in the homes of origin. However, even most of the women who did not have Strong Black Mother role models began to describe themselves as Strong Black Women toward the end or after the conclusion of their abusive relationships. These self-perceptions were created because of their personal dealings with the many social structure and cultural struggles faced by most Black women in U.S. society and because of their fortitude during the intimate partner abuse. Their views of themselves as strong were often solidified through interactions with White women, who, as highlighted earlier, were regarded as pampered and weak. Fittingly, even women without Strong Black Mothers as role models came to view themselves as strong for having lived through unfortunate circumstances. For instance, Wendy was a "special-treatment" child and did not have a mother who fit in the Strong Black Woman characterization. However, she described how her mother eventually displayed strength qualities after years of abuse by her husband (Wendy's father). As evident in her appraisal of herself and her mother a couple of years prior to my conversation with her, Wendy followed her mother's path to the Strong Black Woman characterization: "By this time, I had became my mother: the Strong Black Woman."

Starting with the women's observations of Black mothers' and other Black women's maneuvers in the home, the community, and society-at-large, the formation of many of the women viewing *themselves* as Strong Black Women began at a young age. Forty-five-year-old Helene was one of the women who received special treatment in her home of origin, but she was the only one of the special-treatment girls whose mother fit within the characterization of the Strong Black Woman. Helene discussed her positive view of her own strength when she was a teenager:

> Here I am, my senior year in high school. School started in September. I got pregnant in September, my son was born a week to the day I marched and got my diploma. There was no way I was dropping out of school. Back then, you couldn't even go to school [pregnant]. It didn't matter to me. I wasn't dropping out. There was enough I had to drop out of back then: my debut,[15] I had to miss my prom. . . . That was so embarrassing. . . . I took my senior pictures anyway, though. I stayed in school every day.

Many times the women received verbal confirmation of their strength. Keisha, who graduated from high school only several weeks prior to my interview with her, described how her mother realized and confirmed Keisha's strength: "My mom tells me everyday how I'm the strongest person she's ever seen. She was like, 'For you to be 18, you've been through a lot. With guys, family, and everything, you're very strong.' She's like, 'You're a strong woman.'"

As many of their mothers did before them, a number of the women described how they sustained their strength in spite of an abusive mate. Of course, at times, their strength wavered because of the vicious physical attacks, but more so because of the accompanying mental abuse that diminished their self-worth. Yet the women delighted in their ability to conjure up and rebuild the strength that they acknowledged had been gradually weakened by the batterers. They used their anger, and several used their spiritual faith, to summon and restore their strength. In Chapter 7, I will illustrate that even though the women used interpersonal and systemic resources to aid them in discontinuing the abusive relationships, they ultimately used their own resolve to get to the point where they could leave their violent and otherwise abusive companions. I assert that adopting the notion of the Strong Black Woman appreciably aided the women in leaving. Olivia surmised that once she was able to convey to her abuser that she did not need him—emotionally, financially, or otherwise—much of his motivation to exert power through abuse was eliminated:[16]

> He'd come over, "I've come to see my baby." Or come when it was time to eat, pretend like he really cared. But he was really there to wreak havoc, to see if I was making it without him. I guess I was one of those strong Black women. If I wasn't making it, I wasn't going to tell him. The slapping around was to say, "You're not making it; you have to tell me [that you're not making it]." But it didn't work.

Olivia continued her narrative by describing her strength in the context of dealing with future intimate companions:

> I am the headstrong female. I'm very independent. I don't like people sitting at home, I don't want you cheating. I don't want you staying out on me, cheating on me. . . . You know, lay up with me and I'm not supposed to say anything. I'm not that type of female. . . . So, yes, I'm'a pick a fight with you. And yes, I'm gonna want to know where you been. You got to be accountable.

Similarly, based on her previous experiences with unhealthy intimate relationships, Harriet spoke of how she required even stricter conditions for men's behavior in relationships. Harriet accepted being an independent, assertive woman and maintained that she was not going to compromise herself for a man's sake and ego. She discussed how she believed men responded to women like her:

> I was never, ever a submissive Black woman at all. Never have and never will be. And a lot of men become intimidated by that, I guess. . . . I saw where they didn't think that I was passive enough. I've always been taught to speak my mind. Some men like that when they first meet you. They lie and say they like that. But don't believe it. I'm not goin' change for nobody.

Concerning talking back, the women in this investigation may have faced corporal repercussions when they responded to their batterers with verbal attacks, but they were pleased that they showed their strength by at least letting their feelings about the unwarranted and harmful treatment be known. Olivia emphasized the strength in battered Black women's tendency to talk back:[17] "Black women, we're loud, we're boisterous, we're just out of control sometimes, which is a good thing. 'Cause it saves us." By talking back, the women began to be empowered to terminate or escape the abusive relationships. In a sense, they began to listen to their own rants, which was the foundational stage of providing them agency in taking action against the abuse.

The majority of the women depicted the qualities and consequences of the Strong Black Woman in an optimistic way. However, some women, including some who attributed some positive aspects to the Strong Black Woman classification, identified the negative facets of being a Strong Black Woman. As Harriet's anecdote illustrates, other women also spoke of viewing the strength of Black women in a negative manner and talked about how it may affect their ability to establish heterosexual relationships with men who believe the women are too strong-willed. In trying to determine why she was abused by her intimate partner, 36-year-old Gloria retrospectively reflected, "Maybe I was too controlling or something." Some women also contemplated this view *during* their abusive relationships. Sadly, there are individuals who rationalize that if a woman is outspoken with her male intimate partner, he essentially has a right to aggressively correct her behavior.[18] Some of the women's comments regarding

Black women's strength appeared to blame the women's strong qualities for the abuse by men. Jade described how she repressed her self-assured personality in order to attempt to transform her abusive relationship into a nonabusive one, because she thought her strong and independent qualities exacerbated her husband's behavior: "I was a strong woman. . . . I wasn't one to really invest myself into men and feel like men made me complete or anything like that. But it was like, OK, I really want to try this. His parents never got divorced and I came from a divorced situation. He made me feel ashamed of that."

Thirty-seven-year-old Naomi, whose mother was not identified as a Strong Black Woman, spoke of how certain women (of any race) and a number of Black men perceive Black women and also discussed the effect of embracing this image on speaking publicly about abuse:

> The Black men say, "I'm not gonna date a Black woman because they're mouthy or aggressive." You're expected to be a certain way. You're expected to be strong as a Black woman. Most *women* expect Black women to be very strong. They wouldn't think a Black woman would put up with [abuse]. You're trying to keep that, so people can think I'm strong. I honestly think that. I don't know any statistics, I haven't talked to anybody, but that's what I believe. Because people look at me like, "You put up with it?" I think that's why a lot of Black women aren't coming out, except for the extreme stuff.

Naomi's assertion is supported by Patricia Hill Collins's argument that the "matriarch or overly strong Black woman has . . . been used to influence Black men's understandings of Black masculinity. Many Black men reject Black women as marital partners, claiming that Black women are less desirable than White ones because we are too assertive."[19]

Wanting to be seen as a Strong Black Woman, even by those individuals closest to the women, interfered with their ability to be completely honest about their limitations, thus making them vulnerable.[20] Twenty-eight-year-old Isis discussed why she had not disclosed her previous abusive relationships to her current, nonabusive boyfriend:

> He knows about them because of the kids, but he doesn't know about *all* that stuff. Sometimes I just don't want to open those flood gates. Like I'm crying now, but I don't want him to see me that weak. I don't want him to ever see me being a weak person because of that. And he probably

wouldn't. And maybe if the time is right, maybe one day I will tell him. But I just haven't found it necessary to even talk about it, because we talk about other stuff. I feel like I've built at least a strong exterior where I could deal with these things. I've dealt with them OK at this point. I haven't been on drugs. I've never been arrested. All my kids are healthy.

Caretaking is a major characteristic of the Strong Black Woman. Women with children had first of all the responsibility of caring for those children. However, as many women are socially and culturally obligated to do, there were many other duties for which they were also responsible. These duties are multiplied for women who are unpartnered mothers. Billie's narrative described the caretaking facet of the Strong Black Woman. She realized, with the benefit of hindsight, that because of her custodial obligations at work, to her children, and to her current husband, Odell, she neglected herself:

I think because I got into health care and I was always helping somebody else, I didn't have to worry about Billie. I was always helping somebody else, you see what I'm saying? As long as I was helping somebody else, helping Odell with his seizures and his [medical condition], then I don't have to worry about me. Me will be fine. I'm supposed to be strong. I'm the strong one. I'm supposed to take care of this. This is my job. . . . Babies' daddies were never there to help me and I never really depended on 'em, either. If I got pregnant, I was like, "Oh, well. I'll take care of it." God ain't going to put no more on you than you can handle. I always felt that way. God don't make no junk.

Keisha described the self-awareness process that occurred when she joined her mother, Leah, in a battered women's shelter. Keisha went to the shelter for emotional support from her mother after Keisha was beaten by her boyfriend. Keisha shared the following about loosening the bind of the Strong Black Woman attribute in order to heal:

I'm strong about mine and there was no weakness ever shown in me. I never cried or anything. The time I broke down was when we were at a meeting [in the shelter] and we were all talking about our problems, and that's when I broke down. I lost it. But it took a while for me to break down because I kept it inside, with a whole bunch of other stuff. I was just angry.

Even at the age of 18, Keisha had already developed the unyielding self-image of the Strong Black Woman, which was difficult to set aside in order to address the sources of her distress. Keisha's autobiography, as she reported it to me, and the other life stories presented here demonstrate the damage to a battered Black woman who considers herself a Strong Black Woman influenced by the societal and cultural perceptions of Black women and the element of intimate partner abuse in their lives. Labeling one's self and being labeled by others as a Strong Black Woman hindered the women in detecting the extent of the psychological consequences from the abuse, seeking mental and physical health assistance, leaving the relationship early on, and seeing themselves as "victims" or as a "battered women." Obviously, many battered Black women are able to see the abuse for the destructive action it is, but they may not view it as a mental abscess that will only further infect the women's overall well-being if not treated. Conversely, the espousal of the Strong Black Woman maxim did provide many of the women in this study with the strength to eventually leave the relationships and to cope with the lingering wounds of abuse. The characteristics that make up the Strong Black Woman effectively allow for a theoretical explanation—dynamic resistance—of battered Black women's reactions to their abuse.

Dynamic Resistance

To this point I have regularly used the term "victim" to describe the women as they live through precarious situations in some of their intimate relationships. Yet, in Chapter 6, I expand on the women's general inability to view themselves as "victims" or even as "battered women."[21] A review of the analysis provided at the start of this chapter of the women's opinions of White women in general, and battered White women specifically, begins to offer an explanation for this pattern. The women viewed battered White women as passive or submissive, while seeing battered Black women as aggressive or assertive. They agreed that Black women can survive without a man better than White women. They asserted that, although heterosexual Black women enjoy and welcome stable heterosexual relationships, the problem—both perceived and real—of absent Black fathers and husbands in the Black community leaves Black women with the mindset that there may be an occasion when they cannot rely on these men for domestic assistance. In relation to this, the women believed that White women remain in abusive relationships—that is, *tolerate* these relationships—longer than their Black counterparts. The perceived passiveness of White women, according to many of the women, translated into the White women's incapacity to verbally rebuke the batterers' wrath. The women reasoned that talking back was much more prevalent among battered Black women, building on the stereotype that Black women are loud-mouthed. It was believed, and rightfully so as demonstrated in existing research, that Black women physically retaliate against their batterers at greater rates than White women.[22] Finally, all of these perceptions of White women were grounded in the basic impression that Black women are emotionally stronger than White women. Accordingly, it is difficult for Black women to view themselves as victims of any of life's problems and to incorporate this idea into their identities, particularly when they compare their and other Black women's life histories with those of White women.

Increasingly, in the intimate partner abuse literature, the term "survivor" is being co-opted to describe battered women.[23] Jennifer L. Dunn writes that this term is becoming preferred over "victim" because "[f]raming victims as 'survivors' constructs a different, less pathetic and more reasonable battered woman embodying the cultural values of strength rather than weakness, and agency instead of passivity."[24] In her study of Black women who were physically and/or sexually abused, Traci C. West chose to use the term "victim-survivors" to describe these women in order to "rhetorically remind us of the dual status of women who have been both victimized by violent assault and have survived it."[25] Lee Ann Hoff[26] and Edward W. Gondolf and Ellen R. Fisher[27] argue that battered women are not simply helpless victims but heroic survivors who are skillful women employing calculated strategies to protect themselves and their children. "Even in the midst of severe psychological impairment, such as depression, many battered women seek help, adapt, and push on."[28] Indeed, the women in my study tended to fall within the description of the survivor, as opposed to that of the victim, when considering the extant research on the increasingly preferred and more appropriate term for battered women. To describe the women in my study as survivors would be more in keeping with their views of themselves than describing them as victims.

I contend, however, that "survivor" suggests that the battered Black women's struggles have concluded and that these women are no longer in need of assistance. The women I spoke with were indeed still in need of advocacy—or, at least, acknowledgment of their abuse—from family, friends, clergy, the Black community, and activist allies. In addition, the

term "survivor" in the context of woman battering refers to women's identity as one who has been abused by an intimate partner. It does not adequately allow for how a battered woman truly identifies herself and has a
strong influence on how she views herself. This is particularly important
when considering women of color. As is particular to my investigation,
battered Black women are confronted by many other forms of oppression
aside from being abused by an intimate partner. These women repeatedly reflected on their devalued position in general society, which often
included encounters with sexism, racism, and classism. At the community
and familial levels, the women recognized that within this community, although they are viewed as the mainstay of the Black community,[29] they
face sexism from Black men,[30] discrimination based on skin tone,[31] classism from middle-class and higher classes of Blacks,[32] and intellectual bias
from Blacks who have achieved advanced educational statuses.[33] Hence,
the pressures from the outside, White-dominated society are not always
relieved by interfacing with the Black community and Black family because of the prospect of internal strife within these in-groups. In the face
of these countless pressures and stressors, the women in my study showed
great fortitude and resistance. From their standpoint, battered Black
women are *resisters*.

In part, I compare the use of the term "resister" to Gary Kleck and
Marc Gertz's definition, in their work on gun use as a form of "armed
resistance," of the use of force by victims of crime as acts of self-defense.
Regardless of the outcomes of their research on the use of guns and
their lack of support for organized gun-control, their work provided
a seemingly peculiar fit to explain battered Black women's response to
their batterers. Battered Black women have often not been recognized as
"true victims," and they use terms reminiscent of street or stranger violence to describe their acts of resistance. The responses from the women
in my study are different from the descriptions of many White women
who experience intimate partner abuse. Taking these factors into consideration, it is not problematic to reach beyond *intimate partner* violence research into *street* or *stranger* violence research to draw on such
findings and to develop a more suitable model. Kleck and Gertz contend
that:

> The traditional conceptualization of victims as either passive targets or
> active collaborators overlooks another possible victim role, that of the ac-
> tive resister who does not initiate or accelerate any illegitimate activity,

but uses various means of resistance for legitimate purposes, such as avoiding injury or property loss. Victim resistance can be passive or verbal, but much of it is active and forceful.[34]

Another source for building my theoretical model on battered Black women's responses to abuse and domination in their lives is West's research detailed in her book, *Wounds of the Spirit: Black Women, Violence, and Resistance Ethics*. West interviewed women "victim-survivors" of male "intimate violence," which includes not only intimate partner abuse but sexual abuse (rape) during either childhood or adulthood and perpetrated by acquaintances and strangers. She also analyzed written narratives depicting violence against Black women slaves. Although West's emphasis is on a "theo-ethical assumption of the presence of powerful divine resources available to us for resisting the forms of dehumanization leveled at black women," she provides a secular, sociostructural view of violence and domination against Black women and their resistance efforts.[35] West's main contention is that even when confronted with severe "intimate and social violence," women undeniably engage in endeavors of resistance. She argues that even though resistance does not guarantee healing, it does provide a space where healing can take place. As depicted in her choice to use the term "victim-survivor" in describing Black women who have suffered intimate violence, West suggests an integrated approach to understanding these women's resistance. She concludes that "a resistance paradigm for African-American victim-survivors must include the roles of both victim and agent. These roles should be configured in a resistance framework that allows them to exist as alternating and overlapping dynamics."[36]

Starting from the standpoint of Black feminist criminology and building on Kleck and Gertz's conceptualization of victims of (typically stranger) violence and West's focus on resistance efforts by Black women who have been abused, my evaluation presented throughout this book has led to the theoretical model of *dynamic resistance* to describe the challenging situations confronting Black women who have been battered and their resulting responses. The multiple meanings of the term "dynamic" are equally applied to the women's resistance efforts. Being dynamic can mean that something is ever changing and can have the *ability* to change or adapt, as opposed to being static (fluidity). Being dynamic can involve taking an active stance, as opposed to a passive one (vitality). Being dynamic is an indication of passion and strength, as opposed to disinterest and powerlessness (intensity). A dynamic (used not as an adjective, but as a noun) can also entail interaction with other things or other persons, such as the dynamics between the parties in an intimate couple or the dynamics between Black women and the criminal justice system. These elements of fluidity, vitality, and intensity and the interactional aspect of social and political organisms that explain the term "dynamic" are all functioning within the model of dynamic resistance.

Although a battered Black woman can encompass a multifaceted self, five major aspects of such women include (1) race (Black or African American); (2) gender (woman); (3) sexuality; (4) socioeconomic status (often low-income and undereducated, although there is increasing representation in the higher classes); and (5) experiences with intimate partner abuse. The first three characteristics are considered part of the women's *identity*, while the fourth characteristic, socioeconomic status and education, may or may not be endemic to battered Black women's identity dependent on the extent to which they consider these factors to be part of their identity. However, the fifth item, experiences with abuse, is framed as a "descriptive" characteristic following bell hooks's argument that the "battered woman" term

> is used as though it constitutes a separate and unique category of womanness, as though it is an identity, a mark that sets one apart rather than being simply a descriptive term. It is as though the experience of being repeatedly violently hit is the sole defining characteristic of a woman's identity and all other aspects of who she is and what her experience has been are submerged.[37]

While Black feminism, critical race feminism, and Black feminist criminology proclaim that women have multiple intersecting identities that are all parts of their identity at one time, many other concepts and individuals do not distinguish Black women in this way. Persons who rely on stereotypes to guide their judgment may view battered Black women in a linear and hierarchical fashion. In this hierarchical categorization, *race* is at the forefront or pinnacle, and it eclipses gender, while both race *and* gender overshadow the women as "victims" because of the tendency not to consider Black women as victims of violent acts.[38] Sexuality as part of one's identity is often overlooked, even though *hetero*sexuality is viewed by general society as the default sexual classification for all individuals. However, because of the persistent typecast views of Black women (and men) as hypersexual, the sexuality identity may be part and parcel of the prevailing race identity of Black women by non-Blacks. Regarding socio-economic status, a low-income class status with an inadequate education (or the inability to succeed in educational pursuits) is *assumed* when one is considering the average Black American, despite the few affluent Blacks who receive significant attention from the media.[39] Explicitly, it is regularly suggested that the bulk of Black Americans, by their nature, are poor, government-dependent individuals who are not especially intelligent.

Although many White feminists rally against a number of oppressive behaviors and issues, the *gender* identity is the prominent focus of women's identity. Because of the criticism of mainstream White feminists by many Black feminists, White feminists may view gender as the main characteristic of battered Black women, with race being regarded as a secondary concern.[40] From the mainstream feminist viewpoint, the "survivor" label may be considered *alongside* the identity of womanhood because of the considerable focus by mainstream feminism on issues surrounding women's victimization by men and the patriarchal social order. More recent notions of mainstream feminist thought,[41] however, may provide an outlook in which race, gender, sexuality, class, and violence against women are seen as overlapping or interlinking.

Returning to the concept of utilizing Black feminist criminology to understand battered Black women's experiences with abusive relationships, that Black women have multiple identities that are intricately interwoven was not lost on the women in my study, whose view of their identities in the context of the four basic levels of identity (race, gender, sexuality, and class) encompassed all these areas; the fifth characteristic (experience with intimate abuse) was tangential to this multiplicative identity.

In determining the extent to which battered Black women adopt the three different labels describing the violence in their lives—victim, survivor, or resister—I assert three propositions to support the adoption of only the resister label. First, the idea is not that of a sequential relationship where the battered Black woman starts as victim, moves to survivor, then ends as a resister. Second, the idea is not that a battered Black woman at once considers herself all three classifications. Third, a battered Black woman is not each of these at different times, continually moving between the categorizations in a cyclical manner. (The dynamic concept referring to fluidity does *not* apply here.) It is because of the factors discussed previously that I consider battered Black women's view of themselves not as victims and not as survivors but as resisters. Describing battered Black women as resisters better captures their self-identity because of the women's *in*ability to take on the other descriptive characteristics of victim or survivor as *central* to their Self. In essence, their dynamic lives aided in this rebuff of victimhood. Although they rejected labeling themselves as victims or survivors, most of the women were aware of the negative effects of the abuse on their self-worth.

By using the term "resister," we can begin to combat the "victim blaming" surrounding the occurrence of intimate partner abuse. Women abused by their intimate partners are frequently held responsible for the abuse against them. This often happens because it is difficult for those looking into the relationships from the outside to understand why the women remain in the relationships. Even some women who are abused by their intimate partners blame themselves for the abuse. Because Black women usually are not afforded the same recognition for their "victimization" as White women are, it is highly likely that Black women are viewed even more as responsible for the abuse committed against them, more than their White counterparts. White women are often seen as being in need of protection, and Black women are typically perceived as being able to protect themselves. By renaming "victims" of intimate partner abuse "resisters," we can continue to challenge the culpability placed on *all* women abused by male batterers. In doing so, accountability can be directed toward the abusers and their behaviors and the social, psychological, and other sources driving these behaviors. Additionally, the term "resister" implies that battered women oppose the abuse and violence directed toward them. The term recognizes the fact that battered women regularly employ dynamic efforts to combat and control the abuse against them.

It should be noted that use of the term "resister" does not necessarily or solely reflect the women's propensity to *physically* retaliate against their batterers (particularly in comparison with White women). The term is employed because of battered Black women's experiences and perceptions, including (a) their not seeing themselves as victims and their not being seen as victims; (b) their self-perception as fighters (whether physical or use of other tactics) against abuse by intimate partners; (c) their self-perception as Strong Black Women; and (d) their personal and ancestral history as Black women who have been confronted with and have resisted continuous sociostructural, cultural, and familial obstacles. The intersecting identity of battered Black women and their varied and ever-changing resistive attempts at combating interpersonal and societal domination yield the model of dynamic resistance.

A possible problem with dynamic resistance among battered Black women may be that battered Black women who have not left their first abusive relationship may present differently from the women in this study. This needs to be addressed in future research on battered Black women, specifically considering the sample selection. However, even Black women who are currently in abusive relationships and who are severely dominated and controlled without resisting can still exude dynamic resistance because they are likely resisting other oppressive situations. Despite this unknown effect, none of the women in this investigation were necessarily completely free of abusive relationships in their lives. This idea is based on the fact that the majority of the women had been in more than one abusive relationship. An admonition based on this awareness, then, is that the concept of dynamic resistance may work even better to explain battered Black women in *multiple* abusive relationships. As I discuss in Chapter 5, the women remained in subsequent abusive relationships for shorter periods as they progressed through the bad relationships. In essence, they progressively built up their resistance to withstanding abuse by their male mates.

Among the varied forms of oppression or domination, including those that are institutional, societal, or interpersonal, a question arises: Against which of the oppressive entities do battered Black women find easiest to employ resistance? I assert that the forms of domination in the battered Black women's lives should not be considered through a better-than/worse-than analysis because the forms of domination are often not comparable. For example, how can intimate partner abuse be seen as better or worse than institutional racism? Each of these abuses may cause despondency in the target of the oppression, yet likely in a different way. Further, it is the individual's ability to cope, her history of coping, and her personal coping strategies in the face of varying forms of oppression that dictate how she is able to tackle various modes of oppression. For that reason, dynamic resistance allows one battered Black woman's experiences with forms of oppression to be different from those of another battered Black woman. For instance, a battered Black woman who is middle-class and college educated may find it relatively easier to maneuver in and to resist forms of oppression in the social sphere because of her socioeconomic class position. She may be well informed on how her class privilege, in relation to that of Black women who are situated in lower classes, provides her with the means to avoid the levels of economic oppression that face her lower-income sisters. In this context, the middle-class, college-educated battered Black woman may find her abuser more difficult to combat than the societal-level oppressors.

Since it was developed from a Black feminist criminological standpoint, the concept of dynamic resistance allows for Black women to be viewed collectively, as well as individually, particularly since there is diversity among Black women. Collectively, these women share similar experiences with racism or colorism, sexism, sexualization, and classism from society at large and within the Black community. Individually, the women experience various levels and forms of discrimination, domination, and abuse. They resist this discrimination, domination, and abuse using similar methods as well as personal, distinct strategies.

In summary, the women who opened up their lives to me embraced the Strong Black Woman identity and rarely considered the risks of embracing this identity. Most were familiar with the Strong Black Woman concept starting early in life, and all came to exhibit the characteristics of the Strong Black Woman by adulthood. A strongly positive attribute of this concept is that the women reveled in their ability to endure the many forces of domination and the consequential tribulation that consumed their lives as Black women. However, by living by the code that "Black woman" is synonymous with "Strong Black Woman," they did not easily place themselves in a central position in their own lives. Children, boyfriends and husbands (both abusive and nonabusive), extended family, work, community or religious obligations, and maintenance of the home were placed at the forefront of their existence. The women often put their well-being on indefinite hold or considered their personal interests only after they had cared for the needs of their families. This was even the case for the small number of women who had no children; they spoke of caring for their mothers who were in abusive relationships, providing assistance with childcare of younger siblings, or attending to the needs of battering boyfriends.

The theoretical concept of dynamic resistance effectively takes into consideration not only battered Black women's personal experiences with violence and abuse but their assigned "place" in society and the ensuing struggles resulting from life chances based on the intertwined statuses of race, gender, sexuality, and, often, socioeconomic class. The resistance that battered Black women in the United States display is due to both perceived and real beliefs about Black women's strength, particularly in comparison with the perceived strength of White women and battered White women. The women in this study presumed that White women remained in abusive relationships longer, relied on batterers more, did not talk or fight back as much, and were not as strong as Black women. In fact, some of their presumptions have been supported by academic investigation. The women's deductions were based on their own struggles as Black women in a White, male-dominated society that leads to their best being recognized as *resisters* against all forms of oppression. Indisputably, their resistance was *dynamic* in every sense of the word.

4

Surviving Childhood

"I Learned to Stand up for Myself"

Medea endured a distressing childhood filled with abandonment and mental abuse by her parents. She did not feel that she fit in anywhere, whether it was in her home among her family or at school with her peers. As a result, Medea acknowledged, "I learned to stand up for myself." Medea's poor treatment by several of her family members left an indelible mark on her and, in retrospect, helped her understand how she came to be in abusive relationships and her resulting responses to the intimate partner abuse:

> Using my relationship with my father as a filter, I could understand why I made the choices I made. But I also had to understand that I couldn't continue to make those choices and the only person who could help me be whole was me. And I could get to that place, but I could not depend on having a relationship with men to get me to that place. I had to look at my life and fix what was wrong, the same as if I had a health issue. Ultimately it would be up to me. . . . You have to co-create the life you want.

Medea was a spirited child in spite of the neglect and isolation she suffered. Even though she found herself in a number of abusive intimate relationships during adulthood, during childhood Medea visualized her life beyond her depraved youth: "I felt like the world was bigger than that small space. I was kind of doing time."

At the beginning of this project, I expected that, like Medea, many of the women would have childhood experiences riddled with abuse and neglect. This was indeed a sad reality, as most of the women had suffered from an extensive assortment of abusive experiences during their formative years. Taking into account all forms of exposure to abuse and violence, 33 of the 40 women underwent some type of introduction to violence during their childhood. They experienced abuse from parents, witnessed intimate partner abuse among parents, witnessed other acts of abuse and violence, and exhibited destructive behaviors. To be sure, I do not suggest that battered women cause their abuse because of their abusive backgrounds, but I do wish to move toward determining the significance of the link between childhood trauma and entry into abusive relationships and to enlighten the field of interpersonal violence regarding factors that determine these women's reactions to intimate partner abuse. These experiences helped the women to develop at an early age their dynamic resistance as Black women in a society based in racial, gender, and class inequities.

Individuals who have been the target of intimate partner abuse have often experienced some form of abuse or violence during their upbringings, although this is not necessarily an antecedent to their being in abusive intimate relationships as adults. Researchers on intimate partner abuse have found that experience with violence in the family of origin often begets future family violence.[1] That is, if an individual is raised in a violent and abusive home, some existing research maintains that she or he often learns violence and abuse as a normal event or appropriate response. Further, some scholars have reported that battered women raised in violent family homes are stymied in their ability to recognize warning signs that an intimate partner is abusive.[2] These types of reasoning and findings are based on the concept of social learning theory.[3] But Patricia Tjaden and Nancy Thoennes warn that this link may also be explained by differences in individuals' propensity to disclose their experiences in surveys, because "it is possible that respondents who reported one type of victimization (e.g., child maltreatment) were simply more willing to report other types of victimization (e.g., intimate partner violence)."[4]

Although these prior discoveries on the abusive childhoods reported by many battered women are related to the accounts presented in this chapter, additional investigation based on dynamic resistance must be included when addressing issues of battered Black women specifically. Family dynamics within Black culture, as well as societal pressures outside the family unit, must be given considerable attention in any examination of battered Black women and their childhoods. This is concluded and proposed by Gail E. Wyatt and her colleagues, who have reported that "[f]ew studies have examined associations between domestic violence and exposure to current or past crimes and injustices in one's home or community. . . . [T]here is little empirical documentation of the types of early experiences that may better predict risks for domestic violence among African American women."[5]

Childhood Abuse

Twenty-three of the women in my study experienced a form of verbal, mental, nonsexual physical, or sexual abuse during childhood. Perpetrators of these methods of abuse included parents, stepparents, siblings, other relatives, and acquaintances. To better facilitate the analytic presentation of abuse during childhood, I have separated sexual abuse (9 women) from verbal, mental, or nonsexual physical abuse (20 women); the perpetrators of the latter were parents or stepparents,[6] whereas those who committed the sexual abuse had a greater variety of relationships to the women. These two categories will be discussed separately. Although the women shared stories of neglectful behaviors by those outside their close relations, such as schoolteachers, their most painful, abusive, and noteworthy accounts involved the people they most trusted, who eroded that trust by employing abusive behaviors. This is not to devalue the effect of community- and societal-level violations but serves to place the focus here on interpersonal violation. Accordingly, the abuse addressed here is that committed by parents, other relatives, and family friends.

Verbal and mental abuse of children refers to abuse that degrades, insults, and humiliates for the purpose of denigrating a child's self-worth and for which the intention is not to offer constructive criticism. There is a view, based on widely held perceptions of Blacks, that Black children suffer from greater rates of parental abuse than other children. Although this is reported in a substantial amount of research,[7] other inquiries question the accuracy of these depictions. As with most if not all deviant acts, it is difficult to measure the frequency of child abuse, particularly with regard to racial and ethnic differences. Kathleen Malley-Morrison and Denise A. Hines surmise that the difficulty in measuring the amount and rate of child maltreatment within Black families arises because there has been overreporting of abusive incidents within these families due in part to overreporting by medical personnel. Malley-Morrison and Hines question whether in fact a higher proportion of Black parents do abuse their children.[8] A recent analysis by Blanca M. Ramos and her associates found that Black and White women have similar rates of childhood physical abuse.[9] These contradictory data surprise some researchers, as is evident in the work of Richard J. Gelles and Murray A. Straus:

One of the more surprising outcomes of our first national survey of family violence was that there was no difference between blacks and whites in the rates of abusive violence toward children. This should not have been the case. First, most official reports of child abuse indicate that blacks are overrepresented in the reports. Also, blacks in the United States have higher rates of unemployment than whites and lower annual incomes— two factors that we know lead to higher risk of abuse. That blacks and whites had the same rate of abusive violence was one of the great mysteries of the survey. A careful examination of the data collected unraveled the apparent mystery. While blacks did indeed encounter economic problems and life stresses at greater rates than whites, they also were more involved in family and community activities than white families. Blacks reported more contact with their relatives and more use of their relatives for financial support and child care. It was apparent that the extensive social networks that black families develop and maintain insulate them from the severe economic stresses they also experience, and thus reduce what otherwise would have been a higher rate of parental violence.[10]

There was variation based on socioeconomic status during childhood among the 20 women who experienced verbal, mental, or nonsexual physical abuse by parents and stepparents. Almost two-thirds of the middle-class women endured this type of child maltreatment, while fewer than half of the women within each of the other two socioeconomic classifications (low-income and working-class) did. Nine women experienced verbal or mental *and* physical abuse, but there was no major variation by socioeconomic class among these women, and within this group each socioeconomic class was equally represented. Nine women were subjected to verbal or mental abuse but no physical abuse, and two women experienced only physical abuse but reported no verbal or mental abuse.

Much of the explanation provided by the women to explain why their parents abused them was expressed in terms of socioeconomic status, race, gender, or substance abuse issues. Regarding socioeconomic class, the source of the abuse was attributable to financially unsupportive fathers, the need to acquire and retain assets, and the preservation of the family's general financial interests. The women identified the uneasy feelings experienced by mothers or othermothers who were stressed by financially neglectful fathers and who took their frustrations out on the children. The second area of economic stressors experienced by some of the women's parents that acted as triggers for verbal, mental, or physical abuse was the maintenance of material goods for appearances ("keeping up with the Joneses"). Related to this were the pressures or failures of the parents or their children to become accomplished members of society as evidenced through education and employment. Such pressures were described as catalysts for abuse.[11] Keeping up appearances as a source of tension for the women's parents was evident in all levels of socioeconomic status. Medea described the neglect by her father and stepmother, which took place in their upper-middle-class setting and was based on upper-class measures:

> Their lives revolved around clothes, a big house, cars, that kind of thing. But there was an absence of affection. . . . He never really wanted to spend money on me unless there was instantaneous credit in it for him. For example, when I was a debutante, I remember him saying, "Smile, that looks like a $500 dress." Whenever I accomplished or I achieved anything, it became his accomplishment. He never complimented me. He always criticized me. Nothing I did was ever good enough.

The final theme concerning socioeconomic class as grounds for abuse is the general pressure on the parents to maintain the household finances. Forty-three-year-old Danielle suffered from extreme verbal and mental abuse by her single mother, who used an assortment of techniques to maintain her economic well-being, which included forcing Danielle to leave the family home at the age of 11:

> She hated me. She wished I wasn't born and she used to beat me all the time. . . . I got pregnant when I was 13 and had my baby when I was 14. [My mother] made me move back in when I was pregnant, and after I had my baby she put me back out and took my baby away. It hurt me. She put me out of her house again and told me I couldn't take my baby. . . . It was just so she could get more money from the welfare. It wasn't out of no care and concern. But she grew to love my kids. My grandmother told me [that my mother] gave my kids the love that she couldn't give me.

Billie was pushed by her single mother to secure and maintain employment simply to support her mother's gambling addiction. Similarly, when 33-year-old Victoria's grandmother died, she left several thousands of dollars to each of several family members, including Victoria and her mother. Regrettably, as Victoria and her mother struggled financially and her mother's drug addiction progressed, Victoria's mother used both her and Victoria's inheritance, chiefly for her drug dependency.

Another apparent basis for abuse, particularly verbal abuse, toward a few women was related to racial issues and the hierarchy of skin color among Blacks. Frequently, within the Black family, the Black community, and society in general, Blacks who have lighter skin tones—that is, skin tones closer to those of Whites—are treated with favoritism in many realms of their lives.[12] Bell hooks even argues that "when a child of two black parents is coming out of the womb the factor that is considered first is skin color, then gender, because race and gender will determine that child's fate."[13] Often, dark-skinned Black women face more scrutiny than dark-skinned Black men because of the beauty standards imposed on women, where the idolized measurement in the United States is the White woman.[14] Some of the women in my study were treated better or worse than others in their families because of their skin color, but the focus here is on the women who were *negatively* scrutinized because of their skin tone. Billie surmised that her mother's selective maltreatment of Billie and her siblings was based on skin color:

> She was hard on all of us, especially my sister Sybil. She beat her more than any of us, and I don't know why. My sister Vienna, she treated her like she was a beauty queen, but the rest of us got the crap beat out of us. Anything my sister Vienna wanted, she got. But we had to work to get what we wanted. . . . It just seems like the light-skinned kids, she treats them good.

Medea's experience with the complex issue of Blacks and skin tone was an even more peculiar circumstance within this theme:

> I was told I was ugly, I was everything bad. . . . Skin color was a part of it. My grandmother . . . was half-White. Her father was White. From her pictures, we look exactly the same, except she had blond hair and blue eyes and was very fair. . . . I'm fairer than all of them [other family members], but I was told I was dark because I didn't have [Grandmother's] skin color. That seems weird; but you know, Black people and oppression.

All but one of the 11 women who were subjected to abuse and whose families of origin were headed by two parents suffered their abuse primarily from their fathers (either biological or step). And all but one of the nine women who were abused by parents and who were cared for mainly by their mothers or othermothers were abused by their mothers only, which is not surprising since these women had minimal contact with their fathers. Within the four mother-daughter sets, none of the mothers appeared to abuse the daughters.[15] The women raised in the two-parent homes recounted tales of their mothers relinquishing the discipline of the children to the fathers or stepfathers. The mothers in these families seemed to perpetuate and take on the traditional female role of nurturer, while allowing the fathers or stepfathers to reign over keeping the house in order in an oppressive manner. Jacqueline, who was raised in a middle-class home, conveyed that her mother was never a disciplinarian, so when her mother remarried, Jacqueline recalled of her stepfather: "This man took over." Unfortunately, Jacqueline's stepfather's "discipline" was physically abusive. Fifty-year-old Queen, who was raised in a middle-class White rural neighborhood, also described how her mother relinquished the task of punishment to Queen's father:

> My dad, the discipline was very—if you look at it today, it was abuse. We used to get hit. He'd hold us upside-down and hit us with extension cords, stuff like that. You didn't know it was abuse then. The way we lived, the good things outweighed that type of thing. When you think about it, there were nights where there would be fear. If we did something wrong, my mom would say, "Wait till your dad gets home." . . . So you're up with such fear until he gets home, and then he comes down the stairs and, boy, there it is.

Many of the women who were verbally, mentally, or physically abused or neglected by a parent mentioned their parent's alcohol or drug use as a source for abuse. Twenty-four-year-old Phoebe and her eight siblings were raised in a working-class home with both biological parents. She stated that her parents were so "dazed" most of the time that "they didn't even know if I went to school or not. They didn't check, they didn't care if I was eating. We didn't eat half the time because my parents just spent a lot of money on pharmaceutical drugs. So half the time we would starve." Although the women said that incidences of alcohol and drug use often triggered the parents' abusive behaviors, they were often quick to identify the abusers as good financial providers for the family. This is evident in the experience recounted by Jade, who lived in a middle-class childhood home: "My father used to guzzle a whole gallon of vodka on the way to work and we'd have to cover up for him. He always worked. He was an excellent provider. But mean and cussing and staying out all the time." Queen echoed this sentiment by saying, "My dad was an alcoholic. I didn't know he was an alcoholic because we had everything." As demonstrated to this point in the examination, the common factors precipitating verbal, mental, or nonsexual physical abuse by parents on the women clearly incorporated both social structural and cultural aspects of the parents' lives, and these stressors were evident at some level to the women.

Nine of the women in my study divulged that they had been sexually abused during their childhoods. These women did not have experiences significantly different from those recounted by sexually abused women of other races and ethnicities.[16] Like those who had suffered verbal, mental, or non-sexual physical abuse, these women represented the three levels of socioeconomic status, but the group that reported the higher prevalence of sexual abuse was the low-income group. None of the perpetrators were strangers to the women, which is in keeping with previous research showing that individuals who are sexually abused, particularly Blacks, are often violated by someone they know.[17] The abusers included family members (father, brother, or uncle), family friends, and acquaintances (romantic interest or date). All but one of the abusers were male.[18]

Most of the women who were sexually abused as children kept their abuse hidden from others until they confided in someone during adulthood. In some cases they had suppressed their memory of the abuse. This was the circumstance for 43-year-old Tammy, who blocked her recollection of the assault that occurred by a female babysitter when she was approximately seven years old:

> They say [if] you have problems in your life, sometimes you just lock them out. I do remember now that I was sexually abused as a child. That came out. You know, doors open. . . . All of a sudden these doors started opening up, and the more you open up the doors that you have locked, the more you open yourself up and the better you can become by letting these things go. . . . I can see how a person can develop different personalities from abuse and different things.

Those who did disclose the abuse carried out against them near the time of occurrence were virtually ignored or were not taken seriously. When a few women divulged their abuse to family members or friends, their revelations were disregarded. This was the case for Bev, a 51-year-old who was raised in an unstable, low-income environment in which she repeatedly moved between the homes of her mother and her grandmother. When Bev was raped, she told her mother of the assault but believed that her mother was being paid to allow the assailant to have sex with (rape) Bev:

> I got raped at an early age [by] one of my mother's men. I couldn't understand it 'cause she kept going with him. . . . I don't know if it was for the money or what. . . . He spent a lot of money on her. . . . The next thing I know, my grandmother got wind of it and I started staying with her on the weekends. I held a grudge for a lot of years. Sometimes I have flashbacks. But then I started talking with God and left it up to him and it don't hurt nearly as bad.

Fortunately for Bev, she did have an othermother (her grandmother) there to rescue her.

The sexual abuse of the women resulted in self-blame, confusion about the roles of women and men in healthy relationships, distrust of all men, depression, poor self-esteem, body hatred, and self-destructive behaviors, such as alcohol and drug abuse.[19] Queen equated sex with power, and her flawed assessment affected her negatively when she became sexually active after her abuse. Queen believed that the only value she could bring to a relationship was sex:

> I just wanted him to want me. I didn't care. It was about me in control. Me getting control. Making him want me. Wanting you to want me and not caring. I didn't care about you. I just want you to want to be with me. I just want to have sex. That's what I learned, what I knew, what I was conditioned for. If nothing else, I could do that. That's my calling.

Witnessing Parents' Intimate Partner Abuse

Half of the women reported that they witnessed intimate partner abuse among their parents. For those women who witnessed intimate partner abuse in their families of origin, I specifically consider abuse among biological parents, stepparents, and grandparents. Grandparents are considered because of the significance of extended family within the Black community.[20] The women raised in low-income households were overrepresented in this grouping. Two-thirds of the low-income women experienced this form of exposure to abuse, while fewer than half of the middle-class group and a third of the working-class group witnessed abuse between parents. Although the number of women who experienced child abuse is comparable to the number who witnessed their parents' intimate partner abuse, previous research has shown that being exposed to abuse between parents is the most influential dynamic associated with children's involvement in abusive relationships as adults.[21] The women's experiences of being a part of their parents' unhealthy conflict left unforgettable impressions on them.

The level of exposure to parents' intimate abuse varied among the women. Angie was raised in a household where her mother was the main caretaker and there were intermittent father figures. Angie knew of her mother's abuse, even though her mother attempted to hide it from Angie and her siblings: "She was hoping maybe we didn't know. It wasn't like she was getting beat down right in front of us. We might be in the bed, or they was at a party and he'd drag her home. It was always behind closed doors. She just picked herself up and dust herself off. Kept it to herself, as well." In contrast, most of the women who were aware of their parents' abuse toward each other observed the incidents in an open environment. For instance, Isis spoke of her stepfather's abusive behaviors toward her mother, Doreen, who was also a study participant. These behaviors included "name-calling, hitting, a lot of really just mean things. He would berate her in front of anyone, in front of her friends, in front of my friends." Like Angie and Isis, Toni was also raised in a low-income home. The 44-year-old reflected on one of her stepfather's uninhibited and unreserved acts of maltreatment toward her mother:

My mom was in the bathtub. . . . She had closed the door. My sister and I was in another room. The next thing, the door was being bashed in. That was my stepdad going into the bathroom. He was trying to drown her. I remember her screaming and everything. . . . The police came and took him off. I can't really remember if they arrested him. I just know that night he came back, because my sister and I were in the bed and he broke through our bedroom window and came through there and I remember the blood on the window.

While most of the women who had these experiences reported recurring abuse, a couple of women recalled a single physically violent episode between their parents. Helene, raised in a two-biological-parent, middle-class home, stated, "I never one time seen my father hit my mother. I seen him put her on the ground one time, but just lay her down. But he's never, ever hit her." Twenty-six-year-old Erica, also brought up by both biological parents but raised in low-income circumstances, recalled one incident of abuse by her father and perpetrated against her mother. Even though she concluded that there was love between her parents, the incident left a memorable impact on Erica: "I think I saw him sock her one time. They were arguing over us. I was really young. We were yelling at him, 'Don't touch my mom!' He apologized to all of us. He never touched her again, but they argued a few times. They always got along, they always loved each other." Although Helene and Erica witnessed isolated incidents , the confrontations had a profound effect on them and influenced how they framed their relationships in their adult lives.

As will be demonstrated in Chapter 6, many of the women regularly made efforts to physically retaliate against their batterers. A precursor of this behavior can be connected to their mothers' responses to being battered or to life in general. Wendy articulated her mother's reactions to Wendy's father's and stepfather's abuse: "Reason why my mom left my father, because he was very abusive. Both of my fathers were very abusive to her. I remember as a child that they used to fight a lot. My mom was a little, short woman. . . . But she was very spunky, she didn't take anything from anybody." Likewise, Helene described her mother as "a fighter. . . . She was a tough little toothpick," and Olivia described how her mother and grandmother combated any impending physical abuse from their husbands: "My mother, she's feisty. She didn't go for it. My grandmother didn't, either. My grandfather knew not to mess with my grandmother. He used to holler, scream at her when she didn't do things, [she'd] jump at a moment's notice, but he didn't mess with her too much."

Queen and Billie shared stories of each of their mothers throwing scalding hot water on their abusive fathers. However, these were not instantaneous reactions by their mothers to the abuse perpetrated by their fathers but calculated replies to previous assaults.[22]

Several of the women took on a caretaking role by making attempts to protect their mothers, including during the violent incidents. The women tended to intervene in relationships involving boyfriends, rather than fathers or stepfathers. Keisha, the oldest of four children, was raised mainly by her mother, Leah, who had a few male intimate partners (a couple were abusive) who lived on and off with their family. These men were not permanently situated in the home, and Keisha felt it was her duty to intervene to protect the family. Keisha shared how she intervened when her mother was in the relationship with her second and most recent batterer:

> I tried to be the protector of my brothers and my mom and he really didn't like that. I clashed more with him more than any of my other mom's boyfriends. . . . It's something I just fell into because I would see the way guys would treat my mom. . . . I just tried to be the protector of everything because I thought that was like my job. Because no one knows my mom and my brothers like me.

Toni described one of the occasions when she intervened as her mother was being attacked by her boyfriend: "I know one time he had jumped on her. My sister and I were always trying to get in there. He had pushed me and I fell over onto a glass coffee table and got cut on my shin. . . . We might get hit but we were just in the way because we were trying to help our mom." Toni was also grazed by a bullet when her mother's boyfriend shot at the house she and her mother were staying in. It was then that Toni decided that she did not wish to continue to have the stress of protecting her mother in that manner. She shared, "I almost lost my life because of it. That really scared me. I didn't want to live with my mom anymore, so my sister and I started living with my grandmother and attending school out in that area."

Gloria, who was reared in a working-class home, tried to enlist her two brothers in assisting her with protecting her mother from her violent boyfriend, Jerry:

> Jerry whipped her with a belt like she was a child. She had so many welts and indentions from the back of her knees all the way up from where he had hit her with the belt. My brothers didn't do nothing. I had a knife, and I was going to go out there and stop him. I couldn't do it. I was trying to get my brothers to come and help, they went in their rooms and shut the door.

Gloria's frustration with her brothers and her mother's batterer were instrumental in her forming two negative beliefs about men: she saw them as either instigators of trouble or unwilling participants in family problems and daily life. This outcome is observable in the lives and views of many of the women interviewed, whose experiences helped develop their opinions about men in general, and Black men in particular. Keisha made a concerted effort to *not* date Black boys or men because of her mother's treatment by Black men. However, Keisha realized firsthand that simply shunning Black men was not enough to shield her from becoming a re-sister to intimate partner abuse.

Some of the women also intervened in their parents' abusive relation-ships by attempting to convince their mothers that the relationships were harmful. Keisha revealed that she tried to talk to her mother about how troublesome her mother's boyfriend was, but the traditional mother-daughter relationship was one of the factors that interfered with Leah's ability to heed Keisha's advice:

> She really didn't see what everybody else saw about him. With that, me and my mom really clashed and really didn't get along when they were to-gether. She'll do something, and I'd be telling my mom, "That's not right. What kind of role model are you setting for me?" Me and her would just clash about everything, because I should be a daughter and I should stay in my daughterly place.

A few of the mothers used their daughters as protection, particularly if the mothers believed or knew the batterers would not harm the children in the home. Gloria's mother used her as a shield for defense against her mother's abuser:

> I heard my mother screaming and yelling. She came in my room. She grabbed me. She was shaking really, really bad. She stuck me in front of her. . . . He looked, and he turned around and walked out the door. She climbed out of my window . . . and ran up the street. He came back in with her gun and was going to shoot her.

Although using Gloria as a shield protected her mother for the mo-ment, it failed to prevent the batterer from continuing his assaultive be-havior and left Gloria dealing with trauma and her mother placing her in direct danger by using her as a buffer.

Predictably, the women suffered both immediate and enduring effects as a result of witnessing intimate partner abuse between their parents dur-ing childhood. Most of the women were able to contemplate the damaging effects of witnessing such abuse only as they progressed through adult-hood, but Rebecca, who was reared by both biological parents on military bases, recalled how she felt as a youth in her abusive household: "I often found myself in a shell, 'cause I didn't have a very high self-esteem level because of what I had seen. I was always sheltered from everything else; street life, the reality of everyday life I was protected from, but within my own home I felt like I was entrapped in another world."

Seeing their mothers being verbally, mentally, or physically abused by the women's fathers and stepfathers or by the mothers' boyfriends frequently left the women with mixed messages. There was resistance to the utility of the abuse, even when their mothers were fighting back or the first to strike. Because their mothers remained in the relationships, returned to batterers after leaving them, or continuously found themselves in battering relationships (even when the mothers succeeded in permanently removing themselves from the abusive situations), the women were left with confusion about what is healthy in intimate relationships. Gloria represented many of the women who had witnessed the abuse of their mothers when she described her feelings about one of her mother's boyfriends: "He was just a horrible person. He cheated on her, he beat on her. He and I didn't get along. I didn't like him, so maybe that's why he didn't like me. But I hated him." These sorts of feelings were easier to express when the women were referring to their mothers' boyfriends, as opposed to their fathers, due to the lack of loyalty to the short-term relationships.

As a result of the confusion produced by witnessing their mothers' abuse, the women also expressed ambivalent feelings about the male batterers because of the alternating routine of loving and fighting in the relationships. For instance, Renee, a 45-year-old raised in a suburban middle-class environment, communicated her bewilderment about her parents' behavior after their fights:

> I saw a lot of things. My parents fought, physically. So I grew up seeing him whack her and her whack him when he got really drunk. I also would take up for her. I would jump on him and try to bring him down. Then I would run out in the streets and stay out all night long. . . . I come back home and if they had made up, [they were] screwing and my sisters and brothers watching cartoons and I was made to think that I was the one out of place. So I learned distortion, how to distort reality, at an early age.

Regarding the enduring effects of witnessing her parents' abuse, Rebecca spoke of her uncertainty about healthy relationships: "When you grow up with violence as a child, you don't really understand the dynamic of relationships because you didn't see any healthy ones. But as you get older and you understand the dynamics of what you want in a partner, you've got to be careful. You need to understand the definition of a healthy relationship." Toni echoed Rebecca's outlook:

> I can't remember any of my elementary teachers' names. I can't remember any classmates. I can't remember having any fun. We were always having to go here, go to my grandmother, over to this man's house, over to that man's house. I was wondering if it affected me when I grew up, and I think it did, because of my own unhealthy relationships.

Clearly, each of the women discussed here experienced deficient and sometimes very violent and abusive models of intimate relationships. Granted, other women have been exposed to the same detrimental encounters and have not entered into abusive intimate relationships later in life. But my goal to this point was to complement the research on women who *did* witness violent parental strife and ultimately became resisters to abuse themselves and to demonstrate the additive effect on the women's eventual dynamic resistance in their own lives. Their accounts describe experiences similar to those of battered women across cultures, but I also identified some distinct cultural aspects among battered Black women. In particular, the balance between gender and race regarding Black women is established in how the women were able to view their mothers as Strong Black Women, even though they endured abuse, because of the mothers' efforts at fighting back and their strenuous attempts to keep the families intact. One caveat regarding the issue of how socioeconomic status affects the exposure of the women to their parents' intimate partner abuse is that this form of abuse may be more concealed and less evident to children in middle-class and upper-class families. This aspect is supported in Chapter 5, where I demonstrate the relationship between class and when and where the abusive men committed their abuse and violent acts.

Witnessing Other Acts of Abuse and Violence

Several of the women were also exposed to other forms of violent behavior and its consequences through the experiences of some of their family members. These included brothers who were involved in neighborhood and gun violence and were frequently sent to jail or prison and some of the women's sisters who were abused by intimate partners.

Two women were directly exposed to a sibling's intimate partner abuse during childhood, and several of the women's siblings ultimately were engaged in abusive relationships as adults. In many cases, the women's brothers became perpetrators of partner abuse, while their sisters became resisters of intimate partner abuse. Billie and 43-year-old Grace each witnessed an older sister's abuse when they spent significant time with their sisters during their youth. Billie had direct exposure to violence and abuse at her sister's home. Billie's sister's boyfriend was physically assaultive toward Billie's sister and possibly sexually abusive to the sister's son. Billie had already been exposed to child abuse by her mother and her mother's episodes with intimate partner abuse, but this did not lead her to accept family violence as inevitable. To the contrary, she anticipated that she would avoid abusive relationships in spite of what she had undergone in her mother's and sister's homes:

After I [left] high school I couldn't stand being around my mom any more, so I went to live with my sister. That's when I found out how bad [my sister's boyfriend] was jumping on my sister. I didn't know he was that crazy. He always seemed like a good guy. . . . He would do things to [my nephew] Brian, I remember. He used to pull Brian's pants down. I don't think he ever really fondled him, but I would think, "He's not supposed to be doing that, that's not playing." I couldn't understand why she didn't put this man out of her house. I mean, he's messing with your son, not your daughter, your son. She wouldn't put him out. When I went to live with them, that's when I found out he was abusing her very badly. I mean, he jumped on her like she was a man. She would try to fight back. I would jump in. I would get beat up, she would get beat up. After it was over he'd leave and we'd sit there and drink, get drunk and cry and clean up each other's wounds. Every time he'd jump on my sister I felt like, "I have to do something. I can't just stand here and I know what's going on." So I got abused by him, too, because of my sister. . . . He wouldn't let us call the police or anything like that. My sister, she was kind of scared to do it anyway. She was like, "He'll beat me more if I call the police." I think she called the police on him one time and he went to jail for four or five days. When he got out he really beat her. A couple of days he tried to act like, "I'm gonna straighten up, I'm gonna do right." Once he'd drink . . . [his favorite] whiskey, that was the end of that. He would drink that all the time. That was his drink. He'd beat the crap out of my sister. I would just cry. I'd say, "I'm never going to let anybody do that to me."

Grace had a similar experience with her sister's abusive relationship: "I got to witness it firsthand, and I was part of some of it." Grace was raised in a two-parent working-class home with both biological parents present. Witnessing her sister's abuse was her only significant exposure to violence, and she could not comprehend how it happened that she and her sister each entered into abusive relationships: "You would think it would be, 'I see my mom abused, and my mom seen her mom abused' kind of a thing. But it's not like that."

Some of the women also saw family members engaged in other forms of violent acts. These were typically male members of the family, such as fathers, brothers, uncles, and cousins. Once again, only those occasions where the women's family members were engaged in this behavior during the women's *childhoods* are considered. Phoebe's brothers were affiliated with violent gangs, and she eventually ran away from home to escape the resulting chaos, as her parents appeared unaware of how her brothers' actions consumed and affected Phoebe:

> All my brothers were in trouble from very young ages. . . . They were in and out of . . . juvenile detention facilities and group homes. . . . My brothers went on the street, they had older friends that influenced them to do bad things. . . . It really hurt my mom to see her sons in jail. She couldn't do anything about it, because my dad was a retired veteran and they didn't have a whole lot of income, so they couldn't afford lawyers that really could represent my brothers that could probably have saved them from half the time that they spent in jail. So, the younger ones, we were just kind of left hanging while my parents were being destroyed by this, by my brothers being in jail. I wouldn't say that we were neglected, but we weren't really paid a whole lot of attention to. . . . [My brothers] would come home and bring all these friends of theirs and drink and have parties. My parents never said anything. They never did anything about it. . . . It was crazy. It was just a madhouse. A couple of times the house got shot at. One time my brother had somebody following him and they shot him. It was horrible. I was getting away from all that.

A couple of women suffered from the violent deaths of siblings. Forty-three-year-old Inez reported that her "sister's boyfriend blew her head off, and my little brother, somebody blew his head off." Cicely's brother was killed while he and a friend played with a gun in the basement of the family home.

Women in the low-income bracket were more likely to experience these forms of indirect violence, and those in the middle-class income range were least likely to experience this type. In part, this is connected to the standard of living provided by the parents. Those families with low incomes often lived in government-subsidized housing in urban areas, where violence is more often displayed on the streets, more easily detected, and more easily spread. Undeniably, these women endured significant trauma during their youthful lives as a result of their siblings' involvement in gun and gang-related violence. However, because this form of violence typically involved matters and individuals outside the family entity, and because fewer women were exposed to this type of violence, it is not considered to have a strong effect on entry into abusive relationships for the women in this study.

Destructive Behaviors During Childhood

Some of the women exhibited destructive or self-destructive conduct as youth. I classify this as a form of early introduction to interpersonal abuse because the women began to develop certain harmful strategies at a young age. These tactics involved inflicting their anger on others in a physical manner or turning their anger inward, on themselves. The women who were *fighters* as girls personally learned the benefits, albeit injurious benefits, of using physical aggression to change a situation in order to protect themselves. Cicely, who was taught to fight by her uncles, found that it did not take too many battles to establish a reputation as a fighter:

> Girls used to always want to fight me. In the ninth grade, girls used to pick on me about talkin' country. . . . After I dusted a couple of girls for messing with me, they left me alone. I didn't need a lot of fights. When I got to high school, they didn't like me. They stayed away. After I dusted a couple of guys . . . they all wanted to be my friend.

Kim, a 45-year-old reared by both biological parents in a working-class setting, also described herself as a fighter: "There was a lot of boys in the neighborhood. I was a tomboy girl and I used to fight them all the time, me and my sisters." And Gloria had a similar experience: "I grew up with guys. I was tough and wrestled. They couldn't outwrestle me as much as they tried to." Forty-five-year-old Doreen found it remarkable that she was in abusive intimate relationships during adulthood, as opposed to her sisters, because she often defended them when she and they were youths: "I'm just surprised. I was their protector and I'm the one who got into that kind of situation. I don't understand that myself. Look like they would have been in one before I was."

As is detailed in Chapter 6, most of the women retaliated against their batterers at some time during the relationship. Being fighters as girls was one factor that made it less difficult for many of these women to respond in kind to being assaulted by intimates. Gloria was the only girl fighter who did not physically retaliate against her batterer, but she "felt stupid" and could not understand why she failed to fight her abuser because she knew she "could handle him" because of her experiences fighting boys as a youth.

Several of the women began directing their anger and discontent for their childhood trauma toward themselves. This included using and abusing alcohol and other drugs, engaging in unsafe and premature sexual behavior, and overeating. Isis reflected that as a result of being denied the attention she desired and needed from her mother, Doreen, who was unable to provide the attention because of drug use and abuse from Isis's stepfather, she began to act out sexually:

> I started to use sex as an outlet for when I got mad. That's what I would be using to pacify myself. I started having sex. Before I had my daughter, I'd had an abortion the year before. That was the first time I had been pregnant. I was 13. I had to have an abortion. I was really out there. You talk about the fast girls; I was one of the fast girls. It's something I hate to admit to myself. But I was. I was on a one-way ticket to nowhere with some of the things I was involved in at that time. . . . It's a wonder I didn't come up raped or dead or anything like that. I would sometimes stay out till two in the morning. Half the time my mom was so wrapped up with what my stepfather was putting her through, it was almost like with her sometimes, "Out of sight, out of mind." She didn't focus in on me until I was right there in front of her. I would start to internalize that stuff, "I don't mean anything in this house any more. My grandmother's gone. My aunts had moved out. . . . My granddad's ill. Who cares what I do?" That was the way I thought most of the time.

Max, a 38-year-old who grew up in a working-class home, described her mother as "a mean alcoholic" who was verbally and physically abusive. Max continued to struggle with her own alcohol abuse, which began when she was very young:

My mom used to drink real heavy. So I started drinking when I was eight years old. . . . I've always been with grown-ups. I was the only child. When company would come over, it would be like, "Go over there and pour this much vodka and this much grapefruit juice." So I started fixing the drinks, and after a while you're going to be curious. . . . I started tasting it. Pretty soon I fixed me one while I was fixing them, and I just started drinking. . . . I used to take it to school. From elementary until about my tenth grade year in high school. I can't understand why the teachers didn't smell it.

As a result of her mother's neglect and abuse, Victoria also showed self-destructive behavior:

She would get mad and hit me and I'd cry and make it worse. There was a time when I started hitting myself on the nose. She'd be like, "What's with your nose? I didn't even hit you in the nose." I think I was trying to get attention, make the situation worser. I used to have bloody noses all the time. I would make it bleed so people would feel sorry for me. I was lost for a time. I didn't have nobody.

At a young age, the women who sought out affection and ways to ease their pain formed distorted practices for doing so. I conclude that these imprudent behaviors carried over into adulthood and facilitated the women getting involved in abusive relationships in which they believed they deserved to be abused or took the abuse as long as there was some semblance of affection and love, even if intermittent, by the batterer. These self-destructive behaviors forced the women to resist *themselves* as their own oppressors. This form of resistance continued to require great efforts on the part of these women.

Escaping the Abusive Home

Many of the women felt that the best way to protect themselves from further abuse or to escape the chaos of battering between parents was to leave their home of origin. A number of them repeatedly ran away from their homes. This was Olivia's experience. She stated, "I did well in school, but with all the fighting and the bickering, and everything, I ran away." Olivia and the other runaways usually ran to another relative's home, such as a grandmother's, but Phoebe had a distinctive experience: "I would just hang out on the 16th Street Mall where the rest of the homeless kids were. Just hang out, stay awake for most of the night, and go about my business the next day."

Many of the women left home permanently and had their first child at an early age. Some of these women were told to leave the home, while others were not given "permission" to leave without taking on "adult" responsibilities, such as getting married. Inez, who did not complete high school and was brought up in a low-income household with 13 siblings, left home at the age of 16. Aside from the violence she witnessed, Inez had to care for her seven younger siblings. She shared, "I was tired of it and wanted to get away. My mom said the only way to get away was to get a husband. So I got a husband. He was very abusive to me." Grace demonstrated the pressure to be married that is often communicated within families regardless of whether there is family dysfunction: "In our family it was, if you don't get married by the time you're 25, you're an old maid. They really made a big deal out of that." In fact, it was these decisions and wanting to attempt to seek and make that "perfect family" that pushed some of the women into their first abusive intimate relationship. Queen summarized what many of these women felt and experienced: "I fell in love at first sight. I thought I was going to be rescued."

Lack of Introduction to Violence or Abuse and Special Treatment in Families of Origin

From many of the recollections presented, it is evident that a number of the women did not receive gratifying special treatment within their homes of origin. Indeed, more than three-quarters of the women did not receive special treatment from their parents or guardians, whether in comparison with other children in the home or in terms of general standards of caring for children. Special treatment involved being "spoiled" by caretakers by being offered special liberties, including receiving more approval or less punishment than other children in the family for similar behaviors. Cicely described her situation in her house of origin by relaying, "I was spoiled, being the first, the only girl."

Of the seven women who received special treatment in their homes of origin, six were the middle or youngest child in the family. (Only five of the 40 women were the youngest child in their immediate families, and three of the five fit within the special-treatment category.) Five of the seven women who received special treatment were raised in two-parent homes. Of all the women I interviewed, four of the women raised in the middle-class homes received special treatment, while two of the working-class women and one of the low-income women received special treatment. It appears that special treatment was aligned with socioeconomic class. It is quite possible that parents in more economically distressed homes were unable to dote on their children because of the multiple commitments of an unpartnered parent and/or the tension produced by the need to maintain financial stability.

Of the women who received special treatment, only two were exposed to at least one form of violence during their upbringings; however, neither was the directed targets of violence. Cicely was one of these women; she was taught by her uncles to fight and experienced her brother's tragic death. The other was Wendy, who witnessed the abuse of her mother by both Wendy's father and her stepfather. Of the seven of the 40 women who did not endure any significant incidences of violence or abuse during childhood, 4 received special treatment.

My conclusion that few of the women in my study received special treatment in their homes of origin differs from Beth E. Richie's analysis in which she found that the battered Black women in her study, but not the nonbattered Black women and the battered White women, were in "privileged positions" in their childhood homes. Her definition of this favored status specifies that the battered Black women "received extra privileges, attention, and resources, indicating the families' emotional and material investment in these particular children to meet high standards of success."[23] The battered Black women in Richie's study "had high self-esteem and felt very powerful, and yet their identities were wrapped up in pleasuring others and accommodating the needs of others." This aspect of privileged status women "ultimately left them exposed and more vulnerable to harsh reality" than nonbattered women.[24] The situations of the seven women in my study who received special treatment align with Richie's explanation for battered Black women's preservation in abusive relationships, but not with the remainder (that is, the majority) of the women. To explain the majority of my informants who did *not* receive special treatment in their homes of origin and later entered into abusive relationships, I look to their self-identity. In the previous chapter, I addressed how the women overwhelmingly considered themselves to be strong women or strong *Black* women. I concluded that the detriment of taking on the Strong Black Woman role at an early age (to which they were exposed by their mothers and othermothers) predisposed the majority of the women to

maintain their abusive relationships. Among the seven women who received special treatment, *all but one* had mothers who *did not* exhibit the
characteristics of the Strong Black Woman as the women were growing
up. For instance, Naomi described her mother as "very, very meek. I got
a little bit of it somehow. I took a lot of that into my marriage." I establish that the women in my study who did not receive special treatment
learned at a young age to endure a great deal of hardship and learned that
special treatment from others is not certain, which, interestingly, agrees
with Richie's finding about her comparison group of *non*-battered Black
women. Conceivably, the differences in analysis between my study and
Richie's may rest on the sample. The battered Black women in Richie's
study were all low-income or working class and were being detained in
jail for offenses directly and indirectly related to their batterers. However,
this does not thoroughly explain the deviation, because a few women in
my investigation were jailed as a result of having retaliated against their
abusers or for other offenses, but each of these women still did not have
special statuses in their families of origin as did the battered Black women
in Richie's investigation. It appears that there is some connection between
special treatment by family of origin and participation in future abusive
intimate relationships, and this field of study would benefit from further
investigation.

Two suppositions based on my look into the women's lives can be formulated about Black women who do not enter into or maintain abusive
relationships. First, it might be hypothesized that Black women who received special treatment *and* had Strong Black Mothers as role models are
less likely to be engaged in abusive intimate relationships because they are
accustomed to being treated by others favorably *and* their mothers taught
them that women have the strength to not accept mistreatment in relationships; this attitude is conveyed to potential batterers, who may avoid
attempting to establish relationships with these women because of these
characteristics. Second, it can be theorized, for Black women who were
not treated as special in their childhood households *but* who had Strong
Black Women role models, that perhaps other additive factors account for
their not being in or maintaining abusive relationships. These factors are
(a) not having witnessed intimate partner abuse among parents or parent figures, and (b) not having been physically, sexually, or emotionally
abused during their formative years. Clearly, each of these suppositions
is merely conjecture, and further research would have to be conducted to
determine the validity in these hypotheses.

Surviving Childhood

The title of this section is not intended to suggest that all the women had especially arduous childhoods to survive. Arguably, even the healthiest childhood for girls has to be "survived"; all girls must make it through the trials of puberty and confront the pressure to conform to gendered norms. And for Black girls, there may be the added pressure of maneuvering through a racially stratified and discriminatory society from which they cannot be shielded. Nevertheless, most of the women were exposed to some kind of violent or abusive behaviors during their upbringing. This contributes to the explanation for these women's entry into and preservation of abusive relationships and the development of their dynamic resistance. One question to consider in future research is this: If the abuses against the women had been better addressed during their childhoods, would the women have been able to avoid entering into and enduring abusive intimate partnerships during adulthood? For the seven women who did not have any apparent early experiences with interpersonal abuse, there are other factors that have been identified to explain how they came to be in and sustain abusive relationships, including unfamiliarity with how to deal with battering by a mate. Special treatment during childhood is a subject that certainly demands attention to strengthen our understanding of the association between childhood environment and adult intimate partner abuse.

I have identified many significant factors in my analysis of how the battered Black women in my study received their first exposure to abuse and violence. To begin with, I identified variations related to the class and gender of the women's primary caretakers. The largest representation within the three socioeconomic classes for verbal, mental, and nonsexual physical abuse was those women raised in middle-class homes, while women from lower-income households of origin made up a higher proportion of those in all other categories of introduction to interpersonal abuse. Mothers in single-parent, mother-headed households tended to inflict the verbal, mental, and nonsexual physical abuse on the daughters, while fathers tended to be the abusers in two-parent homes. Regardless of the structure of the parental unit, a good portion of the women witnessed their mothers' abuse by husbands or other male intimates, as well as their mothers' endeavors at physically striking back at their abusers. Another significant means of introduction to abuse was sexual abuse by known assailants. A less influential youthful initiation into violence appeared to be the violence the women witnessed elsewhere, such as within their immediate neighborhoods or greater communities. This is in no way to suggest that I fail to recognize the detrimental effects of state- and government-induced violence on Black women, because I assert that such transgressions affected each of these women's lives and the way they navigated in their abusive relationships and in U.S. society in general. The focus here was on abusive influences of the familial and the familiar, *but* these cannot easily be divorced from the societal pressures that are sources of much of the abuse that was meted out on the women. Further, I have highlighted such familiar abuses because it is what the women directly shared and spoke the most about. Black feminist criminology unavoidably provides a conduit through which the connection between societal sources of pressure and their effect on family and individual (dys)function can be exposed.

The effects of being abused in childhood, witnessing aggression among parents, and being confronted by social structural and cultural pressures typically faced by Black girls and women in the United States led to unhealthy outcomes for the women. The ultimate consequences for them included the development of a distorted or uninformed understanding of the functioning of interpersonal relationships and a tendency to engage in self-destructive and injurious behaviors during their youth and/or as adults.

5

Living Through It

"He Made Me Believe He Was Something He Wasn't"

After Billie quit high school and left her mother's home, she had dreams of returning to school to earn her diploma and romantic hopes of falling in love. However, it was not long after leaving her mother's home that she became pregnant with her first child and found it difficult to survive. She was living in a government-funded housing development and receiving government subsidies when she met her first husband. Billie's desire to be swept away from "the projects" by a man who was holding stable employment, "made a lot of money," and would be a father to her toddler, Nia, had her rushing into marriage. Billie recalled, "The wedding was beautiful. The marriage was a nightmare." The marriage was replete with sexual unfaithfulness and mental abuse on the part of Billie's husband. Her husband's behaviors were emotionally taxing: "I wanted to kill him. I was so hurt. I wanted to kill him. My child is the only thing that kept me from killing him. After that I felt like, ain't nobody ever gonna love me. Ain't nobody ever going to want me. For a long time I was by myself. I would do the three Fs: Find 'em, fuck 'em, and forget 'em. And that's the way it was and I was like that for a long time."

After a few more years of struggling financially, continually being in failed intimate relationships, dealing with low self-esteem, and anticipating the birth of her third child in a few months, Billie met Kobe, a man who would love and support her:

I told him that I was pregnant. He was like, "Are you? I don't mind. I could be the father." That just [melted] my heart. I was like, here's some great man wanting to be my baby's daddy. So me and him got together. I let him move in. . . . After I had [the baby], we brought the baby home, he went and got a job, started working. Our first car was a little blue Pinto.

But we had a car. He wanted me to move out of the low-income [government housing]. . . . I went and got Section 8[1] in [another city]. It took us a little while to get it, but we finally got it. It was just great.

Sadly, Billie's long-awaited relationship bliss was short-lived. Before they could move into their new home, Kobe exhibited his suppressed violent behaviors. The battering incident was preceded by Billie's confronting Kobe in a nightclub about his talking to a White woman. Billie poured liquor on Kobe and tried to hit him with the emptied bottle, after which they were both forced to leave the establishment. Billie describes what occurred upon the arrival at their home:

We got in the house. I went in the bathroom and started taking my clothes off to put my gown on to go to bed. I had kept telling him, "I'm sorry, I'm sorry, I just got upset because men have been going out with other women on me, and I'm sorry, I freaked out." I was in the bathroom. He came in the bathroom and punched the shit out of me. I have never been hit like that in my life. You know how in the cartoons where you see little Tweety Birds going around your head? Sort of like that. Where you see a flash of darkness and then the Tweety Birds. He was like, "Yeah, I'm'a teach you how to embarrass me in the club," and he just started beating the shit out of me. . . . He beat me only in my face. Nowhere else. Just my face. Not my arms, not my stomach, just my face. I kept saying, "I'm sorry, Kobe. I'm sorry." The more I said I'm sorry, the more he would beat me. I got loose from him by hittin' him in his privates. . . . I found out he broke my nose, he cracked my jaw. . . . He had knocked teeth out of my mouth. . . . Just to look at myself in the mirror. That hurt me so bad. And the way he did it. Most guys who are gonna beat the crap out of you, they'll be hollering at you, arguing with you. He was quiet the whole time. Coming home from the club, I thought [everything] was OK. He pulled a rope-a-dope on me.

After Kobe spent three days in jail for the assault, he and Billie resumed their relationship with no major episodes until approximately a year later; Billie never struck first, and Kobe always initiated the physical aggression in the relationship.

The Onset of Abuse

As with Billie, many of the other women in this study were propelled into abusive intimate relationships as a result of having left their abusive homes of origin prematurely and having landed in the initial comfort of their first abusers. Isis welcomed the attention she had not received from previous interactions with intimate male partners, while dealing with witnessing the abuse by her stepfather toward her mother, Doreen. In the initial stage of Isis's relationship with her first abusive partner, he demonstrated the preferred qualities and behaviors that many individuals desire in a mate:

> He took me places. He met my mom. He was always really respectful. He introduced me to his family. It was gradual. It was courting, in the traditional sense of the word. Once we got close enough together, he said, "You know, you don't have to live with your mom and your stepdad, you can live with me." His father was for it. So I moved in with him when I was 17, 18 years old.

Phoebe's experiences in an abusive home and her inexperience with intimate relationships also facilitated her entry into an abusive relationship. Even though Phoebe had spent some time living on the streets with other runaway youths, she was not hardened enough to resist being susceptible to her batterer's charms, and, in fact, her life on the streets served to be an additional reason for moving so quickly into the relationship:

> I was really young at the time. He was 30 to my 17. I was still a virgin and didn't know anything about relationships at all in any way, shape, or form. I had never really been in a relationship. I had little boyfriends to talk to, and went out to movies or whatever, it was very platonic. I think he was very vindictive in what he did to me. He knew that I was really naïve, and he kind of forced the relationship on me. . . . The relationship went really fast, 'cause the type of person he is. So, one thing led to another, and I got pregnant about a year later with my first [child]. . . . [H]e just kind of made me believe he was something he wasn't. I believed him. I realized later on it was all lies.

The few women who had not been exposed to abuse during childhood may not have been attempting to escape the home but may (like many other women) have been receiving messages about their family's expectations of them as women. For instance, 35-year-old Cassandra, who was raised in a middle-class home by both biological parents, spoke of one of the tenets among her family of origin regarding marriage and procreation: "That's another thing I was taught. If you want to get married, definitely do not ever, heaven forbid, my mom told me, don't ever have a kid out of wedlock. [She said,] 'I don't care if you marry the wrong person. You might marry the wrong person, but at least have a kid with someone you're married to.'"

Messages like the one conveyed to Cassandra can guide young women into abusive relationships, even if they know they are abusive, for the sake of the family's honor and reputation. This way of thinking also affects the women's ability to terminate these marriages, because it is their duty to make the relationship work and because it just "does not look good" if a woman is a single mother. However, as Patricia Hill Collins argues, "Black single mothers are not as looked down upon in Black civil society, because most African-American women know that Black men are hard to find,"[2] so being a single mother may be more of an issue among Blacks in the middle class (as was the case for Cassandra) and the upper classes, since they often attempt to emulate and live by the standards of the traditional White middle-class family.[3]

The women's abilities to adequately detect the warning signs of a batterer were often deficient regardless of the women's level of experience with abusive acts. Medea, who suffered mental and verbal abuse by her father, grandmother, and an aunt, demonstrates how this history resulted in an inability to see the warning signs: "I guess I'd been used to so much abuse, and I'd stood up under so much, it didn't jump out at me as it might have." The women who were not directly exposed to abuse between intimates during their upbringing also had difficulty recognizing warning signs, but their inability was generally related to their lack of exposure to such relationships. Although the women had different levels of experience with youthful abuse, from none to multiple and serious exposures during childhood, at some point in their relationships they each were able to figure out that batterers use manipulative techniques to secure women's trust and love. This is demonstrated by Billie in her appraisal of Kobe: "He even cried . . . actual tears. Now that I look back at it, he needed an Oscar. Don't give it to Denzel, give it to [my ex-boyfriend] Kobe Jefferson, 'cause he played it and I fell for it! It took him a year before he did it again. But he did it again."

The women were better able to retrospectively detect the warning signs of an abuser. At the time of my discussions with them, they were able to ascertain that the abusers were at fault and had the captivating ability to manipulate the women into relationships that were bound to turn abusive because of the batterers' inherent behaviors. In their narratives, however, some women demonstrated the self-blame that is often exhibited by battered women,[4] particularly in the early stages of the abusive relationship.[5] Leah expressed this introspective study of herself and of her batterers' behaviors:

I understand I am a dense type of person, but abusers are very charismatic. They put their best foot forward. Once you get sucked in, you wake up one morning and it's like, how in the hell did I get here? An abuser is—they're gonna put their best behavior on to get you. Then once they have you, they show all their ugly shit. That's hard.

Helene, like many others, endorsed this same pragmatic attitude: "You find this shit out after. Not before he's gonna tell you, 'I beat the shit out of my girlfriend, or my ex-wife.' Who's gonna tell you that? You can't even admit it to the person you're married to now when you're wrong. Who starts out dating saying, 'Let me let you beware that I'm abusive.'"

The women sought out idealistic relationships with idealistic men, but many, because of their previous direct experiences with or images of men, pursued mates who met what they considered to be more *realistic* standards. Because of the apparent shortage of heterosexual Black men as potential mates due to incarceration, street or stranger violence, and other reasons, the women wanted everything in a relationship but actually demanded little. Many of the women typically desired that the suitor have a job, not overuse drugs and alcohol, and provide a role model for the children, particularly for any boys already or expected to be born into the family. Unfortunately, if the men met these minimal criteria, the women found it harder to dissolve the relationship once the abuse started. Cassandra's description of how batterers camouflage their abusive persona shows how she measured a "good man" by his employment status: "Maybe some people with common sense know that they wouldn't be with the wrong person, but everybody doesn't know that they're with the wrong person. That person could have a decent job and you still don't know you're with the wrong person." In spite of Cassandra's appraisal, many of the women's companions did not hold regular or meaningful employment. The lower-income women were more likely to accept a man's unemployment, at least initially, if he offered other positive attributes. The women who had children and were raising them by themselves often desired to have a husband as a companion and a father to their children, regardless of his socioeconomic and employment status. Thirty-two-year-old Aaliyah conveyed her acceptance of her abusive husband's drug use prior to the start of his battering, particularly since he was bringing some money into the home. Her reaction to the drug use resulted, in part, from the abusive and neglectful experiences inflicted by her father:

> I started to notice that [my husband] smoked marijuana. I was like, OK, it's not that bad. He's still giving me money. He's still taking care of everything. It didn't bother me. I had my [second] daughter. Things started to change. He'd be gone all night; he'd come home at one or two o'clock in the morning. When I first met him, he'd always be home between six and seven. . . . I was afraid to say something. . . . I was afraid of what he might say because I was always afraid to approach my father. So I was always afraid to approach him, too, just because he was a man and I thought that I couldn't say anything. My dad would never let me talk to him. I could never go to him and say anything. He would either ignore me or give me this look. He was very unapproachable. I felt like if I say something to [my husband], maybe he's going to say he wants to leave or maybe he's gonna ignore me. It wasn't like he was this big, scary guy. Nothing like that. He was actually a pretty nice guy.

As demonstrated, whether or not they had been familiarized as youth to abuse among intimates, many of the women identified precursors to abusive behavior, though typically retrospectively. They were also more willing to establish relationships with men who offered at least a portion of what they desired in an intimate companion. These lowered standards typically are related to the women's desire to be with men of the same race and feeling pity for the Black man's discounted status in the United States.

Whether or not they were raised in a home of abuse, the women showed remarkably similar reactions to abuse from their partners. Each of the women expressed that they were astounded at the time of the first physical strike.[6] The first physical assault usually occurred between the first couple of months and the first couple of years in the relationship. A few of the women recalled that their first assault came on their wedding night, which added confusion and further proved to them that such behavior is sometimes part of married life. It was easier for the women to recall the first physical attack by their intimate partners than the commencement of verbal or mental abuse. Much of this is due to the subtlety of the batterers in their progressively controlling and abusive behaviors. Also, as mentioned earlier, several of the women's ability to initially detect mental abuse was impaired because of the effect of abuse during their upbringing on their ability to recognize the warning signs. Leah was one of the women who was able to retrospectively identify the emotional abuse that often precedes physical abuse:

> When I got with Vic, I didn't even know it was abuse. I just know I didn't like the way it made me feel. At first it was verbal. It's not like he called me a bitch; he never called me a name or cussed at me. Just the way he spoke to me and the things he would say. I didn't even know that was abuse. I just knew that it made me really depressed. It made me sad. It made me cry. He would say I was too sensitive and he would have to watch how he spoke to me. I didn't even know until he got physical with me and we had to leave and the counseling that I got in the shelters, that I realized that it was abuse.

Forty-four-year-old Yolanda is one of the few women who was not exposed to any significant form of abuse during her upbringing, in a middle-class home with both biological parents and five siblings. She was financially reliant on her abusive partner and described the first physical episode as follows: "My children's father slapped me. I was stunned. . . . It came as a total surprise. After that I felt intimidated, scared. I kept going along with it because he was the financial provider." (Nevertheless, Yolanda's financial dependence on this batterer was short-lived and was ultimately not an obstacle when she decided to leave the relationship, which is discussed in detail in Chapter 7.)

In discussing her emotional response to the first strike by her boyfriend, Isis recalled the mental abuse she had suffered from her stepfather and his abuse of her mother, Doreen:

> The first time he hit me was over a real stupid argument, like who was going to do the laundry or something, and it just kind of exploded. He slapped me. I just remember going in the bathroom and sitting there and thinking, "He hit me. How could Tariq do this to me? He never put his

hands on me. How could he do this to me?" I asked him, "How could you do that?" . . . Of course, he tried to apologize. Of course he did what they all do: apologetic, immediately wanted to have sex, 'cause he thought that was gonna some kind of way take my heart off of this big handprint on my face. And it didn't. It didn't at all. It wasn't even a Band-Aid at that point. I started telling him, "You know what I go through, living with my mom and my stepdad, and I don't think I'm coming here if you're going to do the same thing." A long time passed before he did it again, probably about nine months. . . . It wasn't a matter of me thinking he could change. I thought maybe that time I pushed one of those buttons. Maybe that time maybe I kind of deserved it. But I knew the second time that he hit me, I knew I didn't deserve it.

Another response by the women was to "work harder" at being a "good wife" or "good girlfriend," thinking that doing so would remedy the problems in the relationships that they believed caused the abuse. This aspiration to be a good wife or girlfriend was typically rooted in the women's socialization during their childhoods and in the destructive messages girls receive about women's roles in society and in relationships.[7] Along with a few other women, Helene recognized the damage done by childhood stories written especially for girls that continue to penetrate the mainstream children's media. Helene discussed the association between girls' development as influenced by these media, the expected outcomes for adult intimate relationships, and the recurrent realities women encounter in their intimate partnerships: "Those Cinderella stories ruined me. What happened to Prince Charming? What happened to the man on the white horse? I refused to raise my daughter with that mess."

Some Black women may attempt to take on and perhaps overemphasize the traditional role of women in order to detract from the contradictory stereotypes of being unfeminine or being hypersexual, both frequently ascribed to Black women. Wendy witnessed the abuse of her mother by her father and her stepfather and described her mother as a fighter in the relationships. Initially, Wendy attempted to comply with traditional standards of a wife's duties in the home: "I wanted to be the perfect little wife. Do everything right, the Army wife." In her first abusive relationship, Billie's husband was able to provide her a home in a stable apartment, which allowed her to move out of government-funded housing. All of these things, combined with her desire to experience a healthy relationship (something she has still not experienced in her own relationships, nor have the family members around her), led to Billie's attempt to be the ideal wife and mother:

> I tried to do the little wife thing. I tried to cook, clean up, keep the house clean. . . . He didn't want me to work. He was like, "You stay at home and take care of Nia and the house." It was OK at first. I was 21 and he was 20. It was great. It was kind of good there at the beginning. Then all hell broke loose.

It is striking that Wendy, Billie, and some of the other women prefaced "wife" with the term "little." Considering their attempts to conform to the role of the traditional wife, it is as though "little wife" were seen as something less than or subordinate to their desired conduct and role in intimate relationships, perhaps rooted in their resistant and generally independent personalities. This detail supports my earlier inferences with regard to the women's self-perceptions as Strong Black Women and of White women as fitting the more traditional role.

Like Wendy, Naomi was also an "Army wife." In addition, she was raised in the home of her career-military father and her mother, who was not described as the Strong Black Woman. However, Naomi was not introduced to any major forms of abuse during her youth. She described her challenges with appeasing her abusive husband and said that many of her efforts were grounded in the traditional images of womanhood and the tendency to blame the woman for the batterer's behavior. Unlike that of many of the other women, Naomi's conciliation lasted the duration of the marriage:

> All through the marriage I thought, "What am I doing wrong?" My dad didn't hit my mom. Maybe it's because I can't cook. I thought, maybe if I could cook. I had all these recipe books and recipe cards and made a new recipe a week. That didn't work. So something else is wrong. I always kept myself good. I did my hair everyday and my make-up. But I barely wore any make-up; wasn't allowed. The house was sparkling clean. And yet there was something that I was doing wrong.

As many of the women came to discover, their efforts to subdue their abusers' behavior by aspiring to be the perfect wife or girlfriend were futile. Irrespective of socioeconomic status, age, and level of abuse experienced during their formative years, the women each responded with bewilderment to the first physically violent event in an intimate relation-ship. Very few women began physically fighting back upon the first at-tack, but Helene did respond with a verbal threat to her first abusive hus-band: "I was in the kitchen doing something. He slapped me. I grabbed the hot sauce bottle off the counter and cracked it and told him, 'You go there again, it's going to be a war up in here!'" (Unfortunately, Helene's husband continued to be abusive after this event.) As I demonstrate in the following chapter, the majority of the women eventually began to retali-ate, and some even became the initial "aggressors" in battering incidents as the relationships evolved. As the women recovered from their shock at the initial physical assault, they adapted different responses. Often the first physical retaliation by the women occurred during the second physi-cal assault by the batterer. The following comments by Angie and Gloria are evidence of the disbelief produced by the first hit and demonstrate how the desire to fight back was a part of the women's thought processes but was overcome by their stunned reaction:

> I called him out of his name. He hit me. We started fighting. . . . I just kind of let him go ahead and beat me down. He's a big guy, and I wasn't gonna win this. I was like, "OK. What was that? What did I say?" It lasted for a few minutes and it was over. I don't know what actually start that. What nerve did I hit for him to react just like that? When that was done, I'm mad, ready to go [at him], but I'm still sitting there.

> When he slapped me that was the first time he hit me. He hit me so hard that my face—I couldn't believe that. That just shocked me. I didn't know if I should hit him back or just let it go. I just stayed down, I didn't even get up.

Abusive Behaviors

Abusive relationships include various forms of maltreatment by intimate partners. The four types of abuse among romantic couples as recognized by Rosemarie Tong were nonsexual physical abuse, sexual abuse, psycho-logical abuse, and destruction of property and pets.[8] A fifth type of mal-treatment is economic-related abuse.[9] A relationship is "abusive" if at least one of these forms of abuse is present, and in more lengthy relationships batterers may employ all five methods of abuse.[10] These forms of abuse are prevalent across race, ethnicity, culture, sexual orientation, and so-cioeconomic categories. However, it is the methods by which the women respond to these bad deeds that may vary across these characteristics and which were a major impetus for this study. All of the women suffered from both nonsexual physical and mental or verbal abuse by their partners. Other forms of abuse, such as sexual mistreatment, stalking, and property destruction, were also experienced, but not by each of the women. There was no generational variation among the anecdotes of abuse provided by the women, supporting the belief that the methods used by batterers have withstood several decades. The type of abuse inflicted on the women in my study appeared to vary somewhat according to socioeconomic class, which is addressed later.

The women had anywhere between one and multiple abusive relationships, with at least one of each of the women's relationships involving physical abuse. The number of abusive relationships varied according to socioeconomic class. In general, low-income women were in more abusive relationships than working-class women; working-class women were in more abusive relationships than middle-class women. (A detailed description of the number of abusive relationships by socioeconomic class is provided in Appendix A.) Some of the women were in a higher class during their abusive relationships than they were at the time of the interview. In certain situations, it was more beneficial for me to consider the women's socioeconomic status during their abusive relationships or during their youth. In the evaluation that follows, I make these distinctions.

The women's abusive relationships lasted anywhere from a few weeks to 16 years; however, most of the relationships had a duration of less than five years. Socioeconomic status did not appear to be a major factor in the length of time the women remained in the relationships. Linda C. Lambert and Juanita M. Firestone have proposed that it is possible that an abuser will need to utilize fewer methods of control over his mate the longer the relationship stays intact; the longer the relationship, the more the battered woman will be dependent on the abuser.[11] Because most of the respondents in my study eventually used tremendous amounts of force toward their abusers (fighting back) and often were the main sources of income in their households, the relationships were highly unlikely to be long-lasting.

Regardless of socioeconomic status, the women experienced brutal and unforgiving incidents of physical abuse by their mates. There was variation in the batterers' preferences for where they directed their assaults on the women's bodies. Men within the low-income and working-class couples tended to aim their bodily assaults toward the women's faces and other visible areas of the body, while the men in the middle-class couples generally avoided the women's faces. Lola, whom I classified as working-class at the time of the interview, was raised middle-class and was upper-middle-class while she was married to her abusive husband. She described her husband's selective beatings: "If he would be hitting on me, there wouldn't be any way you could see it. Whenever we went out, we always looked good." During Grace's marriage to her first husband, both were professionals in law enforcement and kept a middle-class household. Grace spoke of the deception on the part of her husband, who also fooled his family regarding his abuse:

> Nobody believed what was going on. . . . [W]hen he's in front of other people, he's the nicest guy you'd ever want to meet. He got me several times. His family doesn't believe it. He was the one that was supposed to make somebody out of himself. So they never wanted to believe he was doing any of this stuff.

There were a couple of isolated instances among the middle-class couples where the abuse was more public, but these took place in Africa and in the Caribbean. These two women stated that the cultures in the particular provinces they referred to *allowed* men to control their wives through any means necessary, including the use of physical force. Lola experienced this custom when she and her abusive husband visited his hometown in an African country. Medea's first abusive relationship occurred during her marriage to a man she met when she moved to an island in the Caribbean. Although her husband, Henry, tended to keep his abuse of Medea private, she described the culture surrounding intimate partner abuse:

> There's a culture there. . . . "The more you beat her, the better she likes it." There's a whole culture around abuse of women and marginalization of women. . . . There was a whole culture around it. There were stories. You'd hear, "So-and-so beats his wife." But the man was never stigmatized by that. If anything, he was endorsed by it. I think Henry really bought into that. I really think he thought it would be perfectly OK and I would take it.

As indicated, many of the batterers in the low- and working-class relationships primarily and deliberately directed their attacks at the women's faces. In a relationship with one of her three abusive boyfriends, Danielle described this method of abuse and the motivation of her batterer: "He'd always grab a plant or a statue or anything his hands was close by and he always hit me on my face, or always in my head. He said he was gonna disfigure me so wouldn't nobody want me but him. That's why he knocked my teeth out." Billie's account of her boyfriend Kobe's abuse after their night out illustrates his purposeful assault aimed at marking Billie as his property ("It was like he wanted to fuck up my face"). For Phoebe, her battering boyfriend also directed his hits toward her face but began to focus his attention elsewhere after a seemingly irrational decision-making process: "After a while, after I kept calling the police, he would make sure to hit me in places where it didn't show. I would still show . . . the police. They would always take pictures where it was. It was like some sort of game for him."

In addition to affecting the location on the women's bodies where the abusers would focus their attention, socioeconomic class influenced other aspects of the abuse. The working- and lower-class men were more likely than the middle-class men to employ their abusive behaviors in the presence of family and friends or in other indiscreet settings. This was the case for Max, who was working-class during her abusive relationships. She recounted, "We used to fight at my mom's house, on the street, in the car. He even pushed me out of the car when the car was moving." Victoria, who had a lower-class upbringing and adulthood, was often battered in the presence of her mother. Zora, who was living in a middle-class environment at the time of the interview but was in a low-income abusive relationship, also experienced her partner's uninhibited abuse:

> I remember one time we had company over and he was saying something and I was trying to wave him off. He comes in the room and he was yelling in my ear. It was a time where one of [my] boys had a birthday party. He takes this balloon and pops it right in my ear. I can remember not hearing out of that ear for a long time.

Four of the women were married to and abused by men who were in the military during at least a portion of the relationship and abuse. I categorized military appointments as working-class homes.[12] I expected during the appraisal of the women's stories that I would find that these men's selections of when and where they hit the women would be similar to those of the men in the middle-class households because of the threat of authoritative control by military officials, which could possibly result in getting discharged from military service. However, there was no significant pattern.

These women related that the men were concerned about being sanctioned by military officials if they were officially charged with intimate partner abuse, but, in general, the men did not appear overly anxious about keeping their abuse hidden.

Even though all the women attempted to mask their bruises, cuts, and other evidence of abuse regardless of where the injuries appeared on their bodies, I conclude that the men in the middle-class couplings intentionally made efforts not to mark the women in areas not easy to cover up (such as the face). I surmise that these men behaved this way in order to maintain appearances, as though they were the archetypical middle-class couple, free of conflict, a couple others might strive to emulate. The low- and working-class men also made conscious attempts by where they directed their assaults, but for different reasons. As indicated in the women's narratives, these men essentially marked the women as theirs through their exercise of unremitting control over their lives.

Although all the women were physically battered in a nonsexual manner, not all of them were sexually assaulted in their abusive intimate relationships. For those women who were sexually battered, most of them acknowledged the forceful or coercive sex perpetrated by their intimate partners as abuse. But whether or not the women directly identified the sexual mistreatment as abuse, most of the women did not mention these assaults until I inquired about the sexual aspects of their intimate relationships. When asked to tell about her relationships in general, Gloria did not identify one of her mates as sexually abusive. From her story of his treatment of her regarding their sexual interaction, it is clear that he unmistakably was a sexually aggressive batterer:

> It seemed like when I'd have sex with him, he was always trying to hurt me. It never felt good. Just really, really rough. I would tell him, then he would say, "I'll do better next time." . . . I would tell him and he just didn't care. If I would say something, he would do it harder. Then he would try to do other things. How do you figure? If I can't handle you this way, why would you try to have anal sex with me? That kind of stuff. He didn't care. He would tell me that, "This is the way I want it and this is the way I'm going to do it." . . . Then if you'd be trying to tell him to stop, or you'd push him away, he would try to hold me down or he'd say, "Just one minute." . . . When I kept trying to tell him that he can't do it like this, he would get mad and he would just do it anyway, like he didn't care.

Billie also endured sexual abuse from her malicious boyfriend. Kobe began to demand sex from Billie and to argue with her after they returned home from another night out and after another argument involving their interactions with White people. Billie related that she had stopped having sex with Kobe for some time prior to that night as a result of being mentally depleted from his continuous (nonsexual) physical aggression. Returning home that night, Billie was chastised by Kobe for talking with a White man at the nightclub and was then raped:

> We walked to the house. Got in the house. He was like, "Oh, so you like White boys now, huh?" . . . Sodomized me, choked me, raped me. Like I said, I wouldn't give him sex. So he was just ugly. Just ugly. . . . I was really hurt, because he raped me. I felt like this is my brother molesting me all over again. I just started crying. He sodomized me. He raped me. He choked me so bad I passed out. When I woke up, he had left me in the basement. He did this to me in the basement. Just left me down there. After that I just laid there and I cried and cried. I said [to myself], "I gotta stop this." I got up. I went upstairs, I washed myself up, cleaned myself up, and for the next two days I slept on the couch. I wouldn't even get in the bed with him.

Describing her rape by a boyfriend, Isis displayed the reaction of many sex assault resisters who have been raped by someone they loved and trusted: "I was on my menstrual cycle, and he took me. . . . He held me down and I had to deal with it. That is very humiliating. It's humiliating when it happens with a stranger, but when it's someone you know and you so-call trust . . . that's not right."

Often we are privy to casual discussions regarding the idea of make-up sex after a fight between intimate partners and how it is an effective method for subduing the hurt feelings and mending the relationship. However, many of the women asserted to me that sex after an abusive incident was unwanted, which makes the sexual act itself abuse. This was the case with Zora, who suffered from sexual abuse by her batterer at various times in the cycle of their abusive relationship: "I can remember that there was some aggression towards sex a couple of times. Just kind of being forceful. Or after having a fight, wanting to have sex." Naomi communicated how she came to view sex after passing time in a relationship with her abusive husband:

Sexually he tried to control me, too. He was really into pornography. . . . [He would say,] "You need to learn this and do this. See what they're doing? You need to do that.". . . So that became part of my to-do list. Wash the dishes, clean up the kitchen, have sex, go wash the car. It was a chore to me. . . . I'd wish he'd hurry up and get off of me.

Because physically forceful sex is easier to recognize and categorize than coerced sexual occurrences, it was easier for the women to identify the blatantly violent incidences of rape by their batterers. For most of the women, their lack of love and trust in the abusive men, which developed progressively after constant maltreatment, affected their desire to have sex during more romantic periods in the relationship.

The examples of physically aggressive behaviors by the women's male companions were quite disturbing, as are any stories of violence perpetrated by one person against another. As mentioned, intimate partner abuse is not limited to a particular group of individuals, but there are some differences in the ways in which women experience intimate physical violence depending on their class, race, culture, or other characteristics. While the sexual abuse perpetrated on the women might be similar to that carried out against other women (Latina, White, immigrant, wealthy, and so on), I observed that the physical abuse the women received varied according to their socioeconomic class.

At some point in at least one of their abusive relationships, all of the women were verbally and mentally abused. They reported that most of the abusers employed this form of abuse, but there were a few men whom the women reported as using physical aggression without any verbal or mental abuse. Overwhelmingly, the women described verbal and mental abuse as far more damaging and lasting than physical abuse, a finding that is supported by abundant previous research[13] and that is an important factor to be considered in abusive relationships. This may be particularly significant for the women in my examination since most of them eventually used physical retaliation to combat the physical violence but had greater difficulty contending with the lingering emotional effects of mental abuse. Angie described the impact of mental abuse in comparison to physical abuse: "It sticks in your head. You will get over the physical sometime, sooner or later, but sometime that verbal gets you mentally and it stick around longer." Gloria also expressed this view: "That verbal is hard. You can fight off a fist; you just block it or run away. But when you hear that stuff, I don't forget it. I haven't forgotten any of it." And Isis addressed this topic in one of her experiences with mental abuse:

> He would throw things from my past that he knew that I was ashamed of or that hurt me. He would throw those things in my face. I always thought, that's the worse thing you can do to someone. Worse than a hit, worse than a slap. Don't use my pain against me. He would do that all the time. If I would catch him in a lie, "Oh, you're just going crazy like your granddad went crazy."

A small number of women declared that the verbal and mental abuse did not have dramatic or detrimental effects on them. Twenty-two-year-old Ebony stated that her boyfriend would say things "like bitch, ho. I'll be like, 'Yo' mama!' So that don't even matter to me. I don't care about them words." Even though Ebony expressed that she was not affected by the verbal abuse, other comments she made about her relationships contradicted her statement. It is likely that denying the pain the words caused was part of her dynamic resistance. Consequently, it was apparent that the women were indeed negatively affected by the verbal abuse but that they made their greatest attempts to block the effects of the insults or became anesthetized by the incessant abuse. This is shown in Harriet's narrative: "It did bother me. But I just had a way of blocking things out. I learned how to do that before my mama passed. It's something that I do that works for me."

At the start of the mental abuse, some of the women did not recognize that they were being abused. Earlier I presented Leah's retrospective insight regarding her difficulty detecting mental abuse and her inability to realize that she was being mentally abused at the time it was occurring. But Leah later helped her daughter Keisha identify that one of Keisha's boyfriends was being abusive (Keisha shared her mother's difficulty identifying this form of abuse). Keisha recalled, "He would always try to put me down. I really didn't realize it until my mom would point it out. . . . He never put his hands on me, but it was mental." Renee also was unaware of the verbal abuse directed toward her until she considered the relationship retrospectively: "My limited version of what a crisis was had been narrowed down to physical. So unless I was bleeding or had my eyes scratched out, I didn't think I was in a crisis." Because the mental abuse was inconspicuous and gradual in application, the damage that it did to Renee's and the other women's self-worth was all the more devastating in the end.

The batterers were able to essentially trap some of the women in the ghastly relationships by the use of constant and unscrupulous mental abuse. Danielle equated the mental abuse by her boyfriend with physical abuse when she described that "He'd always want to whup me with his words, making my self-esteem low." Phoebe felt imprisoned in the relationship with her abusive boyfriend because of his verbal abuse:

> He has a mouth like a sailor. He cusses a lot. He would call me names. After I had my second child, not really after but during, he would say I was fat and that nobody else would want me. . . . He was like, "No one's gonna want you like I do. No one's ever gonna treat you or love you as much as I do." I was like, "If this is love, then I'm in a nightmare." Yeah, he was very verbally abusive; he put me down a lot. He would say that I couldn't do anything with two kids. At the time when I met him, I had a lot of little boys that were my age that were interested in me. I had a lot of little friends in the neighborhood. There was a couple of boys that were really cute. He would say things like, "Let's see if they want you now, knocked up."

Jacqueline experienced similar berating from her batterer: "His thing was always, 'You can't take care of yourself. You don't have no education. What are the kids gonna do? I'll take the kids. You won't have nothing.' I believed that." Cicely, who was abused by three of her five husbands, spoke of the process that leads the women to think little of themselves and of their subsequent actions when she said, "I've been called stupid, dumb so much that you get to the point where [you think], maybe I am stupid, maybe I do have problems. What am I doing wrong with men?" Again, though women of all cultures, ethnicities, and races experience similar insults by their intimate partners, some of the battered Black women are further burdened by the social ramifications in the United States of being a Black mother without a male mate (specifically, a husband) in the household. The women often feared being the epitome of the stereotype that all Black women are single mothers on welfare with little education. This was repeatedly demonstrated in the choice of expressions used by the batterers during the verbal assaults.

In addition to using mental abuse to lower the women's self-esteem and make them feel that no one else would have them, the batterers also utilized mental abuse to trap the women in the relationships by promoting *fear* in them. Joanne Belknap and I distinguish the two types of psychological abuse: those abuses meant to demean and those meant to instill fear or terror.[14] Grace described an example of verbal abuse intended to cause terror in her narration of an incident with one of her abusive husbands:

> We go take a ride up into the mountains. I never realized how big the mountains were. I thought he was joking. "I could pull up right here, beat the hell out of you and no one would ever know it." He just said it so matter-of-fact, like it was nothing. That made my blood run cold. I started thinking I've got to get away from him.

The only major association I detected between the women's experiences with mental or verbal abuse and their age, socioeconomic status, or education level was along the dimension of public versus private abuse. As I found in my analysis of the use of physical aggression by the batterers, low- and working-class abusers were more likely to mentally and verbally abuse the women in the presence of others, while the middle-class men tended to conceal this type of abuse.

Behaviors by the batterers also included activities that I have cataloged separately from physical, sexual, verbal, or mental abuse but that were just as perilous. These include (1) maintenance of control and isolation regarding women's work, education, other daily activities, and finances; (2) presence of threatening jealous behavior, infidelity, and stalking; and (3) property theft and damage.

An often-cited reason that battered women stay in abusive relationships is their financial dependence on the batterers.[15] This dependence results, in part, from the common battering behavior of isolating the abused partner and keeping her from obtaining and maintaining employment. This isolation prevents some battered women from gaining skills and confidence in the workforce outside the home. Some battered women have minimal or no work experience prior to entering into the relationship, which adds to their anxiety about leaving the batterers and their ability to support themselves and any children. In spite of this, other literature has suggested that Black women may not be as restrained on this basis because they are more likely to be employed outside the home because of the historical tendency of Black women to be compelled to work outside their own homes (for example, as slaves, sharecroppers, or domestic workers), the need among Black families for a second income as a result of the lower socioeconomic status of Black men,[16] Black women's role as a primary income source in a single-parent household, or the desire to keep up with middle-class ambitions. These characteristics may also apply to other women of color, including immigrant women of color, and low-income or working-class women in general. Frances Beale offered her reflection on Black women's economic situation:

> [I]t is idle dreaming to think of black women simply caring for their homes and children like the middle-class white model. Most black women have to work to help house, feed, and clothe their families. Black women make up a substantial percentage of the black working force, and this is true for the poorest black family as well as the so-called middle-class family.[17]

Many of the women in my study worked outside the home and did not necessarily rely on their abusers for monetary sustenance. Regarding one of her abusive husbands, Cicely stated, "I think I was making more money than he was. I would dish out a lot of money to him. And I would complain 'cause when he'd be at work, he wouldn't bring his money home. We did argue over that." Phoebe similarly described her economic condition while in her abusive relationship: "I don't think he ever had a real job before because he had been sellin' drugs, doin' drugs for so long and he was a musician and that's how he made his money. I supported the relationship from the time we met, 'cause I had always worked." Zora also worked throughout her abusive relationship: "He wasn't that good of a provider. He was in favor of me working. It didn't bother him. He wasn't working. Sometimes I had two jobs. I was very much the head of the household and took care of business as far as our home and cars and everything."

This lack of financial reliance among the women on their batterers may have been a catalyst for some men to control the women in other ways. For instance, Jade's husband would hide her keys so that she could not get to work. Aaliyah longed to begin a career in law enforcement at the urging of her uncles. She described how she came to this decision and her batterer's sabotaging response to her efforts:

> I have two uncles who are correction officers in prisons. They both work at [a state prison], but one's doing death row and the other's a regular correction officer. He's been there forever. I remember being with my uncle and he was telling me that I should do that. I always wanted to be in law enforcement. Then all of a sudden I said, "I want to be a cop." I knew

that I have the attitude and I knew that I can do it. [My boyfriend] was like, "Uh-uh. You already went to school. You're not going to go to school again." But I said I want to go to school. I want to be something. I want to make a difference. I told him I wanted to be a police officer. He was like, "You already went to school. I'm not going to sit around here while you go to school again. You need to be working." I kind of let that drift off. I got afraid. I was like, OK, I can't go to school, because I'm going to be by myself with my kids and that's going to be impossible. He told me he would leave if I went to school, so I decided not to do that.

Aaliyah then portrayed how the batterer attempted to control her by trying to get her to reside in accommodations where he would be permitted to live as well:

I wanted to move, [but] I wanted to keep my Section 8. At that point he was so scarce. He wasn't coming home. We didn't have any money. I was still having to get food stamps. I finally started working so I didn't have to get welfare any more. But I was working and I still wasn't having enough money to buy food. I knew that one thing I wasn't going to do was to get off Section 8. Every time he upset me, I would tell him he had to leave. I was on the lease. It was my Section 8. . . . He got to a point where he didn't want to deal with that any more. He told me I had to get off Section 8. . . . I guess in a way that would have been a good thing, but the reason behind it was not for me, it was for him.

Aaliyah's relationship with the batterer ended soon after this and she eventually was accepted into the police academy, but her participation in this training opportunity that would have moved her toward her ultimate career goal was sabotaged by a subsequent batterer.

In discussing her first abuser's actions, Jacqueline summarized what I infer to be the abusers' rationale for their efforts to control work and education endeavors by the women:

He was stupid. I got a job working as a maid. And he come up to my job fussing and hollering and acting the fool, and they fired me. Then I got another job working as a maid at the [hotel]. He came up there and made me leave immediately. He didn't want me to have anything that I could handle on my own. I think he knew as soon as I could get it together I was out.

As Jacqueline's narrative makes clear, the abusers often seemed to believe that if their girlfriends and wives were to gain too much independence, in the form of a job or additional education, they would have little reason to remain in the relationship. Accordingly, the batterers exerted their power over the women by sabotaging any advancement in the women's professional lives. This behavior was found throughout the sample, regardless of socioeconomic class. But this was the case for only some of the batterers; other men *wanted* the women to work or were already accustomed to the women working, as they reaped the benefits in these situations.

Batterers also may dictate the type of work their female companions engage in. In Jacqueline's second abusive relationship, she was not physically abused until 16 years into the relationship, after which she immediately divorced this abusive husband. However, for many years preceding the violent event, Jacqueline had been coerced into working as a prostitute and exotic dancer, which she identified as a form of abuse. She also explained why she did not leave until she was physically assaulted by her husband:

> Basically he was a drug addict and he used to pimp. That's where the abuse from him was. But more than abusive, he was controlling, very controlling. . . . [But] there was nothing he could do that was wrong. This was my man that was going to take care of me, and he didn't hit me. So whatever he wanted me to do. I ended up working on the streets, taking care of him and my three kids, my sister—the one that was living with me—and her baby. I was supporting everybody. I was twenty years old. . . . [My husband and sister] showed me how to go out on the street, what to look for, how to stop cars, how to get in cars, what to ask for. . . . I actually worked on the street six months, I was in jail eight times. . . . I started dancing in the clubs. He had this reputation to maintain. . . . I didn't want him to look bad in their eyes. . . . I would be afraid that I would get back into another one of those I'm-gonna-beat-you relationships if I didn't do this. I didn't want to go there any more. It was easier to put myself out there than deal with him being angry. He would yell at me. . . . I got a divorce the first time he hit me.

The abusive men also limited other regular activities in which the women were involved. The batterers restricted the women's access to family and friends, and some would not allow the women to attend religious services. The women clearly felt trapped by the restrictions placed on them by their abusers. Danielle described her experience as comparable to that of a slave: "I couldn't do nothing. I had to be his personal slave. I would stay at home slaving. I had to wash clothes on my hands. He wouldn't let me go to the Laundromat. He didn't want me around nobody. He isolated me away from my family and friends, everything." Toni also experienced limited freedom: "Envy, that green-eyed monster appeared. I couldn't go anywhere. Everyplace I went was limited. He was checking my checking account, how many times I went to the ATM machine [*sic*], why didn't I have any money. I didn't have any money because I was paying bills!"

As communicated in Toni's recollection of her abuse, some of the women were also controlled by batterers as a result of their jealousy. In other research, Black women have been found to report more incidences of jealousy within their relationships than have other women. Ramos, Carlson, and McNutt established that 46 percent of the Black women they surveyed, but only 28 percent of White women, reported excessive jealousy by their intimate partners.[18] Lockhart found that middle-class Black respondents reported more disputes over the man's jealousy than middle-class White respondents.[19] The women who spoke with me had been subjected to several forms of threatening jealous behaviors by the batterers. A peculiar illustration of this jealousy was the physical inspections performed by the batterers. On a regular basis, some of the women were forced to undergo body searches carried out by the abusers. These batterers believed they could detect if the women had been with other men by conducting visual and olfactory examinations. Angie experienced this invasion by one of her three abusive boyfriends. She recounted, "We didn't live together, but I would stay over there sometimes with my son. He was just jealous. [He had] to smell me to see if I been with other men." Leah also experienced this form of abuse: "It would get so that when I would come home he would make me take off my clothes. . . . I guess he [thought] . . . he could tell if I was with somebody else. It was all kind of off the wall."

The abusers also demonstrated threatening jealous behavior when they interfered with the women's activities, as articulated in the previous accounts on control and isolation. Grace's second husband/abuser was a White man. She reported that he believed Grace to be engaging in relationships with Black men and tried to control her movements and activities on the basis of this reasoning. Billie referred to one of her abusers as "Mr. Jail" because of his jealous, controlling conduct. Mr. Jail is a name that Celie, the central character in the movie *The Color Purple* (which is based on Alicie Walker's novel), calls the main male character in the movie. Billie's account of her abuser's behaviors explains her and Celie's interpretation of the moniker:

> Mr. Jail. I couldn't go nowhere, I couldn't do nothing. I felt like I was in jail. I used to sit on the couch and look out the window, and that was it. If I tried to go somewhere, [he said] I'd be going to see some men. And God forbid, don't let me put no makeup on [or], honey, I'm going to see a man! He was just weird like that.

Another form of abuse cited by the women was sexual infidelity by their abusive mates. It is possible that the threatening jealous behaviors manifested by the abusers were a result of the transference of their own dishonest behaviors onto the women. Regarding relationship unfaithfulness as abuse, Billie recalled the following about her first husband: "My husband went to women like an elephant goes to peanuts. He never hit me, but he abused me in a different way. He slept with [another woman]. I even think he slept with my kids' godmother. I can't prove it, but I think he did. So I think that was a form of abuse, too."

Stalking, like other forms of dangerous behaviors by intimates, can occur during the relationship or after it has ended. As a result of his stalking, Leah's former husband discovered the location of the battered women's shelter Leah retreated to with her children in order to escape his abuse. Toni discussed her unrelenting anxiety about the possible return of her abusive ex-boyfriend, whom she feared may have been stalking her: "One time I was sitting in church and I had this eerie feeling that somebody was behind me. . . . When I sing in the choir, I sit there and think, 'Could I go out that door? How would I get out of here?'" As with Victoria's experience, the stalking fortunately ceased without further violent incidents for many of the women who were knowingly stalked: "Everywhere I hung out, he'd start hanging out there. He just wouldn't go away. Until I guess he figure there wasn't nothing left and he disappeared."

The women also suffered from the destruction or theft of shared property or property owned or cared for solely by the women. Inez's batterer set fire to her home: "He wasn't living with me. I let my other sister live with me who had two kids. He didn't like that. He said he better stay with me or nobody could stay. . . . He came back to the door and set fire to the door. My little brother . . . was staying with me, he pulled me out. My legs [were] burned." Zora's boyfriend also set her apartment on fire, which, luckily, did not burn down completely, and no one was physically harmed. A few of the abusers took advantage of the women by spending the money they were given on drugs or stealing property out of the home to sell or trade for drugs. Cicely described her experience:

> When he was coming in and out of the house, he was stealing everything out of there. . . . I was out of town, he broke in the house and broke a water line and flooded the whole basement. . . . I would give him money and he'd say he was going to get help; put him in a treatment program and he'd walk away with the money. He would steal stuff that I worked hard to get.

Aaliyah's abuser also had a drug problem that he supported by using resources provided by Aaliyah:

> I don't remember how I found out, but I found out that he was on crack cocaine. Stuff started missing out of my house. Movies, my jewelry, his wedding band. I think I bought him four wedding bands because he'd come home and say he lost it and I would believe in him. And I kept replacing it. I had gold jewelry that I had bought for myself when I was doing really good on my own and I'd let him wear it, but he'd come home and it would be gone.

Perceptions of the Batterers

Battered women are often blamed for their abuse, particularly if they remain in the relationship after being physically assaulted.[20] As part of my study, the women were asked to provide their personal appraisal of why their intimate partners were violent and otherwise abusive. The women mainly spoke of Black men in particular since this was the identity of most of the abusers. Therefore, the majority of the following discussion focuses on Black men as batterers. Some of the women alluded to the possibility that genetic or hereditary factors predisposed the batterers to violence, but they generally attributed the batterers' behaviors to social and psychological factors. In particular, the women tendered their opinions about Black men's predicaments and struggles in society in trying to understand why they became abusive. Cicely elaborated on how incarceration of Black men exacerbates the prevalence of violence perpetrated by Black men: "'Cause [White people] always think Black men [are] animals, they beat you up, they're drug addicts. You keep telling a Black man in prison that over and over and over, when he acts on it, you can't say, 'Why you do this?'" Paula deduced:

> I have this feeling that Black men, after Black boys turn 13 or 14, they're on their own. They're just kind of aloof. . . . I've come to my own little proof that, not all, but most Black men didn't have it so they don't know how to give it and they don't know how to put time in. . . . And I just don't feel that impact that a Black man is connecting with Black children.

And Olivia offered:

> Black men have so many issues. I feel for 'em. I tell my son I'm not a Black man, but I do understand. . . . I do understand y'all got it hard, but still, you gotta break away from that. Quit being so angry and so bitter. . . . So what is the issue? What is it that you did not get when you were coming up? Why is it that you guys don't like us so much? You know, they'll marry you, give you the big house. But then you gotta go fix your boobs and stuff.

These statements speak to what some scholars have identified as plausible explanations for Black men's abuse of female intimates. Bell hooks suggests that because of the compelling stereotypes of Black men as violent, they succumb to this image as a form of self-fulfilling prophecy. She concludes that it is learning to think in a sexist way and practicing sexism that permit men to express their anger in a violent manner against intimates and others. She adds that violence by Black males is not exclusive to them and that their behaviors simply reflect the violence perpetrated by White males.[21]

The women supplied reasons for their boyfriends' and husbands' battering in terms of social and gender hierarchies, employment status and income, and the societal expectations of each of these. These explanations cut through all socioeconomic classes, although there was a tendency for there to be more economic-related discord within low- and working-class couples, since the middle-class couples were those where the male partner typically brought more income into the home. Many Black women are involved in relationships with Black men, as well as with men of other races and ethnicities, in which they attempt to mimic the traditional female gender role in interpersonal relationships.[22] This includes being the family nurturer and allowing the male mate to be responsible for protecting and financially providing for the family. However, this traditional female role may be more typical of White women's lives than those of Black women. Claudia Lawrence-Webb and colleagues suggest that, to their detriment, Blacks follow a White cultural tradition as their reference for intimate relationships, which produces inconsistent results because of Black women's autonomy and independence within the workings of the intimate partnerships.[23] When Black couples attempt to emulate the classic roles of couples, their relationships may suffer from conflict, abuse, and negative views about relationships in general as a result of the role playing.[24] This is demonstrated by Yolanda, who described her abusive husband's typically illegitimate employment and how it began to affect her and the relationship:

> He was the type of person that hustled. He didn't work. I'm more the traditional type, like my family that I had come from. I had started to try to get on him about getting a real 9-to-5 job. That's when the friction came. He didn't want to change his lifestyle. At first it was all fun. But when I had my child I wanted something more traditional.

According to some scholars, when Black women are unable to perform the traditional role of women in relationships, including *not* working outside the home, the recurrent alternative role played by many of them is that of the matriarch, or, at the least, that of an equal participant in an egalitarian family setting.[25] However, the argument goes, the *image* of the matriarch is that of a controlling and often emasculating head of the household.[26] Regardless of whether the image has negative or positive attributes, the matriarchal characterization is in discord with that of a woman's traditionally prescribed role in the family and society. Therefore, many have argued that conflict may ensue as Black men attempt to emulate the characterization of the traditional male in the United States: the patriarch.[27] Various factors can be attributed to the matriarchal roles often taken on by Black women in their households. These are frequently the same factors that have been said to contribute to abuse of the matriarch by her male partner, such as his belief that he is entitled to control her in the absence of economic power[28] and societal power.[29]

Many Black women find themselves initially excusing their Black male batterers' abusive behavior. Beth E. Richie discovered that some of the battered Black women in her study tended to feel sorry for their batterers at the start of the abuse, instead of exhibiting feelings of fear and anger.[30]

In recalling the experience with one of her abusive boyfriends, Billie demonstrated the tolerance many of the women in my study practiced with Black male batterers:

> I was like, you know, he's just always making excuses. He's just upset because he doesn't have a job and he's doing drugs and that's very stressful on him. My sister was like, "Girl, no it's not. You better wake up. 'Cause he doesn't give a damn. As long as you're buying his crack and his liquor, he doesn't give a damn. He doesn't have to pay anything, he doesn't have to go anywhere, doesn't have to buy anything, you're doing everything." Me with my dumb behind, I didn't listen. I kept saying, but you know, he loves me and the kids. He cares about us. He's just going through some stuff. He'll be all right. Soon as he cleans himself up and get a job, everything will be fine.

Richie also asserts that the battered Black women in her investigation tolerated and forgave the batterers' shortcomings because of Black men's degraded status in U.S. society, which made the women sacrifice their own ambitions.[31] The same experiences were reported by a number of the women I interviewed. In addition, the women recognized how their successes, potential or realized, were a source of contempt among their batterers. Harriet, who was a railroad conductor at the time she was in her abusive relationship, acknowledged the complexities surrounding men's economic and occupational standing in comparison to those of women and stated that many men find it difficult to accept a situation in which their female mates are in more lucrative and higher-paying jobs.[32] About her abuser, Harriet said, "He was working for the post office. I was making like $10 thousand more than he was. That's a no-no." When Paula began attending college (at the age of 39 and several years into her abusive relationship), her battering boyfriend expressed his discontent with her educational pursuits. She stated, "I was changing. As far as he was concerned, I was growing into something he considered bad. I think he knew the result would be that I was better than him." Cassandra summarized it this way: "They're probably frustrated that they're not doing anything with their life." Similarly, the women often described their batterers as not being "real men" who took responsibility for themselves, their intimate partners, and their children. Many described the men as "mama's boys" who were too coddled by their mothers, which resulted in an inability to be responsible and benevolent. Olivia concluded:

He's a mama's boy. She never made him do anything. . . . She never made him be a man. If he didn't want to work, he didn't have to work. If he wanted to hang out all day, he'd hang out all day. He's a mama's boy. You know, if you get in trouble, Mama's gonna be there. . . . So he got to the point where he felt he didn't have to do anything. When I got pregnant, he didn't want to take on the responsibility. He wanted to fight and slap me around and tell me I had to stay there because "Mama said you're having my baby and you're supposed to sit here and do as I say do." He was a knucklehead.

Again, many of the respondents worked outside the home and were often the main financial providers. Billie summarized the minimal economic, familial, and social responsibility the batterers assumed and the women's views of how they were not real men: "I had to work, take care of all the bills, buy all the food. I had to do everything because he was smoking so much crack he just stayed at home. I was actually taking care of him, basically, and he's beating the hell out of me!"

A topic that is often a choice of discourse among Black women is the gender-ratio imbalance among Blacks. There are more Black women in need of intimate partners than there are Black men who can (or will) function as the intimate partners of Black women.[33] This "availability factor," which does not appear to be prevalent in other racial or ethnic groups, is occasionally asserted as a reason for battered Black women remaining in abusive relationships with their Black intimate partners.[34] Views of Black men become apparent in casual discussions among Black women about their ethnic brothers, which often evolve into conversations about the scant availability of Black men due to prison and jail incarceration, homosexual orientation, Black men dating and marrying non-Black women, or Black men's higher mortality rate as a consequence of fatal street violence. Contrary to the belief in the availability imbalance among Blacks, some existing research has provided evidence of a statistically *in*significant correlation between availability of Black men and Black women remaining in abusive relationships. Anita Raj and her co-researchers had originally hypothesized that because of a gender-ratio imbalance among young adult Blacks, Black women's ability to form meaningful emotional and sexual attachments with men was thwarted. But, in keeping with their findings, they theorized, "African American men may exert even greater power in relationships in which women *perceive* that they have limited alternatives" (emphasis added).[35] Doreen was one of the number of women who described to me how she felt Black women think regarding the perceived gender-ratio imbalance between Black women and Black men and its relationship to battering:

> Everybody thinks the same thing: Ain't no good [Black] men out here. There's a shortage of men and you better keep what you got. They're scared to lose 'em. . . . They tryin' to keep the one they got 'cause they know ain't nothing out here. That's the way they think. Shortage because of jail and drugs and the White women. Shortage because of a lot of stuff. . . . There's a shortage and you better keep what you got.

The women also spoke of how the pool of Black men shrinks even more if one is looking for a "real man" or a "good man." These are men who hold stable and respectable employment, are drug free, and are socially and morally responsible. Tammy discussed the difficulty of finding a "good man" and of her young adult daughter's situation in today's dating atmosphere:

> She needs to grow within herself and put more love into her children instead of trying to find love out here, because there's not very many men left in this world, especially at the age she's at. It's really kind of hard; especially in the Black community. You don't meet very many real gentlemen or real men any more in this area. There are some, but I'd hate to have to be her age and searching and looking for a man.

The women who were abused by middle-class Black men felt compelled or were pressured by others to remain with the men because of their social status. The batterers' social status categorized them as "good men," regardless of their abusive behaviors, particularly if they kept the abuse quiet, which these men tended to do. To a certain extent, the working-class men were viewed in the same manner because of their capability to hold employment, at least intermittently.

Although many of the women discussed their frustrations with Black men, most of them continued to be romantically involved with them and did not date or marry men of other races and ethnicities. As described by Billie, some women believed, "I just don't think that White men are strong enough for Black women." As already revealed, Keisha was one of the exceptions to the preference to date or marry only Black men. She disclosed that she thought that a White man would be different from the Black men she knew growing up—that is, her father, some of her male relatives, and her mother's boyfriends—who were abusive or otherwise disrespectful and irresponsible. She stated, "When I started dating, I refused to date Black guys." In spite of this, Keisha's two abusive relationships were with non-Black men.

Many of the women shared stories of the batterers' childhood experiences of witnessing abuse or as targets of abuse. The women made connections between those experiences and the men becoming abusive in their own intimate relationships. There were no significant variations by socioeconomic status in the use of this intergenerational explanation to rationalize the men's battering. Olivia shared that "Abuse is a man thing, it's a cultural thing, it goes all the way back to our ancestors. Very few women stepped forth and did anything. I had found out that his parents were abusive to him. His mother was abusive to him. . . . I still say it comes from way back." And Wendy explained:

> His life became the life that he saw his mother was raised up in, that he didn't want, but his life became the way he didn't want. . . . He's always seen his mother go through that. Being abused by every man that she's ever been with. He was brought up in a very abusive household. He saw his mother bow down, cowering to men.

A few of the women believed that if they had known of their batterers' abusive childhoods, this would have served as a warning sign, and they would have not become involved with the abusers. This was explained by Jade:

> Not until I got married did I find out about the abuse he had received from his mother and father. . . . Come later, after I would go to family functions, I found out it was his parents abusing him. I found out that one time his father had knocked him and his sister down the stairs so hard he knocked both of them out. I wish I would have known, but he hid it so, so well.

More frequently, however, knowing of the abuse the batterers suffered as children only aided in providing the women with another incentive for feeling sorry for the men and remaining in the relationships. Cassandra demonstrated this when she articulated, "His mom and his twin brother and himself, they went through so much abuse and so much junk till I just couldn't even believe my ears. I felt sorry for him."

A number of women expressed how they noticed that the batterers, throughout all economic statuses, had a general dislike of women. They deduced that it was these attitudes that made it easy for the batterers to be violent and otherwise abusive. The women typically believed that the batterers' contempt for the women grew out of the men's poor treatment by their mothers during childhood or originated in previous unhealthy intimate relationships with women. Renee explained:

> He had hit me as if he were hitting someone else. As he was hitting me, he was spewing out, "You women are always—!" It dawned on me that I didn't want to die or take an ass beating for a litany of women that were abusive to him. . . . It was my first exposure or realization to the fact that men have issues just like we do. Their abusive childhoods are just like ours. I was actually fighting with this guy for what he thought I had done to him that was similar to what other women had done to him. So he had not been dealing with his issues as they came and went.

Repeatedly, I was told by the women that the relationship between the man and his mother should have been a warning sign to them. They communicated that if a man does not like his mother, then he is not going to like women in general, and this can occasionally develop into violence against women. The women who spoke of this connection typically received advice from their mothers or othermothers, like Wendy: "My mom always told me to look at that situation. She said, 'If the man is abusive to his mother, then he's gonna treat you like he treats his mother. If he's loving and kind and have respect for his mother, then he'll have respect for you.' He didn't have respect for his mom."

Previous research suggested that alcohol and other drug use is correlated with higher levels of intimate partner abuse among couples.[36] The women participating in my study made various connections between batterers' substance use and their abusive behaviors. Some felt that without the presence of alcohol or drug dependency their intimate partners would not be batterers. Others believed that substance use worsened preexisting violent behavior. A few of the women believed that their mates' use of drugs was *the* reason for their getting abused; they believed the batterer to be a good person but for the drug and alcohol use. Inez declared about her batterer: "He was quiet, sweet, loving [when he was sober]. It was the drugs and alcohol." Erica had a similar assessment of one of her abusers:

He was drunk all the time, an alcoholic. He was nice, though. I wouldn't say he was bad. He was a really nice person. . . . I felt sorry for him, 'cause he would call and apologize over the phone, "I'm sorry." I was like, "You need to stop drinking, that's your main thing." He didn't want to stop drinking.

It has been demonstrated that when the women "felt sorry" for the batterers, it hindered their ability to escape the relationship. As is evident in Erica's anecdote, this notion of feeling sorry for the batterer appears again among my respondents. They pitied the abusers for their substance dependencies and the problems that had led to the substance abuse. Accordingly, the women focused on persuading the batterer to be free of substance use and abuse, assuming that the abuse would stop once that occurred.

Some of the women related that as the batterers' drug addictions worsened, they showed more angry and violent behavior when they were between doses. Yolanda found this to be the case with one of her abusers: "At first it was all beautiful. [Then] the crack cocaine came out. He started dilly-dallying in that. He would get more violent when he couldn't get it." Phoebe also experienced this occurrence: "He used to get intoxicated or high a lot. There were times when he was sober, but I think that when he got sober he would get irritated because he needed to get high again. It was a constant circle of madness that I was dealin' with with him." When I questioned Doreen if her batterer would hit only when he had been drinking, she replied, "Nope, he could be sober, it would just come out of the blue. In a way I wished he'd drink, 'cause I kind of know what to expect. But sometimes it would come out of the blue."

While some of the women made a connection between the batterer's substance use and the frequency of battering, another group of women insisted that even if the use contributed to the battering in some way, the violent tendency was already part of the batterer's character even without alcohol and other drugs. Cicely found that "it contributed. [But] it enlightens what already is going on within your mind anyway. . . . It gave you courage to say whatever." Helene concluded, "It can add to it, but those [are] excuses that people use, especially men. 'I was drunk. I was high.' That's not true. . . . That's just an excuse. You can slip without that shit. There is something wrong. Anger. Maybe they're all bipolar." Overwhelmingly, those women who reported substance use by their abusers stated that the abuse was present without alcohol and other drugs but that the use made the battering incidents more likely to inflict serious injury, as demonstrated by Ebony, who stated, "When he was under the influence, that's when he did the most vicious stuff, and when I had to go to the hospital."

Living Through It

Like most women, the women of this study had idealistic ideas about entering into satisfying intimate couplings, free of major conflict. They aspired to secure a man who would be a substantial provider, both financially and emotionally. The majority of the women described circumstances where they were, at the outset, quite happy. The women endured a wide variety of abuse by their male companions. Certainly, intimate partner abuse is not unique to Blacks. The narratives collected in this study, however, emphasize the need to understand the unique aspects of abuse perpetrated by Black men, in particular, and how it is perceived by Black women. The women believed that some of the bases for abuse by Black males are different from White men's motives and that the abuse grows out of social structure issues complicated by gender roles, economic concerns, and racial matters. The women also spoke of the impact of the intergenerational diffusion of family and intimate partner abuse, a dislike of women, and the impact of alcohol and other drugs on abuse.

Starting with a foundation in Black feminist criminology, this understanding of Black women's entrée into and experiences with intimate partner abuse supports the model of dynamic resistance. The model of dynamic resistance can provide a more adequate examination of these women's patterns of abuse in their relationships. The women's experiences with multiple forms of abuse placed them in the precarious position of having to determine how to deal with the batterers. The description of the abuses endured shows the resolve of the women. While they faced ongoing challenges related to being a Black woman in U.S. society, they had to resist recurring abuse in their personal lives and were faced with negotiating the special issue of Black men. The love-hate relationship with male batterers is complicated when the men are Black and are struggling within the confines of a stratified society just as Black women do. This dilemma left the Black women in this study with feelings of ambivalence, torn between upholding one aspect of the Strong Black Woman by continuing to coddle and take care of these men or upholding another aspect of the Strong Black Woman role by using their personal strength to resist their assaults.

6

Fighting Back
"You Want to Fight? We Gonna Fight!"

By the time Medea and her abusive husband, Henry, were approximately five years into their relationship, they were sleeping in separate rooms and Medea was already seriously contemplating getting a divorce. During their relationship, Medea called the police on a regular basis to intervene in Henry's battering toward her. Sadly, the police in the Caribbean town where Medea resided were especially indifferent to woman battering. After what was to be the final battering incident, the police responded but left soon after. Later that evening, Medea took it upon herself to prevent any future battering by Henry:

I waited till he was asleep and I got a knife. I gently turned the [knob] on his bedroom door and the door was locked. I had to take stock, I had to look at what I was doing, look at who I was becoming, look at what was going on with me. I had to look at that, as well as to look at the impact on my children. What kind of children did I want? Who did I want to raise? So I had to really do some introspection. . . . Aside from killing him, nothing would have satisfied me in terms of hurting him. I think he was so emotionally fucked that I think that very little could have hurt him. I really do. I just don't think—I can't conceive of anything that could have hurt him. I think he's hurting now, 'cause [our children] have no contact at all with him. But [back] then, no.

Women respond to intimate partner abuse in numerous ways, and many women utilize several methods throughout the course of the abusive relationship. Initially, women who are confronted with abuse tend to focus on the positive features of the abusive relationships.[1] This was the situation for the women in my study. And, as I demonstrated in the previous chapter, the women were shocked by the first violent physical attacks and were often uncertain as to how to proceed in the relationship. The most common response in the early stages of the abuse is for a woman to placate, accommodate, and/or avoid the batterer.[2] Several of the women demonstrated this indulgent behavior by aspiring to be the perfect wife and mother. Mary Ann Dutton and her colleagues identified that battered women employ these and other "strategic responses" to protect themselves and their children from further intimate partner abuse.[3]

The more resistant and retaliatory strategies of talking back and hitting back are also forms of personal methods for responding to intimate partner abuse. The compelling circumstances that lead battered women to retaliate physically against a batterer may be connected to the severity of an abusive event, the expected outcome, or the battered woman's personal experiences with abuse (particularly that which took place during childhood). The need for battered women to physically fight back has received significant attention in other research.[4] There are many cases where a battered woman has succeeded in putting an end to her abuse through the application of extreme or lethal violence. Though such cases have been profiled in academic literature,[5] it is the popular media that brought women who murder their abusers to the general public's attention. These acts may occur at the time the abuser attacks, or, in a more passive, safer method, while the batterer is incapacitated in some way (for example, asleep or intoxicated) or otherwise not expecting an imminent reprisal by the resister.

A series of studies has demonstrated that the propensity to combat the attacks of a batterer varies between women of different races and ethnicities. In particular, Black women have been found to fight back at greater rates than White women.[6] As most couples are intraracial, a review of statistical findings regarding intimate partner violence against Black men (of whom most would identify as heterosexual, meaning that they have been assaulted by Black women) is important to mention with this analysis. In an evaluation of the National Crime Victimization Survey (NCVS) data, Callie Marie Rennison and Sarah Welchans ascertained that intimate partner violence against Black men was approximately 62 percent higher than that of White men.[7] This survey (and the resultant estimations) is based on interviews conducted with a sample of households across the United States. Individuals age 12 and older in each household were interviewed about offenses perpetrated against them during a specified time period. Black men reported a relatively large number of violent behaviors directed at them by their (mostly) Black female intimate partners. According to James A. Mercy and Linda E. Saltzman's examination of spousal homicide based on the Federal Bureau of Investigation's Supplemental Homicide Reports from 1976 to 1985, Black husbands had a greater chance of being killed by a spouse than did Black wives, White wives, or White husbands.[8] However, recent aggregate calculations show that in the United States between 1976 and 2004, as a group, the number of Black males killed by their intimate partners declined more than the number of Black women or White men or women killed by their intimate partners. While 844 Black men were killed by an intimate partner in 1976, 152 were killed in 2004, an 82 percent decrease. Compare that change with a 56 percent decline in Black females killed by their intimate partners (713 deaths in 1976 vs. 316 in 2004), a 55 percent decline for White males (486 vs. 221 deaths), and only a 5 percent decline for White females (846 vs. 801 deaths).[9] To date, no conceptual analysis has been formulated to explain what appear to be significant variations within groups and between groups. Indeed, it is hoped that such an endeavor is addressed in future research and considering the findings of the study I present throughout this book.

Even though there has been inquiry into women's use of violence in intimate relationships, along with some quantitative analyses of racial variances, the conceptual framing that would explain battered Black women's experiences with the use of violence and their propensity to fight off their abusers is lacking.[10] Accordingly, in this chapter, I first provide a comprehensive discussion of research that has addressed the issues associated with battered women's retaliation in general and then consider Blacks and battered Black women specifically. An extensive look at this research is particularly important in this area of my study because of the unremitting stereotypes that Black women are angry women (and therefore violent women) that is often promulgated by seemingly sound academic inquests. I then supply an assessment of the women's motivations for and incidents of physically retaliating against their intimate attackers, including those thoughts and actions of lethal proportions. The narratives expounded can help us understand battered Black women's use of retaliatory violence against their abusers by causing us to truly listen to what the women have to say and to take into account their position in U.S. society and their perceptions of self. Considered under the dynamic resistance model, their efforts cannot be viewed merely as retribution; the women were not simply "hitting back." The findings imparted here have immense implications for the general well-being of battered Black women, the dissemination of further information about Black women's use of violence in abusive relationships, and the response by criminal justice system workers.

Abusive Women, Mutual Combatance, or Self-Defense?

When women use violence against their intimate partners, their action usually falls into one of three categories: (a) as a form of self-defense, (b) as a participant in mutual combat (also known as gender symmetry), or (c) as a lone aggressor.[11] As reported in research using Murray A. Straus's Conflict Tactics Scales and in arrest reports after the implementation of pro-arrest policies for intimate partner violence, some argue that women do abuse their (usually) male intimate partners.[12] The Conflict Tactics Scales are a quantitative tool used to measure family violence, including violence between intimate heterosexual partners.[13] Straus reports that findings based on the use of the Conflict Tactics Scales as a measurement have resulted in the publication of at least 10 books and 400 articles.[14]

Since the 1980s and in publications using the Conflict Tactics Scales, there has been an impassioned debate about whether intimate partner violence is "gendered," meaning that resisters tend to be of one certain gender (female) and perpetrators tend to be of the other gender (male). The camps in this debate are the "family violence" scholars, including Straus, who argue that intimate partner violence is overwhelmingly *not* gendered, and "feminist" or "violence against women" scholars who argue that intimate partner violence *is* gendered.[15] Feminist critique argues that the Conflict Tactics Scales are lacking in contextual considerations of violence used by women toward their (male) intimate partners, such as the use of force in self-defense.[16] Employing the limited or "narrow" scales approach "conflates acts of violence and aggression and does not examine the context, consequences, motivations, intentions and reactions associated with the overall violent 'event' or the relationships in which the violence occurs."[17] In a rejoinder to feminist criticism, Straus argues that the symmetric results garnered from using the Conflict Tactics Scales bother many feminists not only because they find the outcomes hard to believe but also because feminists are concerned that such results might jeopardize financial support for battered women's services.[18]

With the statistical support of "official" arrest data (such as those compiled by the FBI in the Uniform Crime Reports) and self-report surveys (including the NCVS), feminist-supported research continues to argue that violence is gendered. In much of the research comparing female and male use of violence in intimate relationships, clear gender differences have been established, specifically related to the extent of injuries, the level of fear, and the offending and victimization histories of women and men. Women are targets of more acts of violence and more *severe* acts of violence than men.[19] Males subjected to intimate partner violence feel less threatened by or fearful of their abusive mates than do their female counterparts,[20] and men often find women's violence against men in intimate relationships "comical or ludicrous."[21] Men possess and exert more control in violent relationships than women, and the initial incident of violence in a relationship was reported more by men than by women.[22] Kris Henning and Lynette Feder found that female perpetrators of intimate partner violence were less likely than male perpetrators to have offending histories that suggest a propensity to commit further violence.[23] Eileen Mazur Abel found that women seen as "victims" of intimate partner violence and women who are considered batterers (of male intimate partners) have similar victimization histories, with both groups reporting elevated levels of exposure to violence.[24] Abel found differences between the women in their use of social services related to intimate partner violence; the women "batterers" utilized fewer of these resources than the women "victims." She concludes that the "resource" used by women "batterers" is fighting back, while the other women rely on established social services.[25] Similarly, in their study comparing women's and men's use of violence in intimate relationships, L. Kevin Hamberger and Clare E. Guse found that women court-ordered into batterer intervention programs called the police more often than men under similar court orders but less often than battered women in shelters.[26] These factors support that intimate partner violence is gendered.

Russell P. Dobash and R. Emerson Dobash ascertain that physical responses by battered women toward their abusers fall into three categories: self-protection, self-defense, and revenge.[27] Self-protection includes covering one's face by holding up one's arms to shield oneself from a blow to the head. Self-defense suggests that the battered woman responds in kind during a battering incident. Finally, revenge (also referred to as "retaliation") entails some emotional element, such as anger, and includes a battered woman's violent response after prolonged abuse, though not necessarily during or immediately after an abusive event. In their study of 95 heterosexual couples in which the men had been convicted of intimate partner violence, Dobash and Dobash discovered that while only six of the men said they retaliated against their female partners, they did not frame that behavior in the context of self-defense. However, 75 percent of the women in their study reported that their violence was *always* an act of self-defense or self-protection. Daniel G. Saunders also examined the terms used in reference to battered women's application of violence. He determined that battered women who used violence against their abusers saw "fighting back" and "self-defense" as the same.[28]

To be sure, many studies have determined that a large number of women who get arrested for intimate partner assault report that they were acting in self-defense.[29] Saunders's research established that self-defense was the most prevalent motive among battered women who used violence in their intimate relationships. Suzanne C. Swan and David L. Snow concluded from their research that the motivation for women in heterosexual battering relationships to be physically aggressive varies depending on the type of relationship and the woman's role within that relationship. For women who committed more acts of violence and control than their male intimate partners, referred to as "Abused Aggressors," Swan and Snow found that a desire for retribution and control tended to be the motive for their aggression. These women were categorized as being in a subordinated role, however, because "despite the balance of power being tilted toward the women in the Abused Aggressor group, as indicated by the greater levels of abuse committed by Abused Aggressors in comparison to their partners, Abused Aggressors do not feel a sense of control, autonomy, or agency in their relationships or their lives in general." Conversely, for the women whose partners were more violent and controlling than the women—the "Victims"—Swan and Snow identified defense of themselves (that is, "self-defense") as their likely motive for using violence in the relationship.[30]

It has been supported in some research that women who retaliate against their batterers may intensify their susceptibility to further injury, as opposed to improving their safety.[31] Shamita Das Dasgupta noted that women are not very successful in achieving their desired results when they use violence against their abusers.[32] Ronet Bachman and her co-investigators found that while doing nothing to defy abuse and physically resisting abuse either did not prove effective or increased the probability of further abuse, forms of nonphysical resistance did avert injury or reduce the likelihood of further assaults against women.[33] Nonphysical resistance efforts include verbal threats, reasoning, and calling attention to the assaultive or preassaultive behavior. While physical self-defense efforts may increase the level or severity of violence toward the resister, Dobash and Dobash warn that it is not as simple as directing battered women not to fight back, because the dynamics vary among abusive relationships.[34]

If a battering resister expects that her hitting back will cause the abuser to stop the violence and that she will therefore reduce her risk for future injuries, she may opt for this approach, but negative consequences may ensue. Kathleen J. Ferraro and John M. Johnson contend that when battered women express their anger over their abuse, they frequently feel as though they have done something constructive in combating the abuse and delight in this expression of defense. However, these activities are complicated by the expectation that women should not adopt angry and aggressive behaviors because they do not represent femininity. Therefore, Ferraro and Johnson conclude that finding a balance between defensive acts and prescribed gender roles proves difficult for women.[35] Other emotions resulting from battered women's use of violence toward their abusers include anxiety and fear, which develop from the women's realization that they—like their batterers—also have the ability to be violent.[36] Ultimately, the physical retaliation by battered women against their abusers does not necessarily ensure emotional healing, even if the resisters are successful in their aggressive pursuits.[37]

Much of the research literature summarized here supports that there is *not* symmetry between men and women in relation to intimate partner violence. The feminist-based consideration of this form of violence by women necessarily allows us to consider the context and motivations for the violence. When women do use violence in intimate partnerships, it is likely to be for the purpose of self-protection and self-defense. These studies strongly indicate that women's use of violence is more often a form of safeguarding as opposed to simply being a form of comparable aggression.

Explanations for Race Variance in Battering Resistance

Stereotypical images of Black women have led to a debate in research that addresses battered Black women's success or potential success in using the "battered woman's syndrome" legal defense as it was originally developed by Lenore E. A. Walker.[38] Battered woman's syndrome is a legal application of battered women's so-called learned helplessness and is typically used to explain why battered women kill their battering male mates. The concept of learned helplessness was introduced by Martin E. P. Seligman, who discovered that laboratory animals were unable to escape abusive situations even after eventually being provided an opportunity to flee the abusive environment. Seligman then applied his findings to humans suffering from depression, asserting that depressed individuals feel they have little or no control over their lives.[39] The notion of learned helplessness as it applies to battered women was advanced by Walker and became very well known among the general public and legal community. Walker applied this theory to battered women to explain why—like Seligman's lab animals—these women find it difficult to leave abusive relationships.

It has been argued that battered woman's syndrome fails to be an applicable and practical theory for all women[40] and that there is not a single personality profile for all battered women.[41] Sharon A. Allard asserts that because Walker's battered woman's syndrome is based on the stereotype of the White helpless woman, it cannot be applied to a Black woman who is frequently seen as angry and independent. "To successfully defend herself, a battered woman needs to convince a jury that she is a 'normal' woman—weak, passive, and fearful."[42] Evan Stark reasoned that battered woman's syndrome is not generally found among Black women. Since battered Black women may be employed, respond to violence and abuse with physical fighting, and have criminal histories, they do not match the profile of the battered woman.[43] Even if battered Black women do demonstrate characteristics that fit with those of battered White women, the stereotype of the Black woman may prevail in court settings.

Beyond numerically descriptive differences in the use of resistance methods, there is little research that has attempted to explain the differences by race in the use of resistant violence by battered women, and some research is based on mendacious beliefs about Blacks. One explanation for the disparate use of force concerns the different rates of exposure to violence, that is, that Black women are more likely to live in neighborhoods and family environments where there is purportedly a higher concentration of violence. Other explanations focus on acceptance of violence. Diane R. Follingstad, along with her co-investigators, discovered that Blacks were more tolerant of the use of force in intimate relationships than Whites.[44] This reasoning is similar to the subculture-of-violence theory (and similar propositions), which suggests that a belief in the use of violence among Blacks is normative—more so than among White people, in particular. The theory contends that in certain subcultures, violence is accepted and promoted.[45] It has been hypothesized that the Black subculture is one that endorses or supports violence within its community and among its community members.[46]

The most recognized explication of the subculture-of-violence theory is the work of Marvin E. Wolfgang and Franco Ferracuti from the 1960s.[47]

Wolfgang and Ferracuti attempted to explain the varying rates of violent acts among subcultures situated within the general ("American") culture. They argued that a subculture of violence does exist and maintained that:

> [T]he term itself—subculture—presupposes an already existing complex of norms, values, attitudes, material traits, etc. What the subculture-of-violence formulation further suggests is simply that there is a potent theme of violence current in the cluster of values that make up the life-style, the socialization process, the interpersonal relationships of individuals living in similar conditions.[48]

According to Wolfgang and Ferracuti's thesis, the values perpetuated within the subculture of the Black community, which include the "acceptance" of violence, explain why Blacks have higher rates of homicide and other violent acts than are found in the dominant culture (Whites) of U.S. society.[49] Notably, Wolfgang and Ferracuti provided their racially stereotypic explanation for the fact that Black women commit violent acts, specifically homicide, at a higher rate than by White women in their book *The Subculture of Violence: Toward an Integrated Theory in Criminology*:

> Violent behavior appears more dependent on cultural differences than on sex differences, traditionally considered of paramount importance in the expression of aggression. It could be argued, of course, that in a more matriarchal role than that of her white counterpart, the Negro female both enjoys and suffers more of the male role as head of the household, as parental authority and supervisor; that this imposed role makes her more aggressive, more male-like, more willing and more likely to respond violently. Because most of the victims of Negro female homicide offenders are Negro males, the Negro female may be striking out aggressively against the inadequate male protector whom she desperately wants but often cannot find or hold.[50]

Although this conclusion was pronounced 40 years ago, Wolfgang and Ferracuti's deduction was recognized more than two decades later by Jan E. Stets in her investigation of intimate partner violence. Stets determined that there is indeed a subculture of violence among Blacks.[51] So how might Wolfgang and Ferracuti's conclusion explain the noteworthy plunge in the number of Black men killed by their intimate partners over the past three decades, since a large percentage of Black women continue to play the same egalitarian roles in their personal, professional, and public lives? One could posit that because society has changed since the declarations of Wolfgang and Ferracuti 40 years ago and has become more accepting of the independence of all women, this alleviates the pressures for Black women to be "more aggressive, more male-like." However, Black women continue to be portrayed as being more aggressive, masculine, angry, and violent than White women, and society continues to suggest that such controlling behaviors should be quelled if Black women are to behave more in keeping with established so-called feminine characteristics. In addition, many other factors must be considered and other research can be reviewed to begin to understand race variations in the use of violence in intimate relationships.

Although there have been scholarly inquiries that have continued to support the subculture-of-violence theory to explain regional and racial variations in violent crime,[52] much research has refuted this approach to explaining the differences in violent crime rates between Blacks and groups belonging to other ethnicities and races. For instance, Coramae Richey Mann found that the subculture-of-violence theory is not applicable to Black women who commit homicide because most of the demographic features of women who kill do not vary by ethnicity or race.[53] In their study of female homicide offenders, Melvin C. Ray and Earl Smith surmised that *if* there is a subculture of violence, it is one that affects Black women's and White women's motivations equally, because when they commit homicides, both groups of women tend to kill adult men to whom they are closely related and of the same race.[54] Testing six theoretical models to explain rape, Cynthia S. Gentry found that the racial subculture-of-violence model was not supported but that the crime of rape was supported by the social disorganization model.[55] Regarding the supposed belief system perpetuated by the subculture-of-violence theory— that Blacks value and condone the use of violence more than others— some studies debunked this conclusion by finding that Blacks actually had a *lower* tolerance for the use of violence than Whites.[56]

The conceptualization of the subculture-of-violence theory has been contested because other societal factors were not taken into consideration. Darnell F. Hawkins found that the historical devaluing of the lives of Blacks, the consequences of indigence, and the criminal justice system's responses to violent behaviors of Blacks are causal factors overlooked by the subculture-of-violence theory.[57] Further, Augustine J. Kposowa and colleagues argue that "some previous researchers . . . argued in favor of a black subculture of violence without studying other race and ethnic groups. Because blacks, Hispanics, and American Indians have dissimilar cultures, the subculture of violence thesis is an unlikely explanation for the high rates of criminal participation that characterize these disparate groups." These researchers found that conditions such as urbanity and population density are more credible explanations for violent crime in general, and for homicide specifically, and that additional factors of poverty and divorce better explain the variations.[58] Alternative approaches to the subculture-of-violence theory that include these other influences in their analysis have been introduced to explain the contrasting rates of violence among people of different races and ethnicities.

Accordingly, the subculture-of-violence theory is not adequate, nor are there enough valid data to account for violence that pervades the Black community and Black families. Robert Staples concludes that Black couples are not inherently more violent in their relationships than are White couples.[59] Therefore, it is not sufficient or appropriate to use the subculture-of-violence theory to propose that battered Black women find violence in their lives, families, and communities "normal" and that this explains their being in abusive intimate relationships and fighting back.

Positioning Themselves for Fighting Back

The women in my study shared with me their physical efforts to protect and defend themselves and to be resisters. Their stories demonstrate how they gained agency through resistance against their abusers. Placing these stories alongside their accounts about their self-identification reveals to the academic, criminal justice, political, and Black communities the *complexity* of the world in which these women must function.

There were relationships between the women's exposure to violence during childhood and their propensity to respond in kind to abusive intimate partners and the timing of that action. Of the seven women who were not exposed to any noteworthy forms of abuse during their youth, five of them were especially reluctant to fight their batterers, although a few did make attempts toward the end of the abusive relationships. Naomi typically did not fight back and stated her reason for doing so by replying, "I did what I could at that time, what I knew at that time." Paula also never fought her abuser but felt differently at the time of her interview: "When I see him . . . I feel like pushing him. . . . [H]e's a symbol of something negative to me. So I feel like striking out at him. . . . I feel like he was taking the power and manipulating it. Sometimes I feel like I can do it, too, now."

All but four of the 33 women who *were* exposed to a type of abuse during their upbringing regularly fought back. One of these four women was Gloria, who was a fighter during her youth and did not understand why she did not retaliate against her four abusers. Her background was different from that of the remaining three women who were introduced to violence during childhood and did not typically fight back. Gloria was raised mainly by her mother in a working-class household and was the middle child, with two siblings. The other three women had fairly similar childhood backgrounds. Phoebe, Grace, and Erica were each raised by both biological parents and were middle children. Grace and Erica each have six siblings, and Phoebe has eight. Erica's home of origin was low income, while Grace and Phoebe were reared in working-class homes. Like most of the women who were *not* exposed to abuse during their upbringing, these three women usually did not fight back, and when they did, it was at the close of the relationships. It may be that these three women did not physically react to their abuse because they were making unwavering attempts to cling to the model of parenthood with which they were familiar and for which they were grateful. Phoebe's narrative illustrates that she did what she could to protect herself:

> I started to in the end, but of course he's bigger than me. He's a man. He hits harder. I would try. I would slap him or push him away from me, but I can only do so much. Especially being pregnant, I'm not gonna endanger my kid. I would just try to protect myself from his rage as much as I could.

As demonstrated in Phoebe's account, the women's decision to fight was often dictated by the physical size and strength of their batterers. Many of the women acknowledged these physiological differences between women and men. A few even commented that they now like to be with men who are comparatively small in stature, because the women would have equal footing when the violence commenced or the men would simply be reluctant to introduce physical abuse into the relationship because of their diminutive size. These women tended to recount such stories in a joking manner; however, there was an insinuation of seriousness in their claims. Regarding physical size in prior abusive relationships and the women's attempts at physical resistance, Jacqueline replied, "I tried [to fight him]. He was like The Hulk, and I was a little runt. He would literally pick me up and throw me, and I'd be airborne until I landed somewhere." Although they often described the batterers' physical attributes, this typically did not deter the women from fighting back.

Rejection of the Victim Label

In Chapter 3, I began to speak to the victim labeling issue among the women. This matter has also been addressed in other literature. Carolyn M. West and Suzanna Rose contend, "Perhaps women who do not identify as oppressed by men who use physical aggression against their partners because they perceive themselves as empowered, rather than as victims. Due to Black women's long history of physical abuse and oppression, both within their homes and in the larger society, they had to be prepared to defend themselves against violence."[60] Similar to West and Rose's assertion, Patricia Hill Collins writes, "Because hegemonic ideologies make everyday violence against Black women appear so routine, some women perceive neither themselves nor those around them as victims."[61] Beth E. Richie found that the battered Black women in her study did not identify as battered women either because the women fought back or because they did not feel subordinated by the men they knew.[62] Finally, Barbara Rogers and her colleagues found that battered Black women need help to realize that they have been "victimized," whereas White women are able to identify as "victims" prior to seeking treatment services.[63]

The self-perception among the women in my study that they were *not* victims is based in the issues raised in the previous research and is also the result of the women's internalizing the position of society and the criminal justice system not to regard and acknowledge Black women as victims. It must be noted that there were no leading questions included in my interview guide or asked during the interviews regarding "victimhood." The women's words about their inability to identify as victims or battered women were their own. Their perceptions emerged at various points during our time together. Even though Naomi did not physically resist her abusive mates to the same extent as most of the other women, she offered the following acknowledgment about her first battering situation, expressing the sentiment of many of the women: "I didn't think of myself as being battered." Queen is a certified counselor who was a facilitator of educational and treatment groups for substance abusers and batterers, particularly for court-ordered offenders. Queen's most volatile relationship ended many years ago. She described this relationship in the context of the recognized definition of "domestic violence":

I fought back, but I just got beat down. That's the way I was. That was it. I was just getting beat. No big deal. Still today, I don't see it as domestic violence. I was just getting beat up. I know "domestic" is because it was my partner. If they want to call it domestic violence [they can]. . . . To me I was just getting beat up by a man, by my husband. I was [leading] my substance abuse groups. . . . Now I was going to do domestic violence groups with [my boss]. They were all men. I'd be sitting there with her. Guys would come in. She'd be talking to them about their behavior, beating up their wives. Still, I didn't feel like I'd been a victim. I don't know why. They're talking about beating their wives. I was never like, "Yeah, I know how that is." I never connected that I had been a victim of what they're in there for. . . . Women buy into being a victim.

The inability to view themselves as victims aided in the women's inclination to respond to their batterers' violent acts with corresponding force. This was helped along by the language they used to describe the abuse in their intimate relationships, which has been evident in many of the narratives presented up to this point. The women used terms such as "getting beat down," "getting knocked out," and "getting my ass kicked." But in describing, more specifically, the instances where they were physically resisting the abusers, terms such as "fighting" and "battling" were used. For example, when speaking of the violence that took place in the second of her three abusive relationships, Tammy framed her response in this way: "We had a couple fights. Pretty much, we fought. It wasn't like he beat me, we fought. He gave me a black eye, I bust his lip. It was only a couple of times because I wasn't with him very long. He didn't even last a year." Another example of the distinction in terms is in Ebony's description of an altercation that took place with the first of her two abusive boyfriends: "I was at my cousin's house. We was smoking weed. He didn't want me to smoke weed, so when I was getting ready to put the weed out, that's when he grabbed me by the hair and threw me on the table. Me and my cousins got up and was fighting him, but he was knocking us out."

The semantics of viewing the abuse as fights and battles redefines the circumstance of "woman battering" for battered Black women, making abuse equal to being solicited into physical conflict with a stranger. Although violent crimes against women are most often perpetrated by a person who previously has known the woman,[64] it is accepted, and perhaps expected, in U.S. society that one try to fend off unknown attackers by any means necessary to protect oneself. It is much less clear how one is to handle aggression by acquaintances. Comparatively, by considering the abuse directed at them as equal to being engaged in fights and battles— terms more likely used to describe stranger or "street" altercations—instead of "woman battering," the women enabled themselves to regard the abuse by an intimate partner through a stranger perspective, where it is more acceptable to physically resist.

The Fight Is On

Most of the women fought back on a regular basis. Raised middle-class, Helene related experiences that captured many of the women's contextualization of being beaten and the initiation of counteractive measures against their batterers. She describes her response to her second abusive husband:

> After a while, you get tired. After a few times of me not fighting back because I still don't know what I'm doing. I don't like to fight. I never have. . . . That's crazy. But you have to do what you have to do at a certain point; I don't care how old you are. I stood up. I was so tired. I stood on my toes and I dropped him in the kitchen. . . . You let somebody think that you're afraid, and they'll get away with it and they'll just keep on.

Helene also shared her current attitude about resisting abusers: "I'll fight back. I'll take so much and then I've got to go at it. That's just it. As long as I don't swing first, whatever you get is self-defense. If I hit you first, that's different." Danielle shared a similar attitude when she spoke of why she is cautious when entering new relationships:

> I'm afraid that I'm gonna kill somebody. They come running up on me talking about jumping on me. I'm not takin' no more ass whuppings. . . . I try not to put myself in the positions to where we have to fight. . . . You can't raise me, I can't raise you. Don't hit me, I won't hit you, 'cause now I hit back and I even cut.

The women made their best attempts not to repeat the aggressive dysfunction of their parents and other family members who engaged in violence. Renee made the connection between childhood maltreatment and future experiences with abuse: "Yeah, I was abusive, too. So the abused can become the abuser. . . . I can tell you I was a hitter. I did a lot of knocking brains out. A lot of that was volatile energy because I didn't want to be like my mom." Renee viewed her mother as weak and as a victim of her father's abuse: "My mom was very much like Edith Bunker[65] in behavior. You could peek around the corner and say 'boo' and she would just fall apart." This is a rare perception, maintained by only a few women of their mothers. Typically, as described in Chapter 3, the women saw their mothers as *strong* women, regardless of their relationships with their mothers or whether or not their mothers were in abusive intimate partnerships.

Some of the women would strike first if they thought the batterer was set to hit them. Inez stated, "I started fighting back because I could look in his eyes and I could see he was getting ready to hurt me; then I'll start trying to hurt him before he hurt me." Even though she was the first to hit in certain situations, Inez still framed her behavior as a form of resistance against abuse, not as an unwarranted act of violence. As described earlier, a number of the women were fighters during their youth, including Cicely. When asked if there was abuse in her first marriage, Cicely replied: "I probably was abusive to him. . . . If I couldn't have my way I either hit him or throw something at him. I remember one time I threw a straightening comb at him. I threw the iron and hit him, too. Skillet, too." Cicely's first husband was never physically abusive to her. Even in her first abusive relationship where she was on the receiving end of abuse, Cicely believed she was the first to be *physically* aggressive: "I don't remember the very first time. It started mostly with the verbal stuff. The first time, I probably would have hit him first. You get tired of being called names and stuff." Cicely did make attempts to quell her aggressive behavior but disliked the resulting emotions: "When they attack me first, or pushed me and I didn't retaliate, then I would get angry with myself because I didn't retaliate and I would keep it in myself. I'm saying, 'OK, I deserved that, I'll be cool.' Till it builds up. Then somebody else would get it."

Toni also described herself as a fighter and described how this transpired in her abusive relationships:

I'm a fighter. I'm gonna fight. You want to fight? We gonna fight! We can take it outside. 'Cause I wasn't going to let him just hit on me. When I bulked back up to him, he would back down. But one time . . . I said, "I need to go to the grocery store." I come back and he meets me outside the house. He said to strip. He had a weapon on me, outside in my front yard. I had to take my clothes off. He had a knife. Here I am standing stark butt naked outside, crying. It was during the day. No one was outside. There was a [football] game on [TV]. We didn't stay for the whole game, so everyone else was in the house watching the game. My kids were at a friend's house. Somehow, I can't remember, I ended up getting back in the house. He got very physical. He put the knife up and said, "You want to fight? We gonna fight." So we started fighting. Somehow he had pinned me on the bed, so I took everything I had and kicked him right in the stomach. He bulked down to the floor and we had to take *him* to the hospital.

Discernibly, a number of the women may have stunned their batterers with the ferocity of their resistance. While Billie was with her sister visiting one of her sister's friends (a male Asian American), her abusive boyfriend Kobe located Billie at the male friend's home. In the ensuing altercation, Billie succeeded in astonishing Kobe with the intensity of her resistance:

We was drinking and stuff. Anyway, Kobe must have came home while I was still gone. I don't even know how he found out where we were at. But he came to this guy's house and put his fist through this man's back door window. We're sitting here. You know Japanese people, they make you take your shoes off. We're sitting here with our *shoes off*. Not our clothes. Our shoes, our shoes! He went in there, dragged me the hell out, beat the hell out of me, and then gonna tell me, "Get in the car." Something in my mind was like, Billie, honey, if you get in that car, you ain't coming back. I was like, hell no I'm not getting in this car. I'm not getting in this car. He tried to make me get in the car. Girl, I lost all nails I had, girl, 'cause I was fightin'! I was scared that he would drive off a cliff or run into a pillar. . . . I knew, when you get in that car, uh-uh, something's gonna happen. So I didn't get in the car and I walked back home. Mind you, I'm still drunk, OK? I'm staggering back home. . . . And I forget he had my key. He picked up my key off the ground while he was trying to push me in the car. So I didn't have a key to get in the house. So I sat on the porch and waited for him to come home so I could get in the house. I don't know why I wanted to get in the house. I should have just went to my sister's house. But no, you're drunk, so you don't think correctly. I was sitting there on the porch. He came up and he knocked the shit out of me! He knocked me off the porch. It's kind of a high porch. I fell off in the rose bushes and everything. I had thorns sticking out of my head and everything. He hit me so hard I was sober. I wasn't drunk anymore. I was sober. And I remembered what my sister said: "You got to whup his ass! You got to put a stop to it, or else he's gonna kill you." We had dirt in our yard. I got me a handful of dirt, Hillary, and I threw it in his face! I had on some Dr. Scholl's sandals, with the wood on the bottom of them, with the little strap of leather. I took them shoes off, put them around my hand and I just started whaling on his ass! I was just whaling on him, girl. He called the police on *me*! I had been getting jumped on for five years. I'm tired of this. I can't take it anymore. And they take *me* to jail. He kept telling them, "She's a manic depressive. She refuses to take her medicine. That's why she's out here jumping on me." Girl, I wasn't a manic depressive. I was tired of him kicking my ass!

The women's resistant efforts did not always go without eliciting a threatening response from their batterers. Jade felt she further angered her abuser by fighting back. This was Angie's experience, too, when her efforts at fighting back seemed to cause the opposite effect of what she was trying to accomplish with one of her three abusive boyfriends: "I did [fight back], but then I realized it was futile. You would think when you hit back that they would just stop. . . . But it did end quicker when I didn't fight back. So I learned that. We could be battlin' all day, but when I didn't hit back it was shorter. Couple, five, six punches or whatever." Ebony also had this encounter when she resisted, but she decided to alter her approach:

I started getting weapons when it started getting worse. I had to pick up a vase one time because he was coming at me with closed fists. A broom to back him up off me. I remember I grabbed a knife to back him up off me one time. . . . [O]nce I got like that, he would just keep hitting me like I was a regular person. Once I started getting his routine down, then I would pick up something so that . . . he ain't going to hit me that first time to where he could just continue to hit me. . . . Probably with a frying pan, that was the worst. He had to get stitches for that. I hit him on the side of his head with that.

While generally satisfied that they stood up for themselves, some of the women saw their fighting back as a game employed by the batterer that they were deceived into playing. This was the case for Olivia, who recounted, "I slapped back. . . . I played into that." Medea also considered that she fell into the game of using violence to respond to violence. She declared, "I was a spirited co-combatant." Although Medea referred to herself in a manner that would be consistent with the family violence standpoint (as opposed to the feminist position) on intimate partner abuse, analysis of her entire narrative indicates that she did not consider herself to be the producer of the abuse and violence that existed in the relationship.

Several women seriously thought about killing their abusers, and some of them actually made attempts to do so. Eight women divulged lethal actions and/or thoughts. Of the women who disclosed murderous feelings and actions, three contemplated killing their abusive mates but did not make any serious efforts to do so. Each of these three women was in her respective relationship for no more than three years. Billie described how she began to feel about Kobe after being repeatedly sexually and physically abused by him:

What makes you think after you jump on me I'm going to sleep with you? He would lay down and go to sleep with me. I was like, what if I just get up and get a butcher knife and slit his throat while he's sleep, after he done jumped on me and had sex? I used to think about that.

Also within her private thoughts, Jacqueline planned out the death of her husband, who was the first of two abusers in her life, and why she did not follow through with her strategy:

I remember laying in bed at night thinking, OK, I could kill him now and I can go hide the body out in the field. Literally plotting his death. It was getting to the point where I was seriously thinking about doing it. I didn't want to stay the rest of my life in jail. That's what did it. That was the last straw. If it would have been one more day, I honestly think I would have probably been in jail for murder. I was sleeping with knives under the pillows, knives stuck down in the side of the couch. But whenever it would come to it, if he would hit me, I never did pull them out. I think he would have killed me if I would have. His demise was going to be in his sleep. He was huge. I was scared if he got [the knife] from me, the way he acted he would have took me out, if he was awake during that.

The remaining five women who had lethal thoughts also spoke of having made actual attempts to slay their abusers. For most of these women who made these attempts—including Medea, whose harrowing anecdote opened this chapter—it was by chance that they did not kill the batterers. The women's endeavors ranged from trying to locate the abuser to kill him to being in the act of harming him and hoping for his death. These attempts also ranged from impromptu to premeditated. The members of this group of women were in the last of multiple abusive relationships and/or had been in the relationship for at least five years. Cicely told of how she began to feel with her first abusive relationship (her second marriage), which lasted about five years, then of her actions toward her third abuser (her fifth husband), to whom she was married for seven years:

> When I had gotten to the point where [I wanted to get out of my second marriage], I would lay there in bed trying to figure out how I could kill him without me going to jail. Couldn't ever come up with a lot of it. I couldn't ever come up with a good reason in how I can do this. And that's why I never killed him. One of them I did try. He would come in and he would want to have sex and I didn't want to be bothered. . . . He would force himself and it would hurt. Twice he choked me to where I passed out. I would leave and I would go back. I would keep a gun up under the mattress. . . . I ended up in the hospital, but not because of his hitting me and with his verbal abuse and taking the car and selling it to drug dealers. I got so angry that I couldn't kill him that I tried to commit suicide. They had to put me in the hospital for being homicidal and suicidal. . . . I was trying to kill him, but I couldn't find him. I was goin' kill him, shoot him! Trying to find him, and I couldn't find him. I ended up in the hospital because I was so angry I was going to take it out on myself. I called the [suicide] hotline. . . . I didn't call them to respond; I called them to talk me down, so I could calm down so I wouldn't react.

Danielle was in her third and final abusive relationship when she made her attempt to kill her boyfriend of a year and a half:

> He wanted to whup me like I was his kid, and I told him, "Boy, go sit down!" He's talkin' 'bout, "I whup all my women." I had a can of spray and I sprayed him in his eyes and I just started jabbing him with my knife. . . . I tried to kill him, blind him, sprayed some Raid in his eyes, and I started stabbing him. I didn't know he used to whup his women. And you ain't fent[66] to whup me. . . . That was the first time and the last time that he hit me. . . . I wish he had bled to death. But he didn't.

Wendy was living in Germany with her military husband and children when she reached her threshold of tolerance for her husband's maltreatment and made an attempt to kill him:

We lived up on the sixth floor, and we had a elevator right outside our door. I took off all my clothes. I got stark naked, because I didn't want to get blood on my clothes. I was gonna wash myself off in the bushes. Then dry myself off in the leaves and then tiptoe back up the stairs, and go back in my house. [I did this] so that I would have no bloody clothes or anything. I tiptoed down the stairs at midnight. I hid out, and I had a long butcher knife. I hid outside the compound in the bushes. I waited for him. . . . At that time, American soldiers were being killed over there by Germans. I was gonna say a German killed him. I had planned it all out. The sun was coming out. I said, "Oh my God, I can't stay out here like this." He didn't come home like he said he was gonna come home. I was gonna kill him that night. I was gonna stab him to death. . . . This is how desperate I had gotten. I had got tired of the beatings. . . . He showed up just as I got my clothes on. I had packed his stuff up, I said, "I want you out." He just start kicking me. . . . When he was through, he was sitting on the side of the bed shining his shoes, getting ready for work. I got up, half-crazed out of my mind. I'm in the kitchen, have that same knife I had earlier. . . . He had his back turned, shining his shoes, and I sneak up on him. I went to raise the knife up and to stab him. My daughter just started screaming. . . . When he turned around and he seen the knife in my hand, I said, "She just saved your life. Because if you ever hit me again, I will kill you. I don't care how long I stay in prison. I will kill you." He seen the look in my face, and in my eyes, and he knew that I had had enough. Enough was enough. Then he acted OK—for a while.

As should be evident from these stories of women who thought about or made efforts to take the lives of their abusers, these women had reached a point of great despair. Essentially, these women had reached the limit in their ability to withstand the abuse, even though they had been fighting back in less than lethal ways up to this point. At the time of their deliberations and actions, the women believed that murder was the best way to end the relationship. It was often these most desperate infractions, where the women fought back with brute force or rationally contemplated the outcome of their drastic plots, that finally enabled them to take other actions to end the abusive relationship.

Fighting Back

While the women in this study faced many obstacles in their quests to leave their abusers, they also typically showed incredible fortitude and resilience. According to the concept of Black feminist criminology, where the effects of family, culture, community, and the social structure are simultaneously considered, the women's propensity to fight back can be most suitably evaluated. Fighting is typically viewed as a masculine activity, engaged in mainly by males. However, the women did not view themselves as unfeminine when they fought back but saw themselves as defenders of themselves, their children, and their right to not be abused. The typecast roles of Black women in the United States likely freed the women to resist their batterers without the guilt of feeling less than a woman for doing so.

Because Black women are raised in the United States with the stereotype of being strong, angry, and more masculine than White women, I maintain that many battered Black women can express angry feelings and communicate their anger in a physically resistant manner with less difficulty than other women. This is not because Black women necessarily typify traits of strength, anger, and masculinity but because they are not as constrained to meet a prescribed feminine role within U.S. society. Of course, many Black women are instructed on how to be "ladylike,"[67] particularly by their mothers and othermothers, but, because of compelling societal stereotypes, Black women are less confined by the traditional feminine role than White women may be. Furthermore, most of my informants' mothers concurrently taught them how to be *strong* women, which also aids in battered Black women's proclivity to fight back. If battered Black women choose not to or are unable to fight back, it *may* be because of the fear of subsequent battering, but more likely the reason is the fear of losing their mates, whom they need to provide emotional support, meet societal expectations, serve as full-time fathers, and, occasionally, provide financial assistance. Nevertheless, the women tended to overcome even feelings of great fear of further harm and of being without an intimate companion.

Considering the women's efforts to confront their abusive partners from a Black feminist criminology standpoint, I build upon the concept of dynamic resistance, that is, a form of resistance that can be understood beyond the corporal acts of these women. I conclude that battered Black women typically fight back because they know that they, and all the Black women before them, have labored and persisted through an expansive assortment of struggles, starting with slavery and through present times, and that much of the crusade has not changed in the past several decades. This standpoint allows the women to view their abuse by an intimate as another form of domination that they must fight off on a regular basis. As such, the women do not usually frame their abuse as "battering" or "victimization," but, at the same time, they did not typically consider themselves to be the creators of dissonance and abuse in the relationships. And, as is demonstrated in the next chapter, formal institutions of social control deny or devalue Black women as victims and often see them as *criminals* when they fight back, which denies them a recourse that White women in a similar situation would receive. Effectively, battered Black women are often left to *fight* on their own behalves because these institutions continue to act as though they view Black women as second-class citizens (because of race) or third-class citizens (because of race *and* gender) who are not worthy of all the protections given White women, including protection from the institutions themselves.

7

Getting Out

"We Have to Pray to God and Hope Everything Works Out."

As Billie progressed through her abusive relationships, her dynamic resistance, sowed in her childhood, continued to build. She found it easier to resist the relationships and ultimately found that "Basically, if you just stand up to 'em, stop being such a wimp, stop letting this man do this to you" a woman can stop the abuse or get out of an abusive relationship. In discussing the differences between White and Black women's methods of escape from these relationships, Billie demonstrated the life-long exasperation she believed Black women felt and their more stalwart efforts in abusive relationships: "White women would kill 'em [laughs]. They'd make some poison cookies. Where Black women I think will just [be like], 'I'll kick your ass, but I got to go.'"

However, before getting to a point of leaving, battered women make various attempts to stop the battering. They seek out assistance from family members, friends, religion, and spirituality. In fact, regarding getting out of her relationship with Kobe, Billie asserted:

> Now that I think about it, I'm glad I got away from him. I'd probably be dead and he'd be trying to have sex with my daughter. Who knows what? God only knows. I just thank God. Through all that [God] watched over me and brought me through it. He brought me through it. The only thing I can say is, "Thank you, Jesus, I'm here." I could be six feet under.

This statement by Billie is even more interesting since Kobe left the home soon after the rape described in a previous chapter, when Kobe stole Billie's mother's car and left the home, never to be seen again. Billie's "getting away" from Kobe refers to the stance she took after the rape by sleeping on the living room couch instead of in their shared bed and her certainty that God and her continued belief in the Spirit also contributed to Kobe's being removed from her life. Even though Kobe is finally out of Billie's life, her current intimate partner was physically abusive on one occasion and continues to exhibit verbal abuse. However, Billie believed she had a good deal of control in the relationship and emphasized, "I just thank God that I met Odell. We done had our little arguments and our little go-between. But he found out, she hits back, so we don't have that anymore." In fact, Billie sought out her current husband in order to have him buy her crack:

> I met Odell. I was like, I could get with a little one-night stand, put him out the house and it would be all over with. Actually I was looking at him for a victim. So I can go get some dope. Odell didn't even smoke dope, still don't. He ain't never. After that I made love to Odell and he hasn't left yet.

Further, Billie relayed that Odell has a brain injury that makes him "kind of slow to the draw."

The women also make use of public resources, such as human service agencies and the criminal justice system. While the women had some positive reactions to the support provided by their family and their spirituality, they described less than desirable experiences with religious clergy and public outlets. Billie revealed, "He went to jail for thirty days with twenty-seven of 'em suspended. So he only had to spend three days in jail, and I've got the crap beat out of me!" These encounters, which follow a battered woman's effort to overcome personal obstacles to leaving, can hinder her ability to flee abusive relationships without further harm.

Several explanations for why women stay in abusive relationships have been offered in the research on battered women. To start, these include a combination of the emotions love and despair. At some point at the start of the relationship and prior to the abuse, for example, the soon-to-be battered woman fell in love with her soon-to-be batterer. This love causes much internal conflict for the woman when the abuse starts.[1] Despair comes when the abuse continues and grows in force and all of the woman's efforts to improve the batterer's conduct have gone unheeded. In addition, she may begin to fear her partner because of verbalized or non-verbalized threats against her. Even if the abused woman falls out of love with her batterer—or, in a few cases, never felt any love for him—the fear of further abuse may compel her to remain in the relationship. The differences in levels of fear among the various races and ethnicities of women are not regularly addressed in existing research, but one can speculate on the basis of other findings. For instance, as discussed in the previous chapter, battered Black women have been found to fight back more than other women. Accordingly, perhaps their level of fear is lower than that found in other women and it is other factors that are keeping Black women in these abusive relationships. Moreover, any fear felt by battered Black women may develop into a self-defensive stance, similar to that displayed against unknown violent assailants, as demonstrated when these women talk back and physically attack their batterers to protect themselves. This is evident in Zora's experience:

> I was tearing up the house because he had hit me in my eye. I can just remember just getting up off the floor, just going like a wild woman, just trying to get him out of the house. But I knew that I was not going to be able to get this guy off of me or get to a phone, so I had to get something. I picked up a big, tall vase we had and I threw it at him and it hit a hundred-gallon fish tank, and that's how I got cut. I fell and slipped on the water and my foot was cut. That was how it finally ended.

Lynn M. Short and her colleagues found many similarities between the intimate partner abuse experiences of White and Black women regarding the "rational choice" whether to stay in or to leave an abusive relationship. In addition to staying in abusive relationships because of love and fear, women stayed for many other reasons, including a desire for a traditional nuclear family, financial and emotional dependency on the batterer, and hopelessness.[2] Other reasons that battered women remain in their abusive relationships are denial that it is abuse, a belief the batterer will change his behaviors, no family support, and lack of a place to go.[3]

Although women of all cultures, races, and ethnicities employ similar methods of escaping abusive relationships, some variations by culture, race, and ethnicity exist. In contemplating the ease with which battered Black women depart from their abusive relationships, bell hooks concludes:

> Certainly many black women feel they must confront a degree of abuse wherever they turn in this society. . . . These women often feel that abuse will be an element in most of their personal interactions. They are more

inclined to accept abuse in situations where there are some rewards or benefits, where abuse is not the sole characteristic of the interaction. Since this is usually the case in situations where male violence occurs, they may be reluctant, even unwilling, to end these relationships. Like other groups of women, they fear the loss of care.[4]

Once a battered woman has reached a stage where she realizes the abuser will not change his behavior and that her life, and possibly the lives of her children, may be in danger, she is better able to begin to take steps to leave the relationship.[5] Many battered women begin to devise plans to remove themselves from the home, such as getting a separate and hidden savings account and looking for a place to live. Unfortunately, a battered woman may be more at risk of abuse once she leaves the relationship,[6] and leaving an abusive relationship is rarely a one-time event. Kathleen Ferraro discovered that battered women typically make five to seven attempts at leaving abusive relationships before they do so permanently.[7] It is at this stage that some abused women seek out refuge in battered women's shelters or in the care of family or friends. Utilizing other social service agencies or the criminal justice system is also an option exercised by battered women to assist them in leaving the abusive circumstances or in getting the batterers to change their behaviors. Cicely provided an insightful summation of battered women's difficulties in breaking away from violent intimate relationships, including the rationale for remaining in and leaving the relationships, the judgment by others of the battered woman's choices, and the consequences of the battered woman's responses to the violence:

In order for you to leave an abusive relationship, it has to be you within your own self to make that decision that you want something better. Some women never leave an abusive situation because they come out of a parent relationship, where their parents was abusive, and they feel that's the way it's supposed to be. Some don't leave because they have been brutally injured and the fear and the threat and they stay there or they eventually kill the mate. It's gotten to the point to where if you kill your spouse and you end up in court, the system says, "Oh, you could have left." That's what the system says. So therefore you're a murderer. . . . The next thing they throw at you, "Why didn't you tell somebody?" For one thing, you're afraid. How can you tell somebody when the first thing that will come out of their mouth is, "Well, leave!". . . It's always you, you, you.

So what's the use of telling them? So you keep it to yourself. You got a black eye, put your little make-up on. "What happened?" [You tell them,] "I ran into the door." Why tell anybody? Eventually you get to the point where you retaliate, you kill him, you end up in court. "Why didn't you leave? Why'd you kill somebody? Oh you could have, you should have.". . . You, you, you. What are you thinking in your mind? What are you hearing? It's all my fault. . . . I'm going to prison for 50 years for something somebody did to me because the system is saying it's all my fault. Because they're not looking at how I got from point A to point B.

Paula also provided an insightful account about systemic assistance to battered Black women. Her narrative illuminates the dynamic resistance of battered Black women by showing how life continues after criminal justice intervention (such as arrest of the batterer) and shows that the assistance that battered Black woman (and, likely, other battered women) require sometimes varies from what we believe the women need:

I felt like I was a walking statistic. I was this number out of the sociology books. I felt like, "You really can't relate, leave me alone." My victim advocate, I forget her name, she would ask me questions, go on and on. I was like, "Lady, leave me alone. I'm dealing with trying to pay my rent." I felt like I was part of a group that they had only read about. I felt like [I was] in this category that they looked at under a microscope. It made me feel uncomfortable. I was already embarrassed about the situation that happened, about feeling like that. It hurt my self-esteem and my pride as a woman. I was trying to deal with my circumstance and situation. I didn't want them asking me questions. I felt like I didn't want any help, either. I felt like, "Leave me alone, I've got enough going on. You're not helping me. What can you do to help me? Unless you're going to write me a check, you can't help me. I don't want to talk to you." I was dealing with my own emotions and I still had to get up and cook and do all the things I had to do. They couldn't help me. No matter what they asked me or wanted to let me know, it didn't help me. . . . "Are you going to come over and baby-sit?" What were they going to do? They were just bothering me. Go away. I was just another name on their list, another case number. . . . You would get a paper in the mail about what's going on now [with the legal status of the case]. But when somebody is going through this, they don't want another piece of paper to look at and deal with.

The women used many common methods to remove themselves from their abusive relationships. Before doing so, however, they had personal obstacles to overcome, and they had a variety of motives for finally leaving. The women sought out assistance from family members friends and sought support in religious and spiritual practices and beliefs. The women also described utilizing social services networks, including the criminal justice system, to assist them with terminating their abusive relationships. The services drawn on by the women had varying degrees of effectiveness. While some resources were especially helpful to the women, other means were injurious or, at the least, did not act in the best interests of the respondents. Many of these experiences are endemic to the concept of dynamic resistance. In corresponding with social actors and institutions expected to be available to assist people in need, the women found that they were ultimately responsible for their own well-being. This self-actuation feeds into an aspect of their resistance to life's struggles. Even the constructive support provided to the women built on their dynamic resistance because of their Strong Black Woman identities, which had them not wanting to overburden these positive support networks, and their belief that they could handle their situations with their personal strength alone.

Personal Obstacles and Motivations for Leaving

In reflecting on their decisions to leave the abusive relationships, some of the women often referred to their experiences in their families of origin. In Chapter 4 I detailed that many of the women were exposed to abuse, either as the targets of abuse or as witnesses to others' (typically parents') abuse. The women often considered their abusive upbringings as they were moving toward the process of leaving an abusive relationship. Isis made the connection between her childhood abuse and her becoming "trapped" in an abusive relationship. She discussed how she began to think of her situation as the abusive relationship progressed:

> I know I'm not a child any more. I can take care of myself. I'm an adult. I can get up and leave if I don't like what somebody say. Back then [with my abusive stepfather] a lot of the times I had to just sit and deal with it. I'm so happy I have the freedom now. Something I didn't even know I had with my daughter's dad. . . . Somebody say what you don't like, leave. I never thought I had that with him. I thought I had to be there and

resolve it, clean the relationship. . . . I should have been more concerned about taking care of myself. A lot of times I just didn't.

Isis's revelation that she believed it was her duty to "clean the relationship" and that, in the process, she neglected her own well-being represents Black women's tendency to be nurturers, caretakers, and problem-solvers, while subordinating their own interests for the sake of others' happiness.[8]

The few women who had no early introduction to abuse had few references to being in abusive relationships and perhaps observing ways to maneuver their way out of them. Naomi's two-biological-parent, working-class household of origin provided her with the model of a content and intact couple. She and the women with similar backgrounds relied on this knowledge base to strive to make their own relationships succeed:

> There was nothing in my head that told me to get away. Nothing said, "This isn't right. He doesn't love you. Get away." I always got the guilt gift. He was like, "If you come back, I'll buy you this ring, I'll be there for you." I never came back because of that. I always just came back. And suddenly the whole cycle would start again.

Yolanda was another informant who was reared by both biological parents and who had no significant childhood exposure to violence. She described how her background dictated how she responded to the intimate partner abuse and her method of getting out:

> I was embarrassed. I didn't want nobody to know about it. It made me feel like I was a failure, I'm stupid. . . . My dad never hit my mom. I never had experienced anything like it before in my life. I don't know why, but I never, ever told anyone. I wouldn't have told anyone that one day, except that I was afraid for my kids, afraid that he was really going to kill me that time. That was the only reason why I had mouthed that to the person that walked by. I was really terrified. I thought he was going to really hurt me that time. Now that I'm older, I can see it. Back then, when you're younger, you don't see it like that. . . . I don't have any explanation of why you put up with it. I know for a while, financial-wise, but then I knew that I could take care of myself. I don't know if it was just love, feelings, thinking that he's gonna change . . . and then it happens again and again and again. So finally you've just had enough. That's it. And then I think the classes I went to helped, too. They said, "They're

gonna come back, they're gonna say they're sorry, and then they're going to do it again." I finally realized that. If I had stayed I'm thinking, would he really have killed me?

While fear was an emotion that several women described in talking about the first time they were physically assaulted by an intimate partner, notably, few women said that fear of further physical injury was an obstacle to their parting from the batterers. Danielle demonstrated the trepidation, typically based on threats, that was experienced by these women: "They say, 'When you leave me, I'm gonna find you and I'm gonna kill you.' They say it so often so you really believe that if you leave they're going to find you and they're gonna kill you." Some of the women went through particularly dangerous incidents at the end of their abusive relationships. Jacqueline's escape was one of the more volatile examples of leaving the abusive relationships. This perilous final episode aided her in seeking assistance to end the relationship because of the degree of damage caused by the batterer:

> I was running. . . . [H]e grabbed the back of my head and smacked it on that deadbolt lock and I remember flipping backwards over a chair and landing on the ground. The next thing I knew, he was putting ice on my head. We went over to his mom's house and she made him take me to the hospital. That was the last time he hit me because I left him. I took my kids and went to a shelter.

Thus, fear of the abuser, especially when the woman is trying to leave, was certainly an important inhibitor to leaving the abusive relationships for a few of the women. But, as substantiated by Jacqueline, the increase in violence can also serve as an impetus for finding a way out of the situation; particularly if there are children to consider.

Angie is one of the three women who were in a verbally and mentally abusive relationship at the time of the interviews. She was concerned about not having the resources to secure her own residence. However, she declared that it was *not fear* that was keeping her there:

> I ain't really thinking about it like that. All I'm thinking about is getting away 'cause he's getting on my nerves. And there's my mouth again. When I'm talking bad to him, or somethin' like that, he'll think that's provoking him, but I don't care. I just say what I want to say. I don't put my hands

on you. . . . I just want to get away from him and have my own money. That would help this relationship, is a job.

This lack of fear among many of the women, or at least the lack of acknowledgment of the fear, empowered them to take greater control of the relationship when they reached their emotional limit. As expressed by Isis, this was often exhibited in the women's demanding that their batterers leave the relationship and their home if they were cohabitating: "I told him, 'You come around me again, you're going to jail, even if I have to beat you with my broom to keep you away from me. Stay away from me. Just leave me alone!'"[9]

The financial stability of battered women who leave abusive and controlling relationships is of great concern. The inability of a battered woman to financially support herself is frequently reported as a reason for women to remain in these relationships.[10] Angie continued to discuss how she was stuck in the relationship because of her lack of funds:

I was just thinking, "How am I going to get out of here?" I would go through, "Do I want to go over here?" Then I'd be, "No." I'm weighing. . . . I got to go, but I don't have nowhere to go. I'm trying to think of somewhere to go. I didn't come up with nothing. I wasn't working. I didn't have no money. So I'm just sitting there like a dummy, waiting and biding my time.

In both Naomi's and Yolanda's narratives, presented earlier, they spoke of staying in their relationships because of their desire to emulate the relationships of their parents. That neither stayed out of financial dependence, however, is noteworthy. This was evident throughout most of the sample, and only a few of the women had few resources, financial or otherwise, for leaving. If there was some financial concern, the women's ability to rely on family often aided them in removing themselves from the abusive situation, as is discussed later. Angie described how some of the women felt about leaving their abusive mates, as it related to both financial stability and the intervention of the criminal justice system to stop the battering: "He had a halfway decent job, I didn't want him to lose his job. I know it sounds kind of stupid, but I didn't want him to get in trouble. I still needed him." Angie's account reflects the experiences of the women whose batterers were low- or working-class. One thing to consider regarding Angie's stance is that this is in congruence with the analysis in Chapter 5 regarding the women's feeling sorry for their Black male batterers' devalued position in society. A second and more significant consideration is that the women wished the batterers would financially contribute to the household in order to relieve the women of the burden of being the sole or main financial provider for the entire family. The persistent excuses the batterers made for their abuse and their inability to provide for the women as they desired began to help the women to remove themselves from the volatile relationships. It also aided in the dynamic resistance of the women, who continued or were propelled to gain their financial independence. As already established, Angie's experience was a rare occurrence among the women, but her break from her second abuser was relatively trouble-free once she found a place to go: "I got a shopping cart. I never brought anything in [our apartment], no big appliances or TVs or nothin' like that, so I just had clothes, a little jewelry, and stuff like that. Put it in a shopping cart and went down four blocks and moved in with my current boyfriend."

The long history of employment among Black women in the United States[11] may reduce the pressure on battered Black women to remain in abusive relationships for economic reasons. JoAnn Miller found that battered women who were employed had more personal power than the women who were not employed.[12] As Jo-Ellen Asbury and Peggy S. Plass argue, because Black women have participated in the paid labor force in greater proportions than White women, Black women are better able to support themselves financially, so that finances are typically not a barrier to departure.[13]

Belief in the covenant of marriage and disbelief in divorce, both of which may be influenced by religious beliefs, have also been defended as motivation for remaining in abusive intimate relationships.[14] Black women's fear that they may suffer from the stigma of being yet another single Black mother may compel them to stay in abusive relationships. Their wish to meet traditional relationship standards includes the desire to have a full-time father for their minor children, particularly their male children.[15] In relation to the stigma, Doreen explained why she kept her batterer around: "Even though he was half doing stuff, I was stuck on them having a daddy. But that passed, but it took a long time." Paula discussed this predicament and her resulting feelings when she decided to finally leave her batterer: "So I'm left with four Black children who don't have what they had, whatever that was, to whatever degree."

Several of the women who were mothers made great efforts to keep the children from witnessing the abuse because they knew the damage it could cause. It was coming to the conclusion that the children would eventually become privy to the abuse by being in the same household that aided the women in breaking away from the relationship. Aaliyah, who was recommended to participate in the study by another informant, her mother, Queen, disclosed the following reasons for leaving the second of her two abusive relationships:

> I hated myself. I knew that I had to save not only myself but my kids. My kids look at me as a hero. They don't look at me and say, "Mom, you've done drugs before. You drank. You married a drug addict. You got abused." They don't see any of that, because they don't know. I didn't want them to see that. I didn't want to do that to them.

Medea also contemplated the effects of abuse on children in the abusive home:

> What I had to look at, and this was before any literature on children witnessing, is, "What kind of mother do I want to be? What kind of message do I want to send my sons? What will happen to them if they grow up seeing this? How will that impact them?" Although I put those questions to myself, as I thought about it, I just knew that it felt so wrong and that I couldn't possibly do that to them. And that is what made the decision.

Even though Jade's father was an alcoholic, Jade's mother remained in the trying relationship with him. As a result, Jade did not want to disappoint her own mother by appearing to fail in her own relationship. She shared, "I didn't realize the work you have to put into it, what's healthy and what's not healthy. I think that's why I stuck in the marriage, I wanted to make it work, make my mother proud of me. That's why I think I stuck it out for so long."

As has been found in previous research, many of the women needed multiple occasions to leave an abusive relationship permanently. As the women moved in and out of the relationship, the decision to leave for good became less challenging with each departure. Also, it helped if there was some sort of exposure to how life could be better and healthier without the abusive partner while the woman was away from the relationship. This happened with Zora, who shared:

This is probably the worst decision ever, to get back into the relationship. I felt like I had to do it because it was so abrupt when we broke up. You get back with that person, and everybody's looking at me like, "What's wrong with you?" He came back and trying to be dominant, and at that point I already had come to the conclusion that this was over. I had learned to like me, and I was not about to have all that yelling. I had been involved with an older gentleman for about a year and a half. Even though that didn't work out either, he did teach me how a woman should be treated. So at that point, when [the father of my children and I] tried to get back together, I realized this is not the way. So it didn't take me very long to get him out of my life. And he's still not out of my life, because we have the kids, but to learn that I really deserve better than this, and [he's] never going to change.

Thirty of the women had been in two or more abusive relationships. Just as it became easier for the women to depart a single abusive relationship with each of the multiple partings in the one relationship, I found that as the women progressed through subsequent abusive relationships, it became relatively easier for them to terminate the relationships. For instance, while the first abusive union may last five years, the second one may last two years, and so on. These additional experiences with abusive relationships built on the women's dynamic resistance. That is, while the struggles with moving in and out of the abusive relationship added to the many forms of negative life experiences they resisted, the proliferation of abusive partnerships decreased the amount of resistance they must exert in order to leave. This can be seen in Toni as she described the end of her second and final abusive relationship:

He said, "I gotta talk to you." I went out on the porch and said, "What can I do for you?". . . The hand came up . . . and it came down and it scratched me. . . . It kind of grazed my eye, and I had my contacts in. I was against the neighbor's door and they called the police immediately. He was trying to throw me down the stairs and I held onto the banister and ripped all my fingernails off because I wasn't going anywhere. . . . [Afterwards,] my girlfriend said, "You were so calm." She didn't know I was tired. It wasn't too long ago since I came out of that other situation. I had no more energy to give to this stuff.

Family and Friend Support and Intervention

Many battered Black women are fortunate to obtain assistance from their families—that is, those family members who do not condone intimate partner abuse. The role of family, both immediate and extended units, is of great importance within Black culture.[16] Family is often the support system that is utilized by Black resisters of intimate partner abuse regardless of other services accessed.[17] Noel A. Cazenave and Murray Straus's study on the control of family violence by the use of social networks, such as immediate and extended family embeddedness, found that Black respondents of their study were more rooted in family than White respondents and that this connection is more effective at reducing violence within the Black family than in those of Whites.[18] Research also discovered that battered Black women confide in friends.[19] Isis clearly summarized the importance of family and friend support for battered women: "Sometimes when women get in situations like that, they isolate themselves or the men will isolate them. 'No, you can't talk to your family and your friends.' But that's the first thing that you need in a situation like that, you need your family and your friends."

Lois Weis determined in her study that poor and working-class battered Black women were more open than battered White women in discussing their abuse with others because White women wish to uphold the appearance of the intact nuclear family more than Black women.[20] However, an exception is those battered Black women who do not want to further burden their families with an issue that may seem relatively unimportant and who have chosen or been forced or coerced (by their batterers) to separate themselves from their families. In Beth E. Richie's interviews with battered Black women, the participants recalled gradually becoming very isolated as a result of the abuse, including discontinuing regular contact with family members.[21] For a few of the women in my investigation, I was the first person with whom they shared extensive details about their abusive relationships. Isis was one of these women. She was brought to tears at several points during the interview and shared her thoughts about discussing the abuse she endured at the conclusion of our time together:

> I was thinking, "Hopefully I won't get into the big tears." I'm not a crier. . . . I've never really discussed with anyone in such [detail]. . . . Me and my mom, sometimes privately we'll get by ourselves and start playing,

"Remember that fight? Remember that fight?" We cry and sometimes we laugh. It depends on the day and what kind of mood everyone's in.

As previously indicated, Isis's mother, Doreen, was also in abusive relationships and was ultimately recommended as a study participant by Isis.

Yolanda left her last abusive relationship about 20 years prior to my interview with her, and she reported that she still has not told her mother about the abuse. She revealed to me, "She doesn't know to this day. You know and she doesn't. I've never really told anyone. I've never gotten it out. . . . But it's still so fresh in my memory that it's like it happened last year." When I asked Yolanda whether her adult daughter had been involved in any abusive relationships, Yolanda told me:

> Not that I know of. But she did say, when I told her about [the research project], that maybe if you needed another subject she would talk to you, so I don't know. Maybe she's like me and she didn't want to say. I'll let her know and maybe she'll open up to you if she won't to me. She did say, "Mom, does she need anybody else?" I'm like, "Why? I'll let her know." Maybe she just doesn't want to tell me like I didn't want to tell my mom.

I met with Yolanda at her home and was introduced to her daughter, who then retreated to another area of the home until Yolanda and I finished our discussion. At the conclusion of the interview with Yolanda, I spoke with her daughter, Ebony, and set an appointment for her to share her story with me. During the interview with Ebony, she discussed how she, too, did not share her ordeals with her mother: "I still haven't talked to my mom. . . . I'm more like an inside person. I could tell you, I feel more comfortable telling you than telling a person that I know and that I be with every day. I don't like a lot of people in my business."

Deborah Mahlstedt and Linda Keeny reported that the two major reasons for not informing family members or friends of intimate partner abuse was the belief that it is a private affair and a feeling of embarrassment.[22] Jade discussed the shame that sometimes accompanies being subjected to intimate partner abuse: "I was just embarrassed. I've always been this big, strong woman and a man can't beat you up. I was always like, 'No man's ever going to beat me up.' I'd never been jumped on, hit, or called out my name." This is clearly indicative of the dynamic resistance of the women based on internalizing the concept of being a Strong Black Woman, which is also mentioned in other reasons the women gave for not seeking out family support. At times, the women did not go to their families for help because of their family's inexperience with abuse, as was the case for Naomi: "They don't know I'm getting a divorce right now [from my second husband]. They don't know a lot about me getting hit from my [first] husband. They just know that he probably did put his hands on me. . . . I'm considered the strongest of all the kids. I don't break down. I don't back down. That's what they saw." Cassandra also had reservations about going to her parents because of her lack of familiarity with any major forms of abuse during her upbringing: "I didn't tell my mom, who is a lovable person, a very good person, and my dad, too. They are good people. They never abused us. I always knew that your own parents don't abuse, so how could you let someone else abuse you? That's the reason I never told them."

I have explained that most of the women fought off their abusers and did not typically view themselves as "victims" or "battered women." This added to their difficulty in seeking help from family or other social support networks. The women believed that because of their retaliatory actions, they might be viewed as the producers of, or at least as contributors to, abuse in the home. Jade continued to contemplate why she did not seek out family support. Her self-inquiry about why she did not go to her family was demonstrated in her internalization of the fighter image: "I look back and I wonder myself, Why didn't I go to my family? . . . I didn't want them to see me as a crazy woman, fighting and tearing stuff up all the time. That's what it comes down to; without realizing that it was him triggering the physical and emotional abuse."

Unfortunately, it was evident to some of the women that various family members were not particularly supportive of the women's predicament. In describing the frequency with which she went to her mother and her mother's subsequent reactions, Doreen stated, "Sometimes I'd tell her, sometimes I wouldn't. She would tell me to try to get out of it. [My family] would get mad at me and not speak to me for a while." In addition, some of the women were blamed for the abuse perpetrated by their batterers. Family members often believed that if the women stayed in and continuously returned to the relationships after attempts at leaving, then they were partially to blame for the abuse carried out against them. This was corroborated by Max when she described her mother's response to learning of Max's abuse: "It's not like she went off or anything like that. I'm known to be a fighter anyway. [My mother said,] 'Well, you probably caused it.'" Erica recalled, "My parents got tired of me going back to him.

They just left me alone." Grace described how she learned how her brother felt about her remaining in the abusive situation after she left the relationship: "He thought that if I chose to be in the situation and I didn't say anything to anybody, it was none of his business and he was just gonna leave me alone." However, Grace's brother did provide her with support when she requested his assistance to remove herself from the situation.

Others were persuaded by their relatives to try to make the relationship work. Olivia's mother and othermothers told her: "'That's your baby's father. You need to take the baby to see him. You know y'all can work it out.' And I'm like a nut; I'm listening to this crap." Fortunately, Olivia eventually received some support from her family after she left the relationship: "My family, they became very protective. They were calling all the time, making sure I was never alone, a lot of good things."

Some of the women did find family members who were supportive from the outset and in various ways. Research has determined that when Black women reported their abuse to family members, they tend to reach out to their mothers and their sisters.[23] In addition, Black women reported greater satisfaction with the responses from their mothers, sisters, and friends, and Black women were more likely than White women to tell their brothers of the abuse.[24] In my examination, family members offered advice regarding some of the women's situations. This advice was often not heeded during the early, infatuated stages of the relationship, but the women tended to recall the suggestions as they were fighting back or more seriously contemplating leaving. Billie described how her sister, who had also been in an abusive relationship, provided her with advice: "My sister was like, 'Girl, you're gonna have to stop letting him jump on you and beat you like that.' Because she had already been through it. She was like, 'If you don't stop the cycle, if you don't put an end to this, he's gonna kill you.'"

Reports that batterers were intimidated by the women's male family members, and even by female family members at times, were divulged to me by some of the women. This occurred with Keisha. Her mother, Leah, and one of Leah's abusive boyfriends, Neal, threatened Keisha's batterer. From my conversation with Keisha, I deduced that the details of the confrontation were unknown to her, but it was described to me by Leah:

I would drive Keisha to school and Keisha pointed out where he lived. We went over there and made him piss, literally. It was very fulfilling on my part. We never told her. We just went over there and gave him the business. . . . Even after all this and Keisha broke up with him, he was hanging out at her school. That wasn't cool. So me and Neal went over there and told him that we would fucking kill him, cut his body up in itty bitty little pieces, and bury 'em in his parents' back yard if he don't leave her the fuck alone. And he did.

The women recounted stories about family members who would sometimes go beyond verbal threats and would physically intervene. If this occurred, it was typically while the batterer was being abusive in the presence of family members. As already established, the men in the lower-income and working-class couples were more inclined than those of higher socioeconomic status to display their abusive behaviors in the company of others. Accordingly, corporal family intervention typically occurred among these socioeconomic classes of couples. Angie's recollection included tales of her family members defending her by being violent toward the batterer. Other women believed that if they had informed their family of the abuse, their family, particularly the male members, would have defended them in a violent manner by attacking the batterer. Olivia's first abusive relationship took place approximately 25 years prior to her interview, and her final abusive relationship occurred when her son, who is 28 years old, was an adult and no longer living with Olivia. When asked whether she talked to her son about the abuse by her second batterer, she stated:

> I didn't tell my son because my son's very protective. . . . I felt that that was something he didn't need to know. . . . Anything it would do is it would make him feel guilty for not being here to be able to protect me, being the only child, and being a Black man child. I didn't want that guilt. I'm sure he has his own things he has to go through in life, and the last thing he needed was to be worried about a man jumping on his mother, beating up his mother [and that] he needed to be there to protect me.

Grace described an incident involving physical conflict between her second husband and her teenage son from her first marriage. Grace reflected on the outcome if her son had defended her during her estranged (White) husband's abusive episodes:

> My son, he's always been into karate and boxing. So I don't think my husband was too prepared for that. My son cleaned his clock. That was

one thing that scared me, because I said that if it comes to my defense, he's going to kill him. This man that I brought into my house is going to cause my flesh-and-blood son to go to jail. I can't have that.

As a result, the women feared that family members would enter the criminal justice system as offenders. In regard to letting her brothers know about the abuse as it was occurring, Cicely stated, "I didn't let them know because I didn't want them going to jail. . . . I knew my brothers. They were very protective."

Support was also offered by family members in the form of housing. Several women did not use battered women's shelters because of the protection they received by simply retreating to a relative's home, especially the homes of their mothers. When she needed to get away from her batterers, Ebony recalled of her mother Yolanda's protection and assistance. "I always just came back home with Mom. This is my shelter. They know where she lives. She has sheltered me. She'd say, 'She's not here, don't call here again.' They all just respect my mom. They'd see me on the streets and they'd say, 'Your mom cussed me out.'" And Max described her mother's sanctuary this way:

I've always went to my mom's. I figured, once I got with my mom, they'd prefer to go to jail than go over there and mess with my mom. My mom is a little toughie. They won't go over there and bother my mom at her house. She's a little bitty woman, but she stands her ground. She says what she has to say. We've never had any problems over there.

A number of the women had interactions with the batterers' families as they were trying to determine the future of their relationships. As happened when they shared their abuse with their own family members, the response from the batterers' family members were also unaccommodating, indifferent, or supportive.

The batterers' families occasionally supported or enabled the batterers. Regarding her batterer's mother, Grace said, "She was always covering up for him." Jade's abusive husband's mother encouraged her to stay in the relationship and emphasized the economic reason for doing so. Jade spoke of her mother-in-law's position: "She just more or less said [to] take the beatings. . . . This woman's telling me to stay here just because he's going to be well off." Olivia recalled a conversation she had with her abuser's mother at the end of the relationship:

His mother calls me up to tell me to pray for him and he doesn't mean any harm. I'm like, "You don't know your son." I don't know what he told her. He's a womanizer, he's a charmer. I told her he was crazy, I don't have a thing to say to him. I haven't heard from him since. He would have just continued on with the abuse, if I hadn't stood up and said, "No more."

Zora's discussion with her abusive boyfriend's mother also came with suggestions for prayer: "She told me, 'You guys are a family, you need to keep your family together, you need to pray.' That kind of whining instead of trying to do something about it. . . . He was very much a mama's boy." (Similarly, the suggestion from clergy members to pray away the abuse is addressed in the section on religion later in this chapter.)

When some of the women talked with their family members of their batterers, their ill feelings about the abusers were reconfirmed. Also, instead of covering up or minimizing their sons' abuse, a few batterers' mothers actually encouraged the women to leave. Bev recounted, "His mom told me before she died, she said, 'Leave him. He ain't no good.'" The mother of Gloria's third abuser tried to encourage Gloria to leave the relationship, knowing that her son was not worthwhile as a mate. Gloria recalled, "His mother even told me that he was no good and not to bother. She stuck by me, she did a lot for me. She even told me I shouldn't stay with him." The grandmother of Phoebe's boyfriend was aware of the abuse Phoebe suffered, and the boyfriend's grandmother made efforts to assist Phoebe during the relationship: "She really felt bad for me. She was the only one that really helped me. She would give me money when he would steal [my car] from me so I could go get diapers."

The women's interactions with friends elicited reactions similar to those from family. The women shared their dilemmas with family members more than with friends, but Olivia learned much from interaction with her friends *after* she left her abusive relationship:

I had lots of friends come forward, lots of girlfriends. He had them fooled. They didn't believe it. He was charming. . . . But in the very end it hashed up a lot of old wounds some of them had. Which was a cool thing because they experienced it, and I heard some of the things that they went through. So I didn't feel alone.

Just as the women were advised by the batterers' family members, they also received advice from the batterers' friends, who generally spoke of the women's need to end the relationships. Keisha did not regard the advice of her second batterer's friends: "Even his roommates were telling me that I needed to leave him alone. 'You are too young anyways, you need to leave him alone, he has a lot of issues and a lot of problems.' It went in one ear and out the other. I thought I was in love. I really didn't pay attention to what everybody was saying."

Unfortunately, the women were also confronted with recommendations to remain in abusive relationships, particularly if the (socioeconomic) benefits outweighed the (abusive) costs. Medea was disappointed in and amazed at the reaction she received from her friends on the basis of this cost-benefit analysis:

> I had friends who felt like, "This man is rich. So if he's rich, you can take a little shit, you can take some abuse." I thought that was so wild. Or a friend would say, "Just as long as he was just messing around and it was quiet." I was appalled by that. . . . I was amazed that these intelligent, educated women had such medieval views on relationships and that they could rationalize abuse and battering down to nothing if there were financial perks, if there were social perks to be gained. That amazed me! And that I would speak out about it, do what I've done, they were like, "She's crazy. After all, he's rich, and you have to just make allowances." I was shocked. I was absolutely shocked.

Interestingly, Medea was financially comfortable without the assistance of her battering husband. Lola, who was also in an upper-middle-class marriage, received a similar reaction from her acquaintances and discussed the relationship she had with friends at the conclusion of the abusive relationship:

> When I started trying to complain to people, they thought I was ungrateful. "Look what your husband do. You can go on a trip by yourself any time you want. How can you say he's mistreating you?" The hard part, too, once I left, was that I lost all my friends, my many, many friends, all the people who would go to my birthday parties. If I try to speak to anybody, they will tell me, "Go back home, he treats you good."

The support the participants received from family and friends was sometimes consistent across socioeconomic levels and sometimes varied along this dimension. The socioeconomic variations found in relation to the responses by family and friends hinged on the status of the batterers and the financial (and social) benefits they could provide. As with Medea and Lola, some friends argued that monetary and material possessions compensated for the abuse perpetrated by the batterers. For all the women, regardless of socioeconomic stratum, the connection to family was very important in assisting some of them to leave the relationship; however, in a few situations, family offered harmful advice or were unsupportive. Even those women who had less-than-desirable or even abusive experiences in their homes of origin during their formative years focused on utilizing family support for assistance.

Use of Religion and Spirituality

Religious practices and houses of worship are important cultural components in the lives of many Blacks.[25] Spirituality and the practice of religion have been found to be important methods for Blacks to deal with hardship.[26] Clearly, Black religious institutions serve not only to provide pious enrichment but to foster cultural bonding, as well. Short and colleagues discovered that battered Black women, more than battered White women, find that religion and prayer (along with support from family and friends) are their main resources for dealing with the abusive relationships.[27] The religious and spiritual experiences of the women in my study affected their dynamic resistance in a couple ways. First, the negative religious encounters of some of the women remind them of the many social forces they have had to fight against. Second, the positive religious encounters of some of the women and the spiritual beliefs maintained by the majority of the women gave them all additional strength with which to confront their battles.

Although more of the women were *not* religiously affiliated at the time of the interviews (30%) than during childhood (7.5%), the vast majority of the women relied on their spirituality to help them get through and out of the abusive relationships. Fewer women were involved in formal religion during their abusive relationships, and some saw their being away from the church as a reason for their getting into or staying in the relationship. Max illustrated this point:

> Up until I was sixteen, we had to go to church every Sunday. When I was able to make my own decisions, I got in the choir. I stayed in the

choir for about eight months. That's when I should have stayed in church and left the little boys alone. That's when the chaos with the boys started, when I stopped going to church.

Max believed that being steadily involved in church would have benefited her by providing *additional* support for rejecting abusive male mates. However, while Max discontinued regular church attendance until after her abusive relationships (when she became a Muslim under the guidance of her current, nonabusive husband), she maintained her devotion to a higher power and her belief in the tenets of Christianity throughout her abuse. Similar to hooks's observation on the experiences of enslaved Africans in the United States, the women in my study formed "a spirituality of resistance that would lead to freedom."[28]

Like Max, though they may not have practiced their religion rigorously, many of the women spoke of how they sensed that the spirit or their god was still watching over them and of their continued reliance on their faith. Billie shared her belief in this when she described her struggles with several abusive boyfriends and her eventual involvement in drug use, which led to addiction and her violent street behaviors:

> I've been gone away from God for a while. And even when I was walking around the streets at three or four o'clock in the morning, God was still watching over me. That's why I believe he's still got something for me to do. If I was supposed to die, I would have been gone. There's a reason for me being here. I made it through.

Renee also contributed her being saved from harm because of the presence of a higher power:

> I do a lot of journaling and have for the last fifteen years. I call them "Dear God" letters because it brings me closer to God and helps me share with others. . . . God had been real graceful for me in saving me so many times, and he had put people in my life who had been patient with me . . . or agencies that really did restore me for the moment.

Furthermore, even when they utilized other resources to leave the relationship, such as family support, battered women's shelters, or the criminal justice system, many of the women still placed their faith in the spirit, as alluded to by Renee and revealed by Helene, who involved the police on a few occasions during her abusive relationships. Helene spoke of her thought process while contemplating leaving an abusive relationship:

> You ask the question, "What am I doing wrong?" By then my esteem was gone. Even if you're paying the bills, that shit just strips you. You don't even know better, but it's harder to get out of it than it is being in it, even though you could be at a point where you know you could get killed. . . . I wasn't afraid to die or anything. I do remember praying at times, "God, get me out of this, get me out of this." Looking back at it, when [the batterer] left, my prayers were answered. [God] did get me out of it. It might not have been the way I wanted it. But he rescued me out of it, no matter how it happened. . . . I try to put God first and last. I trusted him to get me out of that situation, even though when I got out of that last situation, I was devastated, like nervous-breakdown devastated.

Most of the women did not seek out assistance from their clergy and other people in their religious orders for help in discontinuing the relationships. While only eight of the 40 women sought counsel from religious leaders, these findings still suggest the importance of clergy in supporting battered Black women. More specifically, given the large numbers of Black women who are battered, particularly in comparison to White women,[29] that one in five women in my sample reported their abuse to a religious leader indicates that many battered Black women do so every day. Seven of the eight women who sought counsel from a religious leader practiced in Christian-based churches. Each of these seven women reported standard support from clergy members during their time of need. Being told by pastors to remain in the relationship and "work things out" was a common occurrence in my own and other research,[30] as experienced by Cassandra:

> I talked to my pastor. My pastor knew the guy was abusive. He's like, "He's your husband according to the Bible. Maybe things could work out." Wrong advice. I'd been a member of the church since my son was three months old. I'm a member of another church now. . . . Obviously it was the wrong advice. . . . Somebody should have helped, done something, even if they prayed.

Wendy was one of the other women who was advised by a pastor to stay with the batterer. While in her working-class abusive relationship, she told of her encounter with the military cleric from whom she sought assistance:

> I went to the [Army base] chaplain. I told the chaplain that I was in a abusive relationship, I wanted to go home, I had all kind of witnesses that will tell you that he beat me all the time. We lived in a housing area. They told me, "If you go home, and you get back with him and we have to send him oversees again, you will never be able to travel with him again." [The pastor] told me, "Now you go home and you think about it." He went on to tell me some other things; he was trying to encourage me to stay with this man. By this time I was so worn down and tired, I just said, "OK, I'll stay." He was telling me, . . . "You better hang on to him." . . . When the questions came to me, "Was he a good provider?," I had to say, "Yeah," because he was. "Was he good to the kids? Have he ever hurt the kids? Have he ever been abusive to the kids?" No, he wasn't. Then they wanted to know what my freakin' problem was! I was tired of gettin' beat up!

As evidenced here, the women who sought out guidance from their Christian ministers became disheartened with their churches during their abusive relationships. They realized that the reverence they had grown to have for the church as children was tarnished when they needed the church and its members most. Jade requested support from the pastor of her and her batterer's church during the abuse. She did not receive the help she needed, and, in fact, the pastor was supportive of the batterer and viewed Jade as too controlling for a wife. Jade later suspected that her former husband was gay because of several incidents that occurred during their marriage, and she learned there were many gay men in their church. Jade was perplexed by the pastor's unbiased openness about and acceptance of homosexuality and by his sexist rejection of independent women:

> Come to find out, the whole pulpit was full of homosexuals. . . . [The pastor would] accept gay men, but wouldn't accept domineering women. . . . He was on my ex-husband's side and we [women] were just making the stuff up and we were just too strong, dominant women. . . . We probably needed to be beat up, put in our places. That's exactly what he said.

Like Jade, when Medea was advised by her minister to remain with the abuser, she realized the misogynist atmosphere that exists in some churches and religions:

The priest advised me to stay, which turned me against the church forever. After that I didn't even attempt it. . . . The Bible's like any other book. It has to be interpreted. The Bible has never said anything to anybody. The misinterpretation and marginalization of women that takes place in religion is just amazing. You know, the man's the head of the household, the man leads his family. So I thought, I ain't doing this, this is not working. That's why I turned to metaphysics, to understand the whys, understand why I invited this experience into my life and what I needed to learn from it and what I needed to do with it. . . . I think [the pastor] looked on it as the lot of women in the world. You know, "This happens and this is what you do, and pray long enough and hard enough, [the abuser will] change."

Several of the women who did not seek assistance from the church also became disheartened with their churches and its members during their abusive relationships. These women's discontent was rooted in (1) their presuming that their reports of abuse would not be believed by their pastors; (2) witnessing how clergy members failed to help other abused women; and/or (3) witnessing how clerics and other church members were hypocritical and aberrant in their faith. In a very small number of cases, respondents were restricted from attending religious services (and other activities) when their batterers invoked isolation on the women. Kim did not go to the church for help with her abusive relationship and spoke of her experiences with this issue, which is why some women do not turn to the church for help with a battering mate:

There's two ways to get close to God. You can get close to God in a church or you can do it one-on-one. . . . But the church ain't like it used to be. Maybe the church was never like that. But when your people are having problems, take care of your people because they'll take care of you. The church is not taking care of people any more. . . . I'm closer to [God] one-on-one. . . . I'm at the point where I won't ask the church for nothing.

Kim was generally speaking of Black churches, as did Olivia, who also spoke of her disillusionment with Black churches and how they should be more supportive to those dealing intimate partner abuse and other issues within the Black community:

The Black churches knew [about the abuse]. They never came and offered a hand. There was a couple sisters that came to me and talked to
me about it, 'cause they had abusive husbands. . . . It was the Catholic
church[31] who really let me know that I had to forgive and that domestic violence is an illness. It's an illness and we haven't touched the
surface of it. . . . Black churches, they collect money. And the crack
house be right next door to 'em. They would not go out there and
picket 'em. . . . They just let it ride. . . . That's not the way it's supposed to be.

Islam was the only other religion besides Christianity that was practiced by the women. The women who practiced Islam experienced much
less religious dissatisfaction than did those who practiced Christianity.
At the time of the interviews, five women considered themselves Muslim. Of these five, only one was raised Islamic, and she continued to
practice that faith at the time of her interview. Only one of the women
was battered by a Muslim man, and, because there were just a few
women in the sample who practiced Islam and were with Muslim men,
no major significance can be gathered from this, especially since previous research has indicated a high instance of intimate partner abuse
among Muslims.[32]

Where my study did find significance is in the general support provided by the mosques and the Islamic clergy to women who are abused
by their male mates. However, the women who practiced Islam described
patriarchal and paternalistic practices and views within their religious experiences. Nonetheless, each of the Muslim women I spoke with described
positive experiences in relation to Islam, particularly concerning how the
religion and its followers deal with intimate partner abuse. Rebecca practiced under the Islamic sect of the Nation of Moorish-Americans. Here
is how she described her experience with Islam and compared it to the
Christian faith in which she was raised:

We help each other. We feel if your brother or sister is down, you help
your brother or sister. . . . It gave me a broader view of what I already
knew and a stronger family foundation, better codes to operate by. I enjoy it. I have more peace. I'm not fighting with fitting in with the Joneses,
like when you go to church. At certain times I have to be covered, at the
beginning of the month or if my [menstrual] cycle is on. Those are the

only times I have to be covered. But I have peace within, knowing that my god is my god. . . . It's such a political game in Christianity. God is supposed to be more godly. You're supposed to be submissive to God, no matter what religion you are. You're supposed to be more Christlike. I wasn't experiencing that in the settings I was in. It was like they were living hypocritical lives. If you believe in something, you should practice what you preach.

Shahida was the sole Muslim to be battered by a Muslim man and was one of the eight women from the entire interview sample to seek clerical assistance. The abuser was Shahida's second husband, and this was her second abusive relationship. That it was her second abusive relationship made it less difficult for her to exit the violent situation, but the assistance she received from her mosque was different from that described by the Christian women who sought clerical guidance. While living in a large, urban city on the east coast with her second husband in a middle-class setting, and soon after a battering incident, Shahida contacted the security faction of the mosque. She said that several men from the mosque, dressed in black, appeared at her home and escorted her husband away. Shahida did not see her husband again until several months later when she arrived home and noticed him sitting on the stoop to her apartment building. She stopped at a public pay telephone, contacted the mosque security group, which showed up shortly thereafter, and she never saw or spoke with that abusive husband again.[33]

As detailed earlier, Max was raised Christian but converted to Islam in adulthood and was married to a nonabusive Muslim man at the time of her interview. Max described the policy at her mosque for dealing with intimate partner abuse, which was evident in Shahida's and the other Muslim women's anecdotes:

They frown on it, I know that much. The Muslim men, they figure they take care of their own. Instead of calling the police, all you need to do is call your Wali. My Wali is like taking the place of my dad, while my dad is not here. If I need anything or have any kind of problems, this guy is the man I call. Call him and all the Muslim brothers will come and handle the individual. So that's the way they handle theirs. . . . If [my husband] has a problem with me, then he needs to call one of his Muslim brother's wives. They'll come and handle the situation; not fight or nothing like that, but come in, take you down and talk to you where you might not want to talk to your husband or wife. That's how they handle that, instead of calling the police. Right when we got married, after the ceremony, we were about to leave and my Wali came and said, "If you have any type of problems, you come and get us. Let the police be the last resort, because a Muslim man is more apt to listen to another Muslim man than the police." If it's a physical violence type thing, they'd probably understand. But if they can get to the situation before it becomes violent, then they prefer to do that.

As reported by Max in a previous section, many of the women spoke of feeling derailed from their religious track during their abusive relationships. They always had faith, but for many, their religious practice waned as they progressed through the relationships. Several began to find their way back to regular religious practice as they made greater efforts to remove themselves from the abusive situation. This is captured in Inez's account: "After I got out of the relationship I started turning my life back over to God."

Notwithstanding any negative experiences with religion, a number of the women continued to rely on their faith and religion to keep them from ending up in abusive relationships in the future, as expressed by Olivia: "I go and I thank [God] all the time, 'cause we would not be able to make it without him. . . . When I went through my ordeal, I asked God never to let that happen to me again. . . . Got to keep the faith in order to keep going." Toni focused on the positive outcomes of being in her abusive relationship, one of which was becoming more religious: "The only blessing that came out of that relationship is that that's when I found God. . . . The Lord can use anybody to reach us. That's how I look at it. To this day I don't have no idea what happened to this man, but the kids and I started doing Bible study."

Some of the women were still inclined to be reserved about what and how much information they shared with members of their religious groups. At the time of my interview with Jacqueline, she stated that she had chosen not to tell her current reverend about her past, particularly her work as a sex worker and exotic dancer, which she was forced into doing by her abusive husband: "If a minister asked me what I've been involved in, I would tell him, but I'm sure I would lose a lot of respect, because they don't have a clue."

Use of Medical Services, Shelters, and Therapy

In addition to the cultural characteristics that may inform battered Black women's opinions about their abuse, and in addition to relying on their own will to leave the relationships, battered Black women access the criminal justice system and other social service agencies at varying rates and with varying levels of success. In general, the women did not believe their lives and their battles were worthy of attention from official institutions situated to assist those in need. Aaliyah declared, "I have not once had anybody be sympathetic to anything that I've been through." Olivia concluded that (White) society listens only for the purpose of controlling Blacks in detrimental ways and that Blacks, especially Black women, are left to fend for themselves: "White America won't say anything unless it will be tragic. *We'll* say something but we're not being heard until something's really, really bad, then you want to lock us all up. We can't afford to get those Prozacs and Thorazines and twenty hours on the couch. We can't afford that. We have to pray to God and hope everything works out." Indeed, many battered Black women often feel as though they are ignored by agents and agencies that can assist them with their substandard relationships and other problems.[34]

Social services used by women while leaving abusive relationships include medical services, battered women's shelters, and (licensed) therapeutic agents. Regrettably, Black women are often reluctant to seek assistance from these services.[35] The barriers to utilizing these resources may not be only the short supply of battered women's shelters and therapeutic resources *in* Black communities[36] or *known* to the Black community but may also be related to the inability of those working in helping professions to deliver adequate culturally competent services to Black women who have suffered abuse from their intimate partners and the lack of trust that this engenders.[37] When asked if she sought help from professionals, Victoria responded: "I didn't know how to reach out to anybody. I didn't know how to share that with anybody I didn't know but my family, and [my family members] were telling me there wasn't anything they could do."

Many of the women received injuries from their abusers that were significant, but several chose not to seek medical help, and those who did frequently experienced unsympathetic retorts by health professionals. For some of the women, not seeking out medical attention enabled them to maintain their denial about their abuse, the seriousness of their battering situation, or their need to rely on others for help. The possibility of bringing attention to their predicament also served as a deterrent from seeking out medical attention. Jade chose not to go to the hospital partially because of the unwelcome attention she would bring to her situation if she did: "No, I was too proud for it. I was afraid I would go to jail because I was fighting back, too." Jade's disclosure captures how many of the women viewed obtaining assistance to heal their wounds and their concerns about being labeled offenders instead of someone who is in need of health care. This is particularly important to consider given that most of the women fought back.

Michael A. Rodriguez and his colleagues conclude that physicians are missing prime opportunities to screen women for intimate partner abuse and that most doctors are not following practice guidelines for intimate partner abuse screening.[38] Many of the women of my study who did seek medical treatment typically lied to medical personnel about the nature of their injuries. Like Jade (even though she chose not to acquire medical help), the women lied to protect themselves from criminal processing, but they also lied to protect their batterers from being arrested and, overwhelmingly, because they felt they could resolve their situations on their own without the help of professional agencies. When Wendy went to the medical center located on the military base where her abusive husband was stationed, she informed the doctor and nurses of the following:

> I told 'em I fell down. They would send a nurse in to talk to me, to try to convince me to tell 'em that he beat me up. There was laws that would protect me, especially in the military. I didn't want to see his career go down, and I knew I loved him enough to stay; that I would be with him. So I lied, and said, "No, no, no, I did fall. I did hit my head. I did hit my face." I get back home, and it was really well for about a month. After that, he started cheating on me. When I asked him about it, he would slap me.

Angie had no medical insurance, so when she was in need of medical services she accessed a local public hospital. She was one of the few women who were actually honest about their abuse when she went to the hospital. Angie spoke of one of her experiences after an attack from her abusive boyfriend and the hospital staff's response to her after she disclosed the cause of her injuries:

I walked down there by myself. They took care of me. They had a counselor that was supposed to come in there, but she happened to be off that day. Yeah, they asked me right away what happened. They said, "Who did this to you?" I said, "My boyfriend." I go down to get the stitches and then the doctor asked me and then the nurse that was attending me also. They all knew, and then here comes the police because they have to follow through. He asked me did I know [the batterer's] name. I didn't want to give his name. So he said there's nothing they could do, which I knew that. I didn't want to mess him up. And then while I'm sitting there, here [my boyfriend] comes. Nobody knows this is the man, right. He just showed up. He waited till they got done, he waited outside, and after they did the stitches, we walked home together. The police had already left.

These experiences with doctors, nurses, and other hospital staff convinced Angie and other women that help is not always readily available even when a battered woman seeks it out. Furthermore, the women were often more concerned about the legal ramifications that might result due to regulations that bind medical personnel. Not only did they fear the arrest of their batterers, they feared their own arrests, as well.

As demonstrated in the discussion on family support, if the women felt they needed a place to go to get away from their abusers, they typically went to their parents' homes or the homes of other relatives. Most of the women did not access battered women's shelters. Much criticism has been directed at the accessibility of battered women's shelters for Black women. Black women have cited their ignorance of these shelters and their discomfort with using battered women's shelters, fearing they are geared toward the needs of other types of women.[39] Indeed, many of the women in my investigation did not use battered women's shelters because they preferred to use other resources and because they believed shelters were intended more for middle- or upper-class White women.

Of the 11 women who did go to a shelter, five went once, four went twice, and two women used shelters three times or more. The majority of the women (seven of the 11) who went to a battered women's shelter were working-class. Keisha was in a battered women's shelter with her mother, Leah, who needed to flee from one of her abusive mates. Keisha took part in some of the group meetings and generally had a positive view of the situation. She summarized, "Overall, I think they do a good job for keeping the women safe, because there's shelters and places you can go if you're in a domestic problem. I think that the [system is] doing a really good job at keeping women safe. I think they're doing a good job with the safe houses and things like that." Unfortunately, as will be seen in what follows, Keisha is alone in her positive assessment of a battered women's shelter.

The reasons provided by the women who used the shelters included the unavailability of family; the unwillingness of family to provide appropriate assistance to the women; or reluctance by the women to have their family see them in poor condition. The latter is exhibited in the dynamic resistance of Renee. In providing her definition of battered women's shelters, she spoke of not wanting her family to see her in a decrepit state:

> These homes, unless you're really ready to change, they're nothing but pit stops. They help if you know how to appropriately take advantage of it. I did. . . . [They] are like people who are stuffing the straw back into the straw man. They polish you up and get you ready for the next round, if there's going to be a next round. . . . I just needed someplace to rest where my people couldn't see me that tired. They knew I was tired, and they probably knew more than I would allow them to tell me, because I think I'm invincible.

The women typically found that they were remarkably unlike the other women (that is, unlike the non-Black women) in the shelters. They spoke of how their situations were often undervalued because the extent of their injuries was often less severe than that of the other women, as described by Lola: "I was the least beaten-up person. I was not as bad as them." Similarly, Wendy revealed, "I thought *my* situation was bad. [But] I seen so many other women who was so much worse." Leah described how she differed from the other women in her second shelter experience:

> Being at that shelter, I met women that were married for 25 years and their husbands beat 'em and women that have lost their kids. I realized it could have been so much worse. If I would have been with him, he probably would have killed me. . . . When we would have group, they would always trivialize what I went through because I didn't have no marks. "How many teeth did you lose?" They said that they didn't think I needed to even be there because they didn't consider what I went through as abuse, because I didn't hang around. I wasn't in it for two years, 10 years, 20 years, 30 years, or whatever. I met women there that had been on the run for months. They get in a cycle. They go from one shelter and when

their time runs up they go to another shelter. Some of them do it just statewide. Some of them do it nationwide. We had women come from all over the country and they would just stay a couple of weeks and just keep on moving because their mindset is, "He's still after me."

In Doreen's shelter experience, she was fortunate to be surrounded by a few other Black women. They were connected by the conditions just described (the undervaluing of Black women's abusive experiences) and their identity as Black women. Regrettably, in group settings, Doreen and the other battered Black women felt stifled by the process and their surroundings and feeling as though they were outsiders, separate from the remainder of the group. Doreen described her disheartening introduction to life in a battered women's shelter:

> The Black woman talked better amongst themselves than [with the] White women. It was like when we talked we were more comfortable with each other. When we had group [with everyone in the shelter], we [Black women] mainly just listened, we didn't participate too much in the conversation. I wasn't gonna go through all that. [The White women] mainly ran the conversation, we would mainly listen. . . . We were quiet. We were mainly listening until we were asked something. The rest of 'em would go on and on.

Other women also felt disconnected from the shelter experience and staff. Lola realized, "It's just that there aren't any Black people there working with Black women." Inez went to battered women's shelters three times and surmised, "Sometimes I would think they would help [White women] quicker. . . . Maybe help them get a place, help them and their kids quicker than the Black women."

As alluded to in Leah's description, most of the women considered shelters to be crutches that made the women too dependent on others. Many of the women's ancestral and personal histories as strong, independent women, though sometimes a form of stereotypical self-labeling, influenced their seeing help-seeking opportunities, such as shelters, as disadvantageous sources of support. Yolanda explicitly described this way of thinking: "It was peaceful, but I didn't want to be there. I don't like to be dependent. I'm an independent person. I didn't want to have to stay there and not have no contact with no one from the outside. What I ended up doing was, I came back out on my own. I had money. I got my own place." Yolanda continued to be harassed by her batterer after she left the shelter, but she preferred her freedom and independence to being confined by the regulations and restrictions of a shelter. Her account also demonstrated the importance of being connected with family during this time of need. The need for a family connection adds to the reluctance of most battered Black women to seek out refuge in a shelter.

The women who had their young children in the shelter with them were concerned about the effect the shelter stay would have on the children. Wendy spoke of her concerns regarding this, which, again, has roots in Black women's dependence on others and their dynamic resistance:

> I learned that this is not where I want to be. This is not where I want my kids to be. Having an idea that they can get with an abusive man and they can run to the shelters. I didn't want to get them in that pattern to show them that this is OK. It's not OK, 'cause I don't want them to even go that direction. I stayed there for a week. Got a job. . . . Got my own place. Put them in a better environment. Counselors were very friendly. I had one lady who took me to the side and told me that I shouldn't have been there in the first place. [She said,] "You're not the type of woman who needs to be here."

Although Wendy's counselor seemed to have good intentions in praising Wendy for her strength and resilience and in distinguishing her from the other women—the White women—in the shelter, these types of messages from counselors also serve to perpetuate the notion of the Strong Black Woman. As I discussed in Chapter 3, even though this perception has its positive attributes, it does a disservice to battered Black women, because it makes it difficult for them to seek and accept help through its suggestion that they are either strong enough to deal with the abuse on their own or because it facilitates their ignoring the effects of the abuse altogether.

Some of the women took advantage of other therapeutic services. These experiences include counseling services that directly addressed the battering victimization and to which the women typically were referred by victims' advocates. A few of the women benefited from the counseling they accessed, but, overwhelmingly, as with the battered women's shelters, they found the counseling irrelevant to their lives and to Black culture. The evaluation presented here extensively overlaps with my discussion of the women's concerns regarding shelter care.

Naomi was one of a small number of women who participated in intimate partner abuse-related counseling. She questioned the lack of Black women clients in counseling: "I just wonder why there wasn't a lot of Black women there in the group. I think a lot of Black women are maybe ashamed because they put up with it. Most of them in my group were White." Traci C. West found similar patterns among women she interviewed who had been subjected to various forms of interpersonal male violence. She recounted, "It seems there is no cultural space for a sad, weak, crying black woman."[40] Lola tried to offer some explanation to why Black women are not getting the help they need to assist them with leaving abusive relationships:

> Without Black women asking for help, they don't get help. The help is there but the help is not acceptable to them. And if they won't ask for help, they won't get the help. And when they do actually go to these places, the people that are supposed to help them, some of them feel inadequate with dealing with a person of color. . . . Some women of color . . . might not be willing in a group . . . to admit to some of the things that they go through because they don't want to make their culture look bad. So instead they might say something pretty. That is a bad thing for them. There aren't enough groups around to support them. For Black women to be stronger, Black women have to work together with Black women.

Olivia described both the positive and (mainly) the negative aspects of the battered women's group counseling she participated in:

> The counseling was good to air how I felt, the anger, the denial. I seen the signs, but didn't pay 'em any attention, like the drinking and the drug abuse and the hanging out. . . . But truthfully, I was disappointed. I was expecting something a little bit different. Prevention, awareness. Not after-the-fact [type of counseling]. After . . . I can't see or hear. I don't want to hear that crap. I have to deal with this pain, I have to deal with those scars. I have to pick myself up and go on. You can't do it for me, I don't care how much you talk to me or what you say. Can you give me the tools to make me not make this mistake again? Awareness, prevention. All we did was sit around and talk about each other and what had happened.

On the basis of this experience, Olivia offered suggestions for improving the services provided to women resisters of intimate partner abuse:

> They gave me all kind of counseling, but if you don't experience it, you really can't counsel. . . . What can you do? I could cry to you, you can cry

to me, pray for me. OK that's fine, but what can we do to prevent it? . . . But [counselors] need more hands-on training. They need to go to the shelters, to the jails, to the hospitals, to see the real blood and guts and the tears and the things that happen to the family, what led up to it. They need to see that. . . . Have you been out there on the battleground? Ride with the ambulances, go to the domestic calls, go do ride-alongs with police officers to domestic cases.

Medea's employment at an intimate partner abuse advocacy agency afforded her a similar outlook: "Counselors are prisoners of their experience or lack of it." Regarding non-Black professionals who assist battered women, she concluded, "These White women here cannot make determinations that involve people of color. You don't have somebody tell you what people of color want. People of color will tell you themselves."

Like Medea, several of the women attributed their healing from the abuse and their ability to depart from the relationships to their employment or volunteer work in the social or human services field. These women entered these professions after having experienced abuse from their intimate partners. Their immediate goal was not necessarily to heal themselves. They sought out social services opportunities to help others with experiences of abuse similar to those they had encountered. In the process, though, the women were able to partake in some self-healing. Isis worked as a medical health counselor at the time of my interview with her and shared her method of personal growth through her education and employment:

Going to school for human services was very therapeutic for me because I learned a lot about relationships and family and dysfunction and reasons why and how. Going to school helped me a lot, especially a lot of the books I read, like *Codependent No More* and *How to Break Your Addiction to a Person*. All the books I read, they actually helped me work through a lot of sadness. I don't feel like I carry it around every day.

Experiences with the Criminal Justice System

Battered Black women and other battered women of color tend to have minimal trust in the criminal justice system's ability to aid them in severing relationships with abusive intimate partners.[41] A history of substandard relations between the Black community and the criminal justice system and its agents, because of biased acts by these agents and agencies, accounts for this distrust.[42] Even with high rate of reporting to the police about the abuse perpetrated against them, battered Black women have not been adequately supported by the criminal justice system.[43] The women in my study made many disapproving comments about the criminal justice system. Most of the unfavorable observations centered on policing, specifically. The women did not restrict their critical comments to the system's dealings with intimate partner abuse; they also shared their feelings about how "criminal justice" negatively affects many aspects of the lives of Black people and the well-being of the Black community as a whole. This is reflected in Cicely's commentary, which captures the sentiments of many of the women:

> There's a lot of *in*justice when it comes to people of color, whether it's drugs, alcohol, or even assault. . . . I mean, no problem, you do the crime, you do the time. But the system is unbalanced. You can have a Black man and a White man in there for the same crime, the same background history of their lives, where they went to school, degree, for the same crime. The Black man'll get 150 years while the White man will probably get five to 10 and out in two. Because the Black man is already stereotyped as, "You're never gonna be nothing. You're automatically a drug addict. You're automatically an alcoholic, and you're not working."

Olivia also discussed the imbalance, based on race, in the treatment of individuals by the criminal justice system: "There's a law for them and there's a law for us. The criminal justice system is not equal like they say. The justice scale is unbalanced . . . and it's blindfolded because you don't know what you gonna get into. I've seen a lot of railroading us, a lot of bad things happening in the criminal justice system to good people."

Because of their belief that the criminal justice system is ineffective in resolving problems and has demonstrated unfairness toward Blacks, the women all suggested that alternative methods of dealing with abuse, including those addressed throughout this chapter, should be employed. In our conversation about using the criminal justice system, Kim proclaimed, "I don't care for it. I'd rather handle it in my own way. . . . We never called the police when we was growing up. It was just something you didn't do. You handle your own business. Handle your own business! What's the purpose of having a person in uniform there?" Likewise, Lola concluded, "If you're lucky enough that the police and the courts will help you, sure, go try that, too. If you can do it a different way, go for the different way."

Voicing disapproval over intimate partner abuse perpetrated by Black men by bringing attention to the abuse in the criminal justice system may be another method of debasing the image of Blacks.[44] Moreover, battered Black women who contact the police and therefore add more Black men to the system's offender population may be seen as a betrayal of the Black community.[45] Because of known instances of poor police behavior toward Black males, Black women are often concerned about how their Black male partners will be dealt with by officers.[46] Building on this previous knowledge about the difficulties of Black men caught in the criminal justice system, I asked each of the women how they felt about the way their Black male abusers might be dealt with by the system and its agents. Certainly, some of the women felt guilty for contacting the police and following through with court procedures. But their guilt was primarily about taking away the fathers or father figures from their children, about angering the batterer by involving the authorities, or about removing a source of extra income. They did not feel guilty about sending another Black male through the criminal justice system. Doreen represents this attitude in her response: "Yeah, because the kids, they kind of wanted to know him, but they didn't. So I was feeling guilty about that. Other than that, about me, I didn't care. But the older they got and the more they saw it, I didn't feel guilty. It was mainly because of them." Also, Angie stated that she had remained with her abuser because she was trying to determine a way to be financially self-sufficient. She shared, "I'm still protecting him. . . . Like I said, he had a halfway decent job; I didn't want him to lose his job. I know it sounds kind of stupid, but I didn't want him to get in trouble. I still needed him."

Some of the women offered insight, based on their interactions with system agents, on how they believed the criminal justice system could better help battered women. Olivia discussed how the system must address the batterer's problems earlier and why in her case her batterer may have been disregarded:

> It's a good old boy association; they'll allow men to get away with abuse throughout years. His record went all the way back to high school, being abusive to women. He didn't get any psychological treatment or help until he damn near killed me and tore up my house. If it wasn't for the victims' advocates—because most of those women had been abused also and they

see these clients all the time—I don't think I would have made it through. Even some of the police officers were finally glad that somebody stepped forward and said something so that they could get him locked up.

Clearly, Olivia's feelings for the criminal justice system wavered because she had had both negative and positive experiences with and perceptions of the system. Though she saw cases handled in different ways, Olivia believed that individuals can make the system work for them. She framed her response around this and her lack of guilty feelings about following through with getting her abuser arrested. In response to my question "Did you feel guilty for turning in a Black man?" she stated:

> No, I felt great! I felt I did a justice not only for me; I helped the justice system, which I really didn't like at first. But it worked for me. I can honestly say it worked for me. . . . So until I had a chance firsthand to really see that it really does work, but you have to hang in there and believe and go through the endurance, the stress and the strain, and rehashing old wounds, stuff like that. I felt great.

A few additional women had positive feelings about and experiences with the criminal justice system. Jade had an overall positive view of the system: "I felt strong that the justice system did the job for me. It worked for me. I thought he was just going to get probation. I didn't know they were going to give him jail time."

Police Intervention

The effect that the arrest of a batterer will have on his possible future abuse of his intimate partner is a chief concern in issues of policing and intimate partner abuse. Only a few women in my study did not call the police due to *fear* of more abuse after law enforcement intervention. The five women in middle-class abusive relationships and many of the women in working-class relationships did not call the police themselves. However, this does not mean there was no police, and possibly court, intervention, since witnesses of the abuse may have called the police to intervene. Despite any consequences to be faced as a result of a batterer's arrest, some of the women considered the removal of the men from their homes as a reprieve. The intermittent periods of respite that resulted from police intervention provided the women time to recuperate and to prepare for continued abuse upon the batterers' return home. Harriet said she "called the police to put him out, so I could go to sleep." Kim shared a similar reaction upon arriving home after a full day of work at a package delivery company to deal with Eli, the last of her four abusive mates:

> I'm trying to get dressed for bed. Eli comes in and starts messing with me. . . . I said, "I've got to be up at seven o'clock. I really, really don't feel like fighting." I called the police. I don't need any more bruises. I'm already bruised from picking up boxes at my job. I grabbed a spaghetti strap t-shirt. I knew what he was going to do and I knew what his temper was like. I got the police there. . . . They [arrested] Eli on abuse on me. . . . They took him to jail. Girl, I got to sleep!

As should be apparent, Kim manipulated the system to work for her—at least for the short term. However, the majority of the women who had interactions with police officers because of altercations with their partners were not satisfied with these exchanges.

At the age of 17, Aaliyah was raped by a man with whom she was romantically involved. She became pregnant as a result of the attack and eventually decided to disclose the assault to police authorities when her daughter was one year old:

> At one point I actually did call the police. I started to feel bad about who my daughter was. I remember calling the [city] police and telling them. They came to my house and I thought, "OK, good, I'm going to take care of this." They told me, "You're just doing this because you're mad at him. Are you doing this because you want child support?" I was so hurt. They was going through my drawers and my kitchen and asking me if I was on welfare. They weren't even asking me what happened. They were like drilling me. So after that I killed it. My whole mind and my body and my spirit, I killed it, and I never talked about it again, until one day I finally told my mother.

Aaliyah's experience demonstrates the complex interplay of race, gender, sexuality, social class, and stereotyping in women's ability to access criminal justice agents for assistance. After Aaliyah was brutally raped again years later by another man, her estranged husband who entered her home unlawfully, she was able to silently persuade her daughter to leave the house and contact the police. When the police arrived at the home, they informed Aaliyah that her husband's only infraction was his violation of the restraining order Aaliyah had taken out against her husband. Aaliyah stated: "I feel like if it was a White lady up in [an upper-class neighborhood], I think the situation probably would have been handled differently. . . . I think she probably would have been treated better. . . . I've never been asked the question, 'Are you OK? Do you need anything?' I don't think a cop has ever asked me if I was OK, ever."

In a few situations, police officers would talk with the women in the immediate presence of the batterer, rather than separating the couple to prevent further abuse and to determine the nature of the situation. These women, including Lola, expressed their dissatisfaction with this practice: "These police are crazy, asking me from the door—he's between me and the police—and the police is asking me if everything is fine. Of course it is! They stayed for a while, but they never asked me by myself. If I was anywhere near that door I would have left with the police." Ebony described a similar situation when the officers responded to her home:

> I think they could have asked more questions. They're asking me questions, and he's standing right here. I think they should have separated us. Maybe they could have got more out of me. . . . It should have been private. And then I don't like to talk in big groups, so if there's two or three police, I'm going to try to rush on. I know they're going to get in the car and laugh at the situation.

Further dissatisfaction among the women was related to police officers' inability to detect evidence of abuse on the women because the color of their skin did not always easily show bruises. If there were no cuts, missing teeth, or other obvious injuries, the police typically failed to take action. Naomi opined, "They're not trained to see what they need to see. . . . They're not looking at the signs, they're looking at physical symptoms." Doreen, who is dark-skinned, spoke of the lack of physical evidence when the police arrived at her home after a battering incident: "They didn't see nothing on me, no bruises or nothing. They would just make him leave the house." Although Renee is fair-skinned, she also lacked physical evidence to support police action after her boyfriend hit her: "They didn't see any marks on me. It was my word against his. . . . Something has to be shown. Something has to be done. Somebody has to be found. And that didn't happen. They didn't see anything." Naomi did not regularly fight back in any of her relationships, but she typically made efforts to protect herself.

In doing so on one occasion, Naomi, who has medium-brown skin, put marks on the batterer, who is a fair-skinned Latino. She discussed what happened when the police officers responded to the home:

> I said, "This man hit me and you're looking at the scars on him because he's lighter than I am. Because of my complexion it's not gonna show up until later." [The officer said,] "No, no, it would show up right now". . . . I could probably touch his cheek and it would turn red. . . . They put me down for third degree assault and put him down for harassment.

Although their experiences left them with negative views of police interaction (both their own experiences and those witnessed among family members and in the community), just as they felt about the criminal justice system in general, a handful of women in my study experienced a positive police experience. Max demonstrated this notion about police officers in general: "Not all police are bad police. There are some that take advantage of being a police officer. You know, just touch you any way they want to. Some of that is unnecessary. But all in all, police are good guys. As long as they're not taking *me* to jail, it's all good." Gloria had a great deal of gratitude for the additional protective measures taken and offered by the officer who responded to her call:

> They took him to jail. The police officer asked me did I want him to beat him up. . . . [The officer] was a White guy. And I had on just my pajamas. He looked at me, he took off his coat and he put it around me. He said, "You know what? You did not deserve this and look how he's got you out here." He put me in the front seat [of the patrol cruiser] and then we sat down and he started talking. He said, "You know what? I can . . . kick his ass if you want me to." I was thinking, "I still love this man! No! No!" And after that, [the officer] would just ride around and just wave. He did that probably for about a month after that. And I thought that was really nice. . . . He was really sweet.

Victim Arrests

The women also discussed how they noticed that changes in the law led to the arrest of more battered women, including themselves, for intimate partner violence-related offenses. To be sure, other research has found that there has been an increase in arrests of women, many of whom suffered repeat abuse by their male mates.[47] Many women who get arrested for intimate partner assault report that they were acting in self-defense.[48] There are indications in previous research that police are exhibiting racial bias in the arrests of battered Black women. Sherrie Bourg and Harley V. Stock discovered that 84.6 percent of the Black women in their study were arrested for aggravated battery, a felony, while the remainder of arrests were for simple battery, a misdemeanor. Conversely, 19.5 percent of White males, 32.3 percent of Black males, and 26.3 percent of White females were arrested on the felony charge. They theorized that the misperception by police of the Black woman as the angry woman may account for the discrepancy in arrest rates related to felony intimate partner violence charges and that women may be more likely to use a weapon because they lack the physical strength of men, thus causing more damage to the partner and breaking with the prescribed feminine role.[49]

As already established, because of the women's tendency to fight back, many of the women feared that they themselves would be arrested when they called the police (or during other interactions with law enforcement agents). They were also aware of newly implemented law enforcement policies that mandate an arrest of at least one party when police respond to intimate partner violence calls. One of the (unintended) outcomes of pro-arrest policies is the significant rates of arrests among *battered* women for intimate partner violence.[50] Even if police officers still had a significant amount of discretion, many of the women in my study perceived that one or both individuals of an intimate couple would be arrested if police responded to the incident. Paula disclosed: "At the time, I thought that I would be arrested also. So I wouldn't call. It was always about my kids, protecting my kids. I thought if there's an altercation then both people would be taken." Tammy also discussed her observation of current arrest procedures:

> Right now they're pretty strict 'cause somebody's going to get a case. . . .
> Sometimes they'll come out and talk, but either one of you are going or
> both of you are going to go. And once you get a domestic violence, that's
> just like a drug case on your record, 'cause people don't want you. Violent
> crimes or assaults, they don't want you in their apartments. Lot of places
> you have to get a criminal background history, and if you have domestic
> violence background a lot of times you can't even rent an apartment. It's
> almost like drugs on your record. It's not good. . . . I don't see no good
> habilitation in the criminal system.

Several of the women were themselves arrested, cited, or threatened with arrest for intimate partner violence, including Naomi, as demonstrated in her narrative in the previous section, and Inez: "When I started fighting him back, I was fighting him back. He wasn't getting the best of me then. I was getting him. And a lot of times they wouldn't take him, they'd take me. I've done a lot of 90 days and a lot of 120 days." Interestingly, Billie spoke of her glee when she was arrested because of the perceived shift in power from her abuser to her brought on by her fighting back: "I went to jail. I was in there for about four days. I wasn't there that long. . . . I just felt so good. I went to jail happy! I've never went to jail happy in my life. I was happy." Even though this facet of violence against Black women has not been detected in other research, Richie found in her study that some of the battered Black women in jail were relieved by their incarceration because they felt safe from further abuse by their batterers.[51] The two women who were (only) threatened with arrest (Max and Zora) negotiated with the police, agreeing that the police would not arrest them if they removed themselves from the vicinity (usually a residence) and from the "batterer-victim." The third woman who was not technically arrested, Victoria, was carted off to a detoxification holding facility until she was sober, then allowed to return home.

Of the eight women who were arrested, cited, or threatened with an arrest, six have dark brown skin tones, one is medium brown, and one has light brown skin. As for their socioeconomic status at the time of the police contact, one woman was middle-class (Harriet, with dark brown skin), three were working-class (one each of light, medium, and dark brown tones), and four were lower-income (all with dark brown skin). The skin tone among all the women in my study spanned the spectrum of shades, and the income levels ranged from middle-class to low-income, so it is especially interesting that the majority of women to be confronted with police action against them for fighting back have dark skin tones and were in low-income or working-class settings when the police made contact. Since there was a good amount of police contact across the sample (even if the women were not the ones calling the police in to assist) and the majority of the women fought back, we can speculate that, again, disparaging stereotypes about Blacks may continue to have an impact. An examination of racial profiling of Black women arrested for defending themselves in intimate partner abuse situations by police officers, taking into account the intersection of race, skin tone, wealth, and living conditions, is obviously needed in future research.

Susan L. Miller argues that if the trend to penalize battered women who fight back continues, the criminal justice system will be ineffective.[52] I agree with Miller's assertion. The arrests of some of the woman in my study (a) mainly served to generate further distrust and reduce the women's faith in the criminal justice system, (b) left the women with criminal records that reduced their opportunities to obtain housing and employment, and (c) opened the women to the stigma and risk attached to being an "offender" within the criminal justice system.

Prosecutorial and Judicial Intervention

Fewer women were involved in official court action as a result of police action than experienced police intervention for their intimate partners' battering. This was to be expected since there is a filtering process as offenders progress through the criminal justice system. Some of this filtering occurs when the women fail to follow through with assisting prosecutors after a batterer's arrest. Phoebe reported a positive experience with the police but said she was angry with herself for her inaction after her boyfriend was arrested:

> They always were very professional and really wanted to help me. They really did. I really wish I had just broke through with prosecuting him. You know, showing up to court and doing my part like I should have 'cause he would have spent some time in jail. I felt bad because they really did want to help, and they really didn't like him at all.

Doreen and a few other women were scorned by criminal justice agents for their decision not to follow through with prosecution of their batterers:

> The police would come and they would get mad at me because they said I was filing reports and I wasn't trying to do nothing about it. So one day when I did call the police, they told me, "You got to testify against him, or we'll put you in jail." I did. I got tired, and I did. They locked him up for a couple of years for habitual domestic.

As with their recollections about police intervention, the women's memories of their encounters with the court process were overwhelmingly disapproving. Court-level intervention includes the use of restraining orders that protect battered women by instructing batterers to stay away from the women. All states in the United States allow individuals who have been abused to secure protective orders against their batterers. Helen Eigenberg and her colleagues found that during the past two decades, legislation regarding restraining or protection orders has been strengthened. These changes included improved access to obtaining orders; a broader definition of "intimate relationships" beyond married parties; improved confidentiality; and increased penalties for repeat violators.[53] Karla Fischer and Mary Rose determined that women who seek restraining orders overcome feelings of fear to do so and feel that they have taken power or control over their situation.[54] Several of the women in my study made use of the opportunity to secure restraining orders. Aaliyah used the restraining order she got against her husband to help protect herself if and when she needed to: "I used it like a shield to protect myself. If I ever felt like I was in danger, I knew that he'd have to leave one way or another." But most of the women said that the restraining orders served no purpose, because they did not deter the batterer from associating with the women or from continuing to abuse the women. Billie described her disappointment with this form of legal intervention: "Restraining order, that don't work. I went and got a restraining order on Kobe numbers of times. And he'd come right over there and talk his stuff and jump on me, and by the time the police came, he was gone."

Even though there has been improvement in the comportment of court officials, Angela Moe Wan observed that legal and court personnel who assist women requesting restraining orders were demeaning and patronizing to the women.[55] Gloria spoke of her irritation with the process:

> I went and got a restraining order. Got the temporary one, then I went back to get the permanent one. I thought that process was tedious. I kept trying to explain to [the judge] that [my boyfriend] kicked me while I was down. I'm mentally drained. I have been doing this for 10 years. Fighting, mentally trying to keep him from lashing out for these 10 years, and you're sitting up here telling me I haven't given you enough excuse for this man to have a restraining order? What's he have to do, beat me down? In that aspect I thought it was hard. I thought, this judge was just thinking that I was being mean, and I wasn't. I was just trying to protect myself. . . . I felt like that was the hardest thing, to get a restraining order. And it was actually worthless, because he could still call and still come by and the police wouldn't do anything, maybe tell him to leave. I don't know how things are today, but I know [with] my mom, and in the

earlier years when it was happening to me, it was no big deal to just go to
jail and get out.

Gloria's mention of "fighting" refers to her attempts, both verbal and psychological, to try to keep her abuser from attacking her. Actually, Gloria
was one of the small number of women who *did not* physically retaliate
against their batterers. Despite that, Gloria demonstrated in her narrative
how the judge in her case may have been relying on a stereotype of the
Black woman as the angry woman ("this judge was just thinking I was
being mean").

Another form of court-level intervention experienced by the women
was the prosecution of their abusers. Even though Blacks have univer-
sally distrusted the criminal justice system both in general and in relation to issues of intimate partner abuse, Hoan N. Bui found that Black
women were more likely to want prosecution in intimate partner abuse
cases than White women,[56] and 65 percent of the Black women in Arlene
N. Weisz's study supported prosecution of their batterers. Weisz argues,
"No matter how strong some women might perceive themselves to be,
they may recognize that legal interventions against batterers are complex
processes best handled by legal professionals."[57] Even while accepting the
court's intervention in their cases, the women in my examination often
found themselves annoyed by the procedures. Isis was willing to cooper-
ate with the prosecution after her batterer's arrest but was frustrated by
the process:

> I had to go to court for my daughter's dad when he pulled that gun on
> me. . . . I was kind of dumb at that point about the whole thing. I just
> wanted to get it over with because it seem to be like such a long, drawn-
> out process. You know he did it. Just lock him up. Do something with
> him. I had to be heard, I had to testify and everything. It was a scary ex-
> perience. But I was honest. And that's what took the fear out of it. I didn't
> have anything to be afraid of, 'cause I didn't do anything. I was in my
> house and he came over with mess. Just being in front of a judge; it's so
> official. And there was a part of me that was worried about him, because
> he had never been to the penitentiary before. He was kind of a pretty boy,
> and that was my daughter's father. I still didn't want him to go to jail and
> get messed over. I just wanted him to serve his time, learn a lesson from
> it. And he did. He came out of prison with a real nasty scar on his fore-
> head that he won't tell anyone where it came from.

Initially, the police charged Aaliyah's husband with violating the restraining order, rather than rape. Once the case reached the district at-
torney's office, additional charges were imposed. Aaliyah was pleased that
additional charges were imposed but discussed her personal conflict and
her disappointment with the outcome of the case:

> He had a rape charge, first degree assault, burglary, kidnapping. It was all
> of that, it wasn't just he violated the restraining order. They told me he
> was looking at 32 years in prison for what he did. All I could think about
> was his kids at the time. I thought, I'm gonna be the one to put him away
> for the rest of his life and he's never gonna see his kids. . . . I said, "Just
> give him a plea bargain. Offer him something, I don't care what it is."
> [The assistant district attorney] called me back and said that he had got
> five years. I was mad. But then I told myself, I can't be mad, I told her to
> do that. I didn't know they were going to go from 32 years to five years. I
> thought he would get 10 or 20 years. He was out in two.

Getting Out

The view of battered Black women as strong and independent Black
women (which is often how they view themselves) interferes with their
wanting to reach out and use medical and therapeutic services, battered
women's shelters, and criminal justice system channels. This view also
negatively affects how social services agents respond to battered Black
women. To a lesser extent, the women's dynamic resistance also interfered, to the extent that they did not want to "burden" their families and
other social relations (including friends and religious companions). However, even when close and private relations were utilized, the women's resistance to daily stressors continued to build.

Overwhelmingly, fear was not a hindrance, or at least not a *major* hindrance, in the women's decision to terminate the abusive relationships.
Other factors were important considerations, such as socioeconomic conditions, the desire for a successful marriage, the stigma of being a (Black)
single mother, the desire for their children to have the regular presence of
a father, family involvement, and spirituality. However, that fear was not a
major element in the abusive relationships of the battered Black women in
this study does not imply that the harm inflicted on the women was less
dangerous than that committed against battered women of other races,
ethnicities, and cultures.

Societal stressors and the structure of U.S. society, in conjunction with typecast images of Blacks and the cultural characteristics considered special to the Black community, all factored into the women's capacity to eventually flee the abusive relationships and the responses these women met as they did so. As there are a multitude of levels to assess how battered Black women get out of these relationships, the multilevel assessment provided by Black feminist criminology is beneficial and necessary. All of the means used by the women to ultimately reject the harmful and unhealthy men in their lives built upon their dynamic resistance to the many battles, including those other than intimate partner abuse, in the lives of Black women.

8

Conclusion

The Response

During my time spent with Billie, her daughter, Nia, was present throughout the entire interview. Nia was generally quiet during the three-hour discussion but did interject periodically. Even though she knew much of her mother's story—and lived some of it—I was aware that some of Billie's recounting was new to Nia and that it caused Nia some pain to listen to her mother's distressing tales. Cassandra was also accompanied by a family member. Cassandra told me she brought along her younger sister (by 15 years) because she wanted her sister to finally learn about her extremely volatile relationships with her first husband and a boyfriend. But, unlike Nia, Cassandra's sister never spoke during the interview and left about a third of the way into the four-hour encounter, as it was a lot for the sister to take in. A good number of the remaining women wished to share the detrimental effects of intimate partner abuse, as well. They wished for other Black women and Black girls to learn from their experiences. A couple of hours into Billie's interview, Nia asked with curiosity: "Can I ask you a question, Hillary? What are you doing with these stories people tell you?" Aside from the academic explanation of "analyzing the data for similarities and themes," I shared with Nia that I had a broader, yet firm, goal: to communicate to the Black community and society-at-large that we must address the problem of intimate partner abuse against Black women.

Addressing this problem will allow us to draw attention to Black women's contribution to and role in society in general and to the many struggles in addition to intimate partner abuse that Black women face on a daily basis. Now that we have an even greater understanding of Black women's experiences with intimate partner abuse, how are we to confront the abuse and the way in which others respond to abuse against Black women?

In Black history and culture, the "call-and-response" feature has compounded and significant meanings. The call-and-response is an African-derived process of communication that involves verbal and nonverbal exchanges that are reflexive in nature, where "all of the speaker's statements ('calls') are punctuated by expressions ('responses') from the listener."[1] As one of the few traditions retained from African cultures among Africans trapped and enslaved in American colonies, call-and-response was predominant in the Black church, including during the period of slavery when "'church' was anywhere black people were: in the fields, back in the woods, in the 'new ground' areas (uncultivated, unplowed land which had to be made ready for seeding)."[2] In current times, call-and-response remains an important communicative factor in Black churches but has extended to general communication within Black culture, as well. Call-and-response communications can be found in dialogue, music, and literature. In and out of the church, verbal examples of responses include "Amen!," "Speak on it!," "Go 'head!," "Teach!," or "Preach!" Nonverbal responses comprise feet stomping, raising the Black power sign (balled fist held on high), head nodding, and "giving skin" (hand-to-hand slap).[3] Geneva Smitherman concludes that call-and-response "seeks to synthesize speakers and listeners in a unified movement." While the use of call-and-response is not limited to Blacks and the Black community,[4] it undoubtedly has significant meaning within the interactions of the Black community, a community in the broadest sense and not one restricted by geographical boundaries. Maggie Sale asserts that call-and-response patterns "both value improvisation and demand that new meanings be created for each particular moment."[5] Moreover, in the African and Black American tradition of call-and-response, Adisa A. Alkebulan writes that the "absence of audience participation invalidates the event."[6] Through the lens of these explanations for the call-and-response method of communication, we can reply to the "What's next?" inquiry regarding intimate partner abuse perpetrated against Black women. I use this special and cherished call-and-response aspect of Black culture to heed the passionate admonitions given to me by the women represented in this book.

One of the distinctive attributes of feminist research is that which Shulamit Reinharz identified as a *political connection*. She reported that the design and purpose of feminist research is grounded in political activism. Indeed, Reinharz concludes that many feminists believe that research qualifies as feminist only if it is associated with social action that seeks social change.[7] As follows, I press upon, first and foremost, the Black community to respond to the call of the women's battle cries. During my time with Medea, she conveyed instances when the alliance among the few people of color working in advocacy settings to stop violence against women was threatened by the inability of the advocates of color to be unified in their common goal of underscoring the need to make violence against women *of color* visible and to establish cultural competency in services afforded to battered women of color. Internal strife among Blacks working in areas that deal with violence against Black women and within the Black community in general is disadvantageous. Certainly, many other individuals, groups, and institutions must also answer the call, but, as a (Black) community, we must rally to set in motion and to lead the effort to alleviate intimate partner abuse among Blacks in conjunction with our activism to assuage the many other challenges confronting Black Americans.

Theoretical Contribution

With the coming of the Second Wave of the mainstream feminist movement in the 1960s and 1970s, intimate partner abuse against women was identified as a significant social problem. The development of the concept of this abuse and the recognition of it as an all too frequent phenomenon is attributed to the grassroots work of women activists who fought against violence against women and to intellectual research into the subject by academicians. Investigations that specifically study the lives and experiences of battered women of color, however, are still scarce. By employing a theoretical base formulated to specifically consider Black women's position in U.S. society (Black feminist criminology) and by sampling battered Black women from diverse backgrounds, the study described in this book provides an essential analysis of battered Black women's experiences with intimate partner abuse and support networks. Although many of the findings in this book are consistent with patterns, themes, and reports from existing literature on intimate partner abuse, a great deal of the information resulting from my investigation does not exist in other published works.

Black feminist criminology was an appropriate theoretical foundation to consider in analyzing intimate partner abuse against Black women, their reactions to this abuse, and the responses to these women by unofficial and official support systems. Black feminist criminology is chiefly based on Black feminist, critical race feminist, and feminist criminology theories. Black feminist theory stresses that the Black woman encompasses many components that frame her identity. These elements include the general categories of race, ethnicity, gender, class, nationality, and sexuality. Moreover, the Black woman identifies not as one or the other at different times and places in her life but with all components at all times. Black feminist and critical race feminist theories maintain that oppression and discrimination directed against any or all of these parts of the Black woman's identity can occur at the structural or societal level, within the Black community, and within interpersonal relationships. Feminist criminology brings a gendered approach to the field of criminology. Feminist criminology seeks to demonstrate how women in particular are affected by and react to crime, violence, and the law. Using Black feminist criminology to understand Black women's experiences with and reactions to intimate partner abuse provides a more comprehensive evaluation and understanding of these women's lives. In addition, Black feminist criminology considers how battered Black women are supported within informal and formal settings, as demonstrated in the women's experiences with these sources of support. Using Black feminist criminology as the foundation to investigate the experiences of battered Black women, I was able to develop a theoretical model specific to these women's encounters. The concept considered what Black feminists and critical race feminists have established about Black women's experiences, as well as the women's personal appraisals about their lives as Black women who had been abused by intimate partners.

The women in my study continuously referred to themselves and other Black women as Strong Black Women because of their lifelong struggles growing out of being Black *and* female in the United States, as well as other identifiers, such as being a mother and self-sufficient. The women often compared their social position to that of White women, whom they believed to be privileged and delicate. The women added that battered White women with whom they had interactions stayed in abusive relationships longer, spoke out more about their abuse, were more passive with batterers, made fewer attempts to fix the abusive situation, fought back less, and relied on the batterers more than did Black women in similar situations. The stereotypes of Black women as fighters, emasculating, and more masculine than White women liberated the Black women from the restrictions placed on White women, thus allowing them to fight back. The women did not necessarily consider their actions masculine in nature but saw them as inherent in their right to resist domination in order to protect themselves, their children, and their property. This resistance occasionally resulted in the women contemplating or planning to kill their abusers.

To describe the women in this study as victims or survivors—the terms usually used to describe battered women—does not accurately describe how the women situated themselves in the context of their entire life experiences. The women typically did not consider themselves to be "victims" because they never saw themselves as passive; they fought back most of the time, and being a "battered woman" was not a part of their *identity*. The term "survivors" is more fitting to describe how battered Black women view themselves because being a survivor typically connotes taking an active role in leaving the relationship. However, because battered Black women continue to confront racial, class-based, and other struggles, such as the need to avoid entering subsequent abusive relationships, the use of the term "survivor" assumes that their struggles have concluded. The women continually face the need to resist all forms of abuse, whether institutional or interpersonal. Accordingly, the women are best described as "resisters," even though they frequently *reacted* to events, because the focus is more on the *resister's* actions than on the actions of others. Although the view of themselves as Strong Black Women sometimes interfered with the women seeking assistance with combating the abuse, they overwhelmingly embraced the *idea* that supports this term. They embraced the idea that they have exhibited *resistance*—either physical *or* nonphysical force—in many aspects in their lives, not only their abusive relationships. This concept of *dynamic resistance* encapsulates the whole of battered Black women's distinctive life-chances, influenced by race, gender, sexuality, class, violence, abuse, and other characteristics, and their dynamic responses to these life-chances. The women exhibit their dynamic resistance to being beat down, knocked out, and kicked around by (a) their intimate partners, (b) their social and religious communities, which ignore the abuse, and (c) the criminal justice system, which disregards their battles with abuse. The outcome of this study, using Black feminist criminology as a backdrop, alerts us to the notion that these findings can be applied to the broader spectrum of Black women's lived experiences. Although not every Black woman in the United States is a resister of intimate partner abuse, most, if not all, Black women face one or more forms of oppression or bias because of their dynamic identities. Battered Black women, along with many other Black women who have not been in abusive relationships, are resisters of racism, colorism, sexism, heterosexism, and sexualization in the Black community and in general U.S. society.

Formation and Role of Abuse, Gender, Race, and Class During Childhood

There are variations and similarities among battered Black women's childhood experiences. Their construction of racial and gender identities, positions within the economic hierarchy, and encounters with abuse and violence were important variables for the investigation of the women's entrée into abusive intimate relationships. The formation from Black girls into Black women involved the struggle to live up to prescribed womanly duties and femininity while simultaneously being socialized to become Strong Black Women, which often challenges society's notion of what it is to be a "lady."

More than half of the women were verbally, emotionally, or physically abused by their parents or guardians. Also, half of the women witnessed intimate partner abuse among their parents, and a smaller number of women were sexually assaulted by a family member or acquaintance. Several women were exposed to other forms of violence and abuse, such as witnessing siblings in abusive relationships and observing neighborhood violence. Sometimes the women had experienced several of these types of abuse, and the majority of the women had experienced at least one form of maltreatment. These abuses significantly affected the women's emotional well-being and were partly responsible for their low self-esteem and their destructive behaviors in their intimate relationships.

The explanations the women provided for unpleasant childhood experiences were typically given in the context of race, gender, and class themes. The women reported wealth and class triggers as reasons for abuse, including their parents' frustration with the difficulties of financially stabilizing the home and securing material possessions. Other important patterns related to race, gender, and class also emerged. Subordinate treatment based on skin tone hierarchies among Blacks was offered as a racially based explanation for unfavorable treatment. Regarding class differences, the few instances of sexual abuse were more prevalent among women raised in lower-income homes. Interestingly, verbal, mental, and nonsexual physical abuse were more prevalent among the women raised in middle-class homes, which were mainly two-parent homes where the abuser was most likely to have been the father or stepfather. The single-parent homes of origin were overwhelmingly run by mothers; therefore, mothers were the main perpetrators of verbal, mental, and nonsexual abuse in these homes.

Women who were witnesses to abuse among their parents (that is, intimate partner abuse) absorbed the idea that couples sometimes attempted to solve their problems in an abusive or violent manner. However, the women were distressed by the abuse, which was frightening and left them with confusing and conflicting images of intimate relationships. This often led to the women taking on a caretaker role, making attempts to physically protect their mothers or persuade their mothers to leave the abusive relationships. The women also saw their mothers retaliate against the batterers and described their mothers in positive terms for making dynamic and physical attempts to protect themselves. Prior to becoming involved in abusive relationships, some of the women had already begun to exhibit behaviors they would carry into the relationships. These behaviors during girlhood included fighting, using alcohol and other drugs, and engaging in risky sexual practices. In order to escape their unstable and chaotic home environments, several women left their homes of origin and went directly into the relationships with their first abusers. These women, as well as those who had no significant exposure to abuse during their youth, had difficulty in determining the clues that would suggest their batterers' pending abusive behaviors.

All these actions, both those of the women during girlhood and those of their mothers, affected how the women would react to their own experiences when they found themselves in abusive intimate relationships. The women either fought hard to resist being like their mothers or mimicked their mothers' responses to abuse. That they had witnessed male violence against their mothers left the women with less than favorable opinions about Black men in general. At the same time, however, the women were sympathetic to Black men because the women knew personally of the struggles and injustices that Black men face in the United States. Moreover, they often reported feeling empathy for Black men because of their gendered struggles and how these intersected with racism, such as their failure to live up to the traditional expectation that a man is to provide for and be the master of his family. Because the majority of the women were abused by Black men, this view was solidified as they progressed into adulthood and entered into relationships with these abusive men.

Sociocultural Consideration of Forms of Intimate Partner Abuse

All the women in this study were abused mentally and physically (in a nonsexual manner) by intimate partners, but to varying degrees. Mental abuse was overwhelmingly reported as being more destructive than physical abuse, as it struck at the core of the women's self-esteem. Sexual aggression, via coercive threats or physical force, was an integral part of the physical abuse encountered by some of the women. Other forms of abuse included stalking, property theft or destruction, infidelity, and control over daily activities. Women classified as low-income and working-class during their youth and up to the time of the interviews were in more abusive relationships than the women from the middle-class. However, I identified no patterns that linked wealth status and the length of time spent in these relationships.

Another economic class difference concerned the site where the batterers struck the women on their bodies and the setting in which the batterers physically and mentally abused the women. Batterers in middle-class relationships were more likely to keep their abuse hidden by not inflicting scratches, bruises, or other marks on parts of the women's bodies where they could readily be seen and by not committing the abuse in front of others. Low-income and working-class batterers tended not to restrict their abuse to the privacy of their homes or to places on the women's bodies that were typically hidden. In fact, these men in the lower classes often beat the women in their faces with the intent of marking them as chattel.

Regardless of class status, the women in this study tended to be employed, at least intermittently, during the abusive relationships. A few batterers made attempts to restrict the women from working outside the home or to keep them from advancing in their professional careers, but the batterers typically did not restrict working, because the women's incomes greatly aided in financially supporting the household. Furthermore, some of the women worked while their batterers did not, and some women reported higher earnings than their abusers. Yet, if it appeared the women were advancing professionally, the batterers tried to place some limits on the women's employment. I speculate that these batterers did this out of fear that the women would become too independent. The men appreciated that the women's work provided economic benefits, but the batterers did not want the women to become too accomplished because they would be less motivated to remain in the relationships. However, attempts to meet even the most traditional wifely standards did not appease the batterers' wrath. The batterers also sought to control other movements and contacts the women had, such as access to family, friends, and religious activities. This control, in addition to coming from a need to control others, often grew out of the batterers' jealous attitudes.

The women had much to offer about the factors that motivated their male companions to be violent and otherwise abusive. The explanations generally focused on environmental and psychological dynamics. The women found themselves feeling pity for their Black male partners, stating that the men battered because of their devalued status in U.S. society and their difficulties finding and maintaining suitable employment. Many of the women simply believed that their batterers had a basic dislike of women. It was clear that the women recognized the gendered and sexist nature of intimate partner abuse. Several women attempted to imitate the role of the traditional wife in their intimate relationships. However, since they often described the batterers as not being "real men" or as being "mama's boys" because of their limited success in the world, the women were taking on more nontraditional, matriarchal, or egalitarian roles inside and outside the home. Undoubtedly, negotiating the sexism, racism, and class struggles was confounding for both the women and the abusers.

The women described how their Black batterers' racial status within the U.S. social structure was an added factor in their diminished position in U.S. society. The sex-ratio imbalance between Black women and Black men was cited as a reason for remaining with a Black male batterer if he was able to offer something to the household finances. At the time the batterers' abusive behaviors became obvious to the women, many of the women were aware of the shortage of desirable Black men, partly due to high incarceration and mortality rates among Black men. These beliefs made the women decide that if their mates at least partially met the criteria for a "good husband," they would endure a certain amount of abuse. Friends and family of the women in middle-class abusive relationships often pressured the women to stay in the relationships because the monetary benefits outweighed the tumultuous costs. The women who were abused by non-Black men recognized no major differences between Black men and non-Black men, and, moreover, they personally discovered that battering is not a behavior exhibited only by Black men.

As the women acknowledged the effect of their own exposure to violence during childhood, they identified it as a factor for their batterers, as well. Many of the batterers used or abused alcohol and other drugs that affected their abusive behavior. Some said that the level of violence increased when the batterers were intoxicated or when they craved the drugs during a sober moment. However, many of the women stated that the violent tendencies were present regardless of the level of drug use. It may be that the problems that lead to excessive and problematic alcohol and other drug use are the problems that also lead a (Black) man to be abusive.

Sociocultural Consideration of Seeking Support

Motivations that led the women in the study to remain in or to leave the abusive relationships were often dictated by the sociostructural and cultural factors to which they were subjected and by their access to supportive entities. There were few economic class variations among the women in this area. To start, fear of retaliation was seldom reported as a reason for staying with a batterer. Reasons for continuing the abusive relationships related more to (a) the shame of being a single, unpartnered mother whose children had no stable father-figure, (b) urging by family members to make the relationship work, (c) religious teachings, (d) embarrassment, and (e) to a lesser extent, advice from friends that the financial benefits were worth enduring some abuse.

Because the entire group of women had severed at least one abusive relationship at the time of my interviews with them, they were able to speak of and conceptualize their motivations for terminating the unions. Some of the women who had been exposed to abuse during childhood recognized that their own children's exposure to abusive relationships might increase the likelihood that the children would become abusive with or be subjected to abuse by intimate partners. Even those women who had not been introduced to any forms of abuse during childhood recognized the effect the abuse could have on their children. Therefore, the women left the relationships before their children were able to fully recognize the abuse or removed the children from the abuse and tried to rectify any damage that might have already been done.

The women had several methods of support available to them as they sought to leave their abusive relationships. The most salient of the methods among battered Black women in this study was family support, particularly from mothers. Even in instances where mothers were unaware or not aware of the extent of the abuse, the women's use of mothers as a support system was important in helping them out of the relationships. Support from mothers was therapeutic; in addition, mothers' homes served as some women's personal "battered women's shelters." When male family members provided assistance, it was typically to intimidate the batterers or to seek physical retribution. Because some of the women believed male family members would physically retaliate on their behalves, because of perceived or actual experiences, the women often refrained from alerting the men in their families of the abuse for fear their loved ones would encounter the criminal justice system as offenders. Dependence on this belief, whether true or not, kept some women from seeking emotional support from some family members.

The majority of the women were raised in the Christian faith, and most of these women still had a strong sense of spirituality during adulthood (that is, at the time of the interviews), even if they were not formally practicing a religion. Many of the women's religious or spiritual convictions became dormant during the abuse. The women who sought counsel from Christian clergy members each reported that the experience was unhelpful, typically to the point of being damaging. These women received recommendations that they remain in and pray for the relationships and that they work harder at being a "good wife." The Muslim women received more satisfying clerical responses to wife abuse than the Christian women. Even though both Christian and Muslim women described their religious experiences as patriarchal in practice, the Muslim women described how clerics and other members of the mosques employed a more intervening and proactive perspective about intimate partner abuse.

Secular and nonfamilial services were also utilized by the women. The women's experiences at medical facilities, in battered women's shelters, and in other therapeutic interventions yielded mixed outcomes but tended to be more negative than constructive. Most of the women did not seek medical attention unless it was absolutely necessary. In part, they did not want to bring formal attention to the battering. Most of the women were aware that medical personnel are part of "the system" and have official responsibilities. This was particularly the case for the low-income women and some of the working-class women who had had involvement with government assistance agencies, who knew that these agencies must comply with legal reporting requirements, and who were more likely to use public health facilities. Another reason for not seeking medical attention was the self-image of these women, who saw themselves as Strong Black Women who can take care of themselves and who must subordinate their needs to those of their intimate partners, children, and other family members.

Assuming the role of the Strong Black Woman, as well as being perceived as a Strong Black Woman, also had implications for shelter and counseling services. The women who used shelters and therapy to assist them with terminating the abusive relationships were often singled out because of their distinctive experiences with abuse and as Black women. When the women's experiences with intimate partner abuse were pointed out by other clients, it tended to be done for the purposes of placing battering and abuse in a hierarchical sequence and served as a perverse source of competition for the other battered women. When the women were singled out by counselors, it was for the purposes of benefiting the battered Black women, to highlight how they are stronger than the other women (specifically, stronger than the *White* women) and strong enough to get out of the relationships. Even if these assertions by other battered women and service providers were true, they often served as a deterrent to battered Black women's efforts to leave abusive relationships. Undervaluing the impact of battered Black women's violent encounters because Black women are not in abusive relationships as long as White women or because their injuries are not as severe as other women's justifies battering to a certain degree. Further, it perpetuates battered Black women's impression that they do not need to seek alternative assistance to supplement their familial resources.

The criminal justice system and its history of ineffectively dealing with Blacks was often cited by the women, even though they occasionally used the system when they believed it would benefit them. Police and court interventions in intimate partner abuse were usually viewed as temporary solutions to the women's battering. Such intervention provided a form of respite or retreat from the batterers, giving the women time to rest before the next battle. It also allowed the women opportunity to reflect on the relationship and on their next course of action. Regrettably, the women were sometimes considered to be perpetrators or aggressors and not resisters or defenders of their person or property. This left these women bewildered about the role of the police and the courts in stopping intimate partner abuse. Stereotyped and biased views about Black women may form the basis for the opinions of police officers and court personnel about intimate partner abuse between Black couples, including stereotypes about inherent abusiveness among Blacks along with the idea of Black women as Strong Black Women or angry women.

The Academic Response

Even with the outcomes of this investigation, it is clear that more research is needed if we are to understand the unique experiences and perspectives of battered Black women. This study provides a theoretical basis for guiding further research on intimate partner abuse among Blacks, and, perhaps, for comparison across cultures, nationalities, races, and ethnicities. In addition, the analysis clarifies and supplements findings from survey and other research in this area. For instance, previous research determined that battered Black women physically resist their batterers more often than other women. My study provides a conceptualized analysis for this finding. Other quantifiable research that has been supplemented by my investigation includes (a) the variations and similarities in socioeconomic class among battered Black women; (b) insight into battered Black women's early exposure to violence, with an alternative way to view its effect on these women; (c) the differences in the types of abuse by intimate partners among Black couples; (d) the justification for staying or remaining in abusive relationships, including the awareness that fear is *not* a major barrier to remaining in the relationship; (e) the justification for using or not using options for assistance in ending abusive relationships, including reliance on mothers, responses by clergy members, and reactions from staff and clientele in battered women's shelters; and (f) the view among study participants and others that they are Strong Black Women. Accordingly, future research should entail returning to survey research to convey these factors through structured questionnaires for further exploration and to determine their generalizability among a larger sample of Black women who have been in abusive relationships.

Future research samples in research on intimate partner abuse, particularly that involving Black women, should also include Black women who may not personally initiate a response to an advertisement that solicits study informants. Specifically, regarding participant recruitment, extended outreach should be instituted within the Black community—as well as beyond the Black community to reach battered Black women not embedded in this community—in order to locate Black women who are more discreet about the abuse against them and who are not especially ready to reveal their lived experiences without urging from researchers. In conducting this research, it is also important that the gender and race of interviewers be seriously considered. This assertion is based on my experiences in the field with Black women. It is questionable whether the respondents to my study would have been as forthright with their race- and gender-based opinions, in particular, if I had been of another race or gender. I strongly believe this interpersonal dynamic yielded the rich data collected in this investigation.

In addition to improved and expanded inquiry into the lives of battered Black women, further research is needed on intimate partner abuse experienced by other marginalized groups and individuals. This includes surveying and conducting in-depth interviews with immigrant women,

Latinas, Native American women, Asian American women, lesbians, and teenage girls. Also, the literature on intimate partner abuse within inter-racial couples is remarkably scant; therefore, research on abuse within interracial couples is particularly important to determining whether women and men in these relationships have any distinctive experiences or needs. To continue to perpetuate theories and research that address intimate partner abuse from a belief that the experiences of this abuse are similar across races, ethnicities, cultures, nationalities, and sexual orientations is problematic. Further, one area that has yet to be examined is what appears to be a statistically significant decline in intimate partner homicides of Black men during the past 30 years. This plunge is not as dramatic as the drop in the rate of homicides involving Black women, White men, and, especially, White women. That fewer Black men have been killed by their (mostly) Black female intimate partners over recent years unquestionably calls for academic attention.

The Systemic Response

This study raises several procedural issues related to battered Black women's access to support agencies and how and when they use these agencies. To begin with, the examination presented in this book serves as a starting point for debunking myths—whether they are actual fables or traditions based in some truth. Such ill-conceived beliefs about battered Black women and their lives do them a serious disservice. My investigation provides improved knowledge of how battered Black women's cultural distinctions and their position in U.S. society may explain why they experience and respond to battering differently from women of other races, ethnicities, and cultures. Incorporating these varied experiences in agencies' guiding principles will improve their delivery of services to Black women confronted with intimate partner abuse. Areas of public policy that may be affected by the dissemination of my results include the social service, medical, psychological, and legal fields.

Fortunately, many battered Black women are able to use their family members' homes as shelter from their batterers, but this resource is not always accessible to battered Black women. Therefore, an improved approach is needed to help battered Black women who are in severe and life-threatening situations to get to *existing* shelters and medical clinics. Facilities located in local communities and small in size will help the women feel more comfortable and find satisfaction in these services. Further, it is crucial that shelter personnel consider how battered Black women are stigmatized in society and how workers in the shelters may themselves accept these stereotypes. Although the maintenance of security and anonymity are main concerns of shelters, because battered Black women's continued contact with family is important to their recuperation, a review must be conducted to determine how the conflict between maintaining security at the shelter and battered Black women's best interests can be resolved.

In addition to improved and specific instruction to shelter staff regarding Black women's responses to intimate partner abuse, training is also required for police officers, court personnel, social workers, victims' advocates, members of intimate partner abuse coalitions, and any other counselors and service providers who work with Black women. Both patrol officers and detectives in units that deal with assault, homicide, and intimate partner abuse ("domestic violence unit") should receive regular updates regarding the problems many Black women face in abusive relationships. While the violence-against-women movement is fortunate to have brought about the advent of "domestic violence investigations units" in police departments and some level of specialized training for intimate partner abuse in police academies, we must ensure that the training is adequate and not laden with stereotypes about intimate partner abuse in general and Black women (and men) specifically. As such, the focus of the training must be on assisting police personnel in exposing their own biases that affect how they see Black women involved in intimate partner abuse. This training should be significant, interactive, and, I would hope, mandatory.

Similar forms of training should be made available to and impressed upon the other workers and agencies mentioned earlier. Judges and magistrates, prosecutors, and defense attorneys could all use improved education in the concerns presented throughout this book. The difficulty, however, is in implementing training—and especially in mandating that such training be completed—for already overburdened public officials. Nevertheless, concerted and organized efforts must be made in this area so that we may work toward better outcomes for women who are regularly stereotyped and left to their own defenses, that is, Black women who feel they must utilize dynamic resistance to protect themselves and their children from abuses by their intimate partners.

With regard to others who are presumed to assist women in need, to assume that those working as advocates or counselors are immune to racial bias and are well versed in issues facing Black women will only continue to be deleterious to battered Black women. In many instances, fortunately, these advocates are typically amenable to receiving new or advanced findings that will help them in their support and therapeutic work.

The Community Response

Because of the discounting of violence against women, the increased advocacy and the introduction of innovative justice policies that began in the 1970s were sorely needed. But now that we have experienced the unintended (or seemingly unintended) consequences of get-tough policies on all forms of violent and abuse-related crimes throughout the United States, it is important for us to focus on another approach: community intervention.

Just as the African adage stresses that "it takes a village to raise a child," it also takes a village (community) to hold batterers accountable and to support resisters of intimate partner abuse. While, admittedly, there is use for a criminal justice system that must seek to control the violent behaviors of batterers, I advocate that we simultaneously bring the Black community together to confront intimate partner abuse in our communities. This should be our principal goal. But this goal should not be limited to confronting intimate partner abuse. We must increase informal community control over other transgressions among Blacks, including child abuse, youth violence, street violence, illicit drug sales, substance abuse, and behaviors that lead to high rates of transmission of HIV/AIDS. Along with community intervention, we require community education in order to prevent our children from carrying on these behaviors that will continue—at least for the time-being—to affect future generations of Black Americans. Much of what has been disclosed in this book draws attention to a problem that persists within the Black community. Essentially, *Battle Cries* "airs our dirty laundry." However, as implicated in the title of this book, the Black community must heed this rallying cry to address the abuses directed at Black women.

Grassroots community outreach to combat various forms of violence within Black communities is already occurring to some extent in urban settings with sizable Black populations. We can consult these efforts as a starting point for ideas on how to implement similar efforts in other communities and for other outreach purposes. Many of these outreach endeavors focus on youth violence, particularly gang-related violence. Of course, such efforts must continue and proliferate. These community outreach models often involve individual activists who respond to locations of gang-related shootings and hold vigils, rallies, and truces that demonstrate the community's condemnation of such violence. These activists also visit wounded gang members in hospitals or in their homes or in jail soon after their release from hospital, believing that the turning point that will help gang members leave the gang is most likely to arrive at or near the time of this traumatic event. Is a similar model possible for intervention in intimate partner abuse?

A call for structured community outreach is not a new concept.[8] Recommendations for increased Black community involvement have been advanced through the Community Insights Project of the Institute on Domestic Violence in the African American Community.[9] Efforts are also being made to improve responsiveness to intimate partner abuse by individuals closely involved in the Black religious community, as evidenced by the work being conducted by the Reverend Aubra Love through her direction of the Black Church and Domestic Violence Institute.[10] This institute provides education and spiritual training to clerics that addresses intimate partner abuse and sexual assault among Blacks. In describing her motivation for the work she is doing to combat intimate partner abuse in the Black community, Reverend Love stated, "I wanted to stay in community with other black people, to talk about the experience of my own healing and recovery, to break the silence for women in the pews who felt nobody would listen to what they were talking about."[11]

The community outreach model as it applies to intimate partner abuse among Blacks needs to be a collaborative effort between Blacks who (a) have educated knowledge of the issues of Blacks and intimate partner abuse, (b) have been resisters of intimate partner abuse, (c) are part of local houses of worship (ministers, deacons, and so forth), particularly those educated on issues of intimate partner abuse, (d) have specialized training in counseling and performing therapy with Black people, and (e) are committed to the cause of liberating the community from intimate partner abuse. As with antigang grassroots interventions, incorporating Black men into this model is extremely important. Support from Black women in this collaborative model is surely needed, but Black men are especially desirable to provide positive guidance for Black male batterers. This model does not preclude non-Blacks from being part of the partnership, but such individuals would serve as support allies. A necessary aspect of this collaboration is liaison with criminal justice agencies and agents. The goal is to have police officers who work within police precincts or districts with a large number of Black residents (or, at the least, intimate partner abuse advocates who work with these police departments) routinely reach out to a collaborative community outreach group to respond to the scene of the intimate partner violence call. This is a necessary function of the community outreach model. Such intervention by the outreach group would include follow-up with visits to the arrested parties in jail or at another location. Another function would be to interface with court personnel, including prosecuting attorneys and judges. In essence, the outreach group would become an integral part of the legal process and serve as *the* expert entity on how a particular Black community should deal with intimate partner abuse among the members of its community.

Beyond these efforts, I suggest that each outreach group work painlessly to determine its own best ways to confront intimate partner abuse among Black men and women. This includes developing safety plans for all parties involved, including the resister, the batterer, and outreach workers. It includes developing various methods by which to intervene when instances of intimate partner abuse are made known. The approaches should be individualized to each community. As established through my investigation, men in low-income and working-class living situations are more likely to exhibit abusive behaviors in the presence of others, so community intervention may be more feasible with these groups of men than it will be for middle-class (and other) men who tend to conceal their abuse. Nonetheless, great efforts must be made in all Black communities and with all Black couples, whether low income or upper class. The community outreach model also must reach beyond the geographical notion of "community" in order to counter abuse that takes place in Black families living in predominantly non-Black neighborhoods, towns, or cities.

Community-level publicity about the existence and objectives of the outreach group is also important. This could be conducted by (a) word-of-mouth, (b) billboard advertisements, and (c) information postcards and posters placed in neighborhood and community public settings, such as local stores, community centers (recreation and health centers, libraries), houses of worship, schools, barbershops and salons, and government offices.

Just as silence around issues of gang-related and youth violence in the Black community may represent tolerance of the violence, continued silence about intimate partner abuse serves to condone the behaviors of batterers. Intimate partner abuse in the Black community needs to be viewed as a major community problem exacerbated by Black people's placement within U.S. society. Likewise, we must pay heed to the connection between intimate partner abuse and nonintimate violence among Blacks and in Black communities, instead of considering intimate partner abuse as a stand-alone problem. Although many of the individuals working in community agencies, churches, and mosques are Black, this does not guarantee that they do not possess and perpetuate damaging stereotypical ideas about battered Black women and Black women in general. The examination provided in the preceding chapters will serve to further educate Black communities about Black women's experiences with and responses to intimate partner abuse. While the Black community can utilize government-established resources to confront the ills of the community, it is the Black community that must unite to fix its problems. Working from the inside, and using ourselves as situated knowers,[12] will likely prove more effective than reliance on a system of criminal justice that, at present, focuses more on conservative notions of retribution than on advantageous efforts to address future behavior.

The Black Woman's Response

In addition to improving awareness of the problem of battered Black women, this study appeared to profoundly benefit the women interviewed. Many of the women who participated in the study seemed to leave the interviews with a better understanding of their circumstances or, at the least, with a willingness to pursue avenues that would assist them in their recovery from the trauma or, for the few women still in abusive relationships, in making the decision to leave the precarious environments. For battered Black women to assume (or continue to identify with) the Strong Black Woman maxim does not have to mean that they must forgo support from others. Although playing this role has been found to leave us Black women with unmet and unaddressed mental, relational, physical, and social needs, in other instances it has been found to provide us with the wherewithal to persist in meeting our life's goals. As Black women, we must find our personal healthy balance in the strength of self that acknowledges the need for various forms of support. As Black women, we should relish our unique standpoint and our ancestral and personal histories, but not at the expense of our well-being. Accordingly, establishing and supporting a forum where battered Black women can discuss their ordeals is key to sustaining these women. Several of the women who contacted me upon learning of my need for informants asked whether (and *hoped*) the solicitation was for a conference about and for Black women who had experienced abuse in their intimate relationships. They hoped to share their experiences with those similar to them and who had experienced intimate partner abuse as they did. These women were disappointed to learn that my request was simply for one-on-one exploratory and intensive interviews, but they were delighted to offer their assistance with my investigation into their plight. Undoubtedly, this demonstrates battered Black women's need to discuss their life (her)stories and their dynamic resistance in comfortable, welcoming, and familiar settings that will begin or continue the healing process for these women. The cries have been heard, the calls have been made, and our reinvigorated responses are awaited.

Appendix A

Research Methods and
Demographics of the Women

Feminist Research

Feminist research methods, as specified by Sandra Harding and Shulamit Reinharz (along with other proponents of these techniques), support a common research paradigm.[1] These methods support the idea that, historically, women have been ignored as both research participants and effective researchers.[2] Evelyn Fox Keller argues that science became associated with masculinity and domination.[3] Francesca M. Cancian asserts that the use of traditional, positivist research methods promotes inequality for women and other marginalized groups. She concludes that the hypotheses and findings of social researchers who are mainly White, upper-middle-class men frequently represent the viewpoints of "elite" groups of managers, businesses, and government agencies. Therefore, Cancian encourages and supports the use of a feminist method of research not only to obtain and interpret data from a different view but also to empower women and other marginalized individuals.[4] Along these lines, the social world has been viewed by these challengers to mainstream traditional social research as being interpreted through a "male voice and gaze," which also equates masculinity with objectivity and femininity with subjectivity.[5] Typically, subjectivity in science has been, and in many instances still is, deemed unreliable. Therefore, any "feminine traits" of subjectivity in research have historically been avoided. Keller further argues that gender and science are socially constructed and, therefore, change through time.[6] Harding also supported this socially constructed view, agreeing that all societies are transitional and suggesting that being bound by one epistemology tends to suppress newly emerging ones.[7] Accordingly, it is these social constructions that must be examined in relation to their effect on findings in sociological research.

Fundamentally, "[f]eminist research is guided by feminist theory,"[8] whose focus is generally on women (that is, bringing their experiences to the forefront with those of men). But some feminist researchers maintain that the study of women also enhances our understanding of the male experience, though perhaps from a different perspective. This method seeks to understand how gender is related to social inequalities and conflict.[9] Although the discipline is referred to as "feminist research methods," Reinharz asserts that feminist research is a *perspective* on an existing method, not a research method in itself.[10]

In essence, Patricia Hill Collins's concept of Black feminist epistemology supports the qualitative research technique of ethnography and expands on the feminist research perspective. Collins's work was helpful to my investigation because it provides additional epistemological and methodological considerations specific to Black women's issues. Collins's approach assists in understanding and validating the Truth of Black women's experiences and stories. She asserts that traditional epistemologies are laden with the vested interests of elite White men, resulting in the misrepresentation or exclusion of Black women's experiences as "knowledge." According to Collins, this Black feminist epistemology involves four points: (1) the lived experience of Black women is central to understanding knowledge; (2) dialogue is an important factor in evaluating new knowledge claims; (3) individuality, emotions, and empathy as components in the "ethics of caring" is useful in validating knowledge; and (4) individuals are held accountable for their knowledge claims. "[W]hen these four dimensions become politicized and attached to a social justice project, they can form a framework for Black feminist thought and practice."[11]

The Research Setting

For three interrelated reasons, I found that the Denver metro area was the ideal research site of choice for locating participants for this study. Although the Black population in the state of Colorado—3.8 percent of the state's approximately 4.3 million citizens—is not equal to Blacks' 12.3 percent overall share of the U.S. population, approximately 11 percent of the city of Denver's population of 554,636 is Black.[12] In addition, Aurora, a mid-size city adjacent to Denver, boasts a Black population of 13 percent of its 276,393 residents. As such, the Black population of the Denver metro area was fairly representative of the national Black population. I also chose the Denver area because of my proximity to the research setting and because I had limited monetary resources to fund this project. The possibility of going to cities where there is a larger Black population, thus giving me a larger pool of participants to choose from, was severely restricted. Last, because I am a Black woman who was born and reared in a Denver neighborhood with a significant Black population, I am especially familiar with the community as a whole and the Black community in particular, and, therefore, knew how to best access potential informants.[13]

The Sampling Process

Two nonprobability sampling designs were utilized to gather informants for this project: purposive sampling and snowball sampling. The goal of utilizing these two recruitment sources was to secure a variety of Black women for the study. Purposive sampling is appropriate when one wishes to look at a small, select, and possibly hidden population; when one is looking for cases that are especially informative; and when one is looking to identify particular types of cases for in-depth investigation.[14] The purpose is less to generalize and more to gain deeper understanding. Originally, the procedures that were to be attempted to gather participants through purposive sampling included (a) posting and distributing flyers advertising the study to individuals and groups in the Denver metro area who may have had interaction with women who fit within the study parameters; and (b) placing an advertisement in at least one community newspaper with sizable Black readership. I made the decision to focus my early efforts on the latter and then proceed to conducting outreach to various agencies and organizations.

I anticipated difficulty in enlisting participants for my study because of the reticence and shame attached to being a "battered woman."[15] This speculation was supported by those I spoke with in academic and Black communities. We predicted that, because of the reluctance to discuss this form of abuse and the relatively small number of Black women in the Denver metro area (compared to cities with larger Black populations), there would have to be concerted and diligent efforts to find the proposed sample population of 40 to 50 informants.

During the process of establishing a contract with a community newspaper in late April 2003, I placed a flyer on one of the hallway bulletin boards assigned to the academic department (Criminal Justice and Criminology) at the college where, at the time, I was employed as an assistant professor. It was from this posting that I received the first call from a potential contributor, 41-year-old Paula. After verifying that Paula met the criteria for participation, I made arrangements with her, and we had what was my first of 40 interviews. Only one other woman, 39-year-old Rebecca, contacted me as a result of the bulletin board flyer.

As stated previously, I wanted to place an advertisement in a community newspaper to "jump-start" data collection for the project. I chose to advertise in the monthly Denver-based publication called *Urban Spectrum*. At the time of the data collection, this newspaper had been part of the Denver Black community for 16 years. It is a well-known, well-circulated publication. The *Urban Spectrum* reports a readership of 60,000 people, of which 69 percent are Black, 21 percent are Latino, 5 percent are Asian American and Native American, and 5 percent are White. It overwhelmingly publishes articles and advertisements concerning Blacks. Approximately 25.2 percent of the readers make $20,000 and under per year, 40.3 percent earn between $20,000 and $40,000, and those making more than $40,000 annually make up 34.5 percent of the readers. The *Urban Spectrum* reports that 42.7 percent of its readers have at least a college degree. Most of the readers are between the ages of 25 and 49, and 58 percent are female.[16]

I planned to publish the solicitation for participants in the *Urban Spectrum* for two months and then determine if I should discontinue the solicitation, continue to advertise, or intensify other methods for locating informants. The advertisement—a quarter-page ad midway through the paper and priced at $376 per month—first ran in the May 2003 issue. I received the first call as a result of the notice on May 6, 2003. By May 30, 2003, 23 potential participants had responded to the *Urban Spectrum* solicitation or upon being told of it.

The placement of the flyer in the *Urban Spectrum* proved to be especially successful. By June 30, 2003—the end of the second month of advertising—I received a total of 44 calls, 12 of which were based on snowball sampling from women who were told of the study by an acquaintance who saw and responded to the ad and had participated in the study herself. Snowball sampling was especially needed to acquire the stories of younger women. If I learned during an interview that a woman was acquainted with a younger battered Black woman, at the completion of the interview I strongly encouraged the informant to tell her acquaintance of my project and my need for more participants. This method of sampling reached those women who otherwise might not have been reached through the other sample selection methods. Six of the first 22 interviews (which were completed by June 17, 2003) were with women who were 39 years of age or younger. Nine women were ultimately interviewed as a result of snowball sampling, four of whom were under the age of 39; their interviews were completed after June 17, 2003.

I completed 32 interviews by the end of June 2003. In mid-June, I determined that I no longer needed to advertise in the *Urban Spectrum* and requested that the notice be discontinued. For reasons unknown to me, the advertisement continued to be published in the paper through November 2003, for a total of seven months. I was not charged advertising fees beyond the initial two months. As grateful as I was for the benevolence extended to me by the publication, the volume of calls I received because the ad continued to run for several months was unmanageable. From the start of the advertisement through December 1, 2003, I received a total of 93 known inquiries.[17] This number far exceeded my initial assumptions about the likelihood of my securing an adequate number of eligible participants.

The other proposed technique to obtain informants (another form of purposive sampling) was to distribute flyers to workers in law enforcement agencies, district attorneys' offices, battered women's shelters, and other social services organizations. Contact was to be made directly with agency personnel, as opposed to sending mass mailings, to improve participation rates. I also planned to post and distribute flyers in community centers and among community groups frequented by a high proportion of Black individuals. However, because of the volume of inquiries that resulted from the newspaper advertisement and because the time and monetary constraints that I faced meant that I could not afford to conduct more interviews, I did not utilize the additional sample selection tactic.

When the women called (or were called back after they left messages stating their interest in participating in the study), they were told (a) that the purpose of the study was to learn more about Black women's experiences with intimate partner abuse; (b) that the interview would be conducted in one sitting, lasting from one to three hours; (c) that they would determine where the interview would take place (with suggestions from me); and (d) that they would be paid $50 in cash[18] at the completion of the interview. Typically, an interview was arranged once this exchange occurred, and only once did a potential informant decide not to participate in the study when I returned her call. (I later learned from a participant who recommended the woman who declined that the potential informant was no longer interested in participating in the project because she had returned to her batterer.) In addition, five women did not return the messages I left for them. Seven women were "no-shows" to the interview site; I rescheduled interviews with a few of them, only to have them fail once more to appear.

The Demographics of the Women

A short questionnaire on demographics was used to help me keep track of the basic characteristics of the women. However, much of this information was elaborated on and confirmed during the interview. This was important for establishing nationality and particularly for determining socioeconomic statuses for each of the women. Table A.1 presents the demographic characteristics of the sample along several dimensions, including age, socioeconomic status, education level, and religious affiliation. Other important demographic characteristics include family of origin, intimate relationships, and parental status.

Nationality

As this study involved an examination of Black culture in the United States, it was important that the women identify themselves as African American or Black as opposed to my making that determination. All of the women considered themselves *American* citizens at the time of the interview, but there were a couple of variants in nationality. One woman, 42-year-old Lola, was born on an island in the Caribbean and raised there until she moved with her mother to the northeast United States at the age of 10. Another woman, 37-year-old Naomi, was born to a Black American father and a Central American mother of African descent in her mother's country of origin. Because of her father's military status and his posting to a U.S. military base in Central America, Naomi was considered a U.S. citizen, but she identified with both nationalities. Naomi began living in the United States when she was nine years old. Although several of the other women had multiracial and multinational ancestry, all of them confirmed that both birth parents were Black Americans, and, aside from Lola and Naomi, the remainder of the women were born and raised in the United

TABLE 1. *Demographic Characteristics of the Sample: Age, Socioeconomic, Education, and Religious Statuses*

	Household of Origin		During Abuse		At Time of Interview	
	n	%	n	%	n	%
Age						
18–19					1	2.5
20–29					5	12.5
30–39					11	27.5
40–49					16	40.0
50–59					7	17.5
Socioeconomic Status						
Low-income	15	37.5	10	25.0	15	37.5
Working-class	12	30.0	25	62.5	19	47.5
Middle-class	13	32.5	5	12.5	6	15.0
Level of Education						
Middle school					1	2.5
Some high school					7	17.5
High school/GED					9	22.5
Some college					14	35.0
Associate's degree					5	12.5
Bachelor's degree					3	7.5
Master's degree					1	2.5
Religious Affiliation						
Christian	36	90.0			23	57.5
Baptist	18	45.0			9	22.5
Catholic	1	2.5			2	5.0
Jehovah's Witness	1	2.5			0	0.0
Methodist	1	2.5			0	0.0
Mormon	1	2.5			1	2.5
Multiple Christian	3	7.5			0	0.0
Pentecostal	3	7.5			1	2.5
Protestant	2	5.0			1	2.5
Seventh Day Adventist	2	5.0			1	2.5
Non-denomination Christian	4	10.0			8	20.0
Islamic	1	2.5			5	12.5
None	3	7.5			12	30.0

TABLE 2. *Mother-Daughter Participant Sets*

Mother	Age	Daughter	Age
Doreen	45	Isis	28
Leah	38	Keisha	18
Yolanda	44	Ebony	22
Queen	50	Aaliyah	32

States. While all the women lived in Colorado[19] at the time of the interviews, many of them had previously resided in a variety of other states and countries.

Age

The sample was limited to adult women—those 18 years old and older—to avoid complications that would have arisen had I interviewed minors. Interviewing women under the age of 18 would have required the acquisition of parental permission. The purpose was not to devalue intimate partner abuse against girls but to assess battered women who are adults, who therefore likely have better coping strategies than minors. Of course, the women were free to (as well as encouraged to) speak of intimate partner abuse that occurred when they were minors. Three of the snowball sampling women under 39 years of age—Keisha, 18; Ebony, 22; and Aaliyah, 32—are daughters of women I had previously interviewed for this study (see Table A.2). The fourth, 27-year-old Nicole, was the next-door neighbor and friend of 47-year-old Harriet. By the conclusion of the 40 interviews, I had interviewed 17 women under the age of 39 and 23 who were between the ages of 40 and 60.

Socioeconomic Class

I considered various measures to determine how to gauge socioeconomic status among the women. The government and other official bodies usually measure class by income alone.[20] The U.S. Census Bureau reported that the overall median income in the United States during 2002 was $42,409.[21] When separated out from these figures, the median income of Black Americans was $29,177. Carmen DeNavas-Walt, Robert W. Cleveland, and Bruce H. Webster admittedly stated that income data in Census

Bureau reports do not include other measures of economic comfort such as the effect of taxes, partial payment of health insurance provided by an employer, or government-furnished school lunches or housing assistance.[22] Melvin L. Oliver and Thomas M. Shapiro argue that *wealth* should be measured when determining class level, rather than *income*. "Income refers to a flow of money over time, like a rate per hour, week, or year; wealth is a stock of assets owned at a particular time. Wealth is what people own, while income is what people receive for work, retirement, or social welfare."[23] Accordingly, many other pecuniary factors aside from work income must be taken into account when categorizing individuals by economic class.

The socioeconomic status measurement I chose is that which is supported by Robert L. Harris, Jr., in his article "The Rise of the Black Middle Class."[24] Along with income, I took into account home ownership, education, occupation, and work stability as factors in determining the women's socioeconomic statuses at the time of the interviews, during their abusive relationships, and in their households of origin. In determining the socioeconomic class levels of the women during their youth and in adulthood, I often inquired directly about class level. But I overwhelmingly relied on my interpretation of the information they provided throughout the interviews, such as stability of employment and ability to meet basic needs. I developed operational definitions for three different classes among the women.

I defined the *low-income* household as one where the residents were not regularly working and received government assistance as a major means for survival. The *working-class* was the next class up in the socioeconomic hierarchy. Working-class individuals maintained regular employment, but in typically unskilled or lower skills professions or in professions that did not provide adequate incomes. These individuals often faced challenges paying bills and affording necessities or material goods. I classified those in the military as working-class, particularly since the women's fathers and husbands[25] were "enlisted personnel" and not "officers."[26] My definition of *middle-class* provided that members of this class be working in professional, highly skilled, or college-level occupations. The jobs held often provided a stable environment and included benefits such as health insurance and retirement plans. I also considered home ownership as an additional salient factor in identifying middle-class status. All of the measurements were based on the combined incomes of all members of the household.

On the basis of my classification of socioeconomic status during up-bringing, 15 of the women were raised in low-income households. Twelve of the women were raised in working-class environments, including the four women whose fathers were in the military and who lived on U.S. military bases during their childhoods. Thirteen of the women were reared in middle-class settings. This includes 54-year-old Medea, who communicated that she was raised in an *upper* middle-class home, where college-educated and debutante family members were in abundance. The distribution among the three socioeconomic groups at the time of the interviews demonstrates a dropping off in hierarchy for a number of women. The middle-class decreased to six women, while the working class increased to 19. Fifteen of the women at the time of the interview met the criteria for the low-income category, the same as the proportion of women who were in lower-class settings during childhood.

During the abusive relationships, only five women were in middle-class households, but 25 women were in working-class households. The remaining 10 women resided in low-income households. For the women who were in more than one abusive relationship, all abusive relationships for each of these women were consistent along class lines. (In a subsequent section, I provide the number of abusive relationships by socioeconomic class.)

Twenty-one of the women in the sample were employed at the time of the interviews. (One unemployed woman, 18-year-old Keisha, had only recently graduated from high school at the time of the interview in June 2003 and planned to attend college that fall; therefore, she was still considered a dependent of her mother.) Seven of the 19 women who were unemployed were in that category because of a documented physical disability. Three of these women attributed their disability to the enduring effects caused by the violence perpetrated by their former batterers.

Education

The sample was well dispersed across varying levels of education. Eight women discontinued their studies between eighth and twelfth grade and did not graduate from high school. Nine women reported that they received a high school or general education development (GED) diploma. Another 14 who finished high school or its equivalent proceeded on to complete some college courses but did not have a college degree or had not yet earned a college degree at the time of the interviews. The remaining nine women of the sample had earned college degrees: five had an associate's degree, three had a bachelor's degree, and one had earned a master's degree. Eight of the nine women with college degrees were classified as working- or middle-class at the time of the interview, and all of the women who were classified as middle-class at the time of the interview had completed at least a high school education.

Religious Affiliation

An additional basic demographic variable documented among the women was religious affiliation, both during childhood and at the time of the interview. As expected on the basis of earlier research regarding religious affiliation and Blacks, the majority of the women were affiliated with a Christian denomination. Also consistent with previous findings, the most frequently reported Christian affiliation was Baptist.[27] During youth, 90 percent of the sample was of the Christian faith, with half of the Christian women practicing as Baptists. There was a significant flight from Christian affiliation between childhood and adulthood. Twenty-three of the women were practicing Christianity at the time of the interviews, compared to the 36 in childhood.

Another noteworthy shift in religious affiliation occurred among the women who identified as Muslim. Five women identified as Muslim at the time of the interview, including Aaliyah, who was raised Muslim during her youth. As mentioned earlier, Aaliyah was referred to the study by her mother, 50-year-old Queen. Queen converted to Islam in adulthood and raised Aaliyah in the same faith. Notably, despite the existence of the Nation of Islam faction of the Muslim faith in the United States, which was founded by Black Americans and supports Blacks and their causes, none of the women were associated with the Nation of Islam. In fact, most Black Muslim women in the United States belong to traditional Muslim groups.[28] Four of the women practiced in traditional mosques, and the fifth practiced in the small and fairly new sect of the Nation of Moorish-American, which has teachings similar to those of the Nation of Islam, with a focus on Black Americans.

There was also a change from youth to adulthood in those women who did not practice a religion. Only three women indicated that they were not affiliated with any religion or house of worship during their youth. This number quadrupled by adulthood: there were 12 women in this grouping at the time of the interview.

Family of Origin

The birth order among siblings and the parental composition of the women's families of origin are interesting enough to merit mentioning. The majority of the women were either the oldest child (15 women) or a middle child (17 women) in their homes of origin. Only five women were the youngest sibling, and three women were the only child. Regarding the parentage of the women, 23 of the homes of origin consisted of two-parent families, and 10 of the women were raised with both *biological* parents. Not surprisingly, of the 13 women reared in middle-class homes, 11 lived in two-parent households.[29]

Intimate Relationships

It was anticipated that the abusive partners of the women would predominately be male, but before I began conducting the interviews I decided that I would include any women who responded to my solicitation, whether their current or former batterer was male or female. (Moreover, the advertisement did not specify that the abuser had to be male.) However, all of the women reported that their abusive partners were male, and no women identified as bisexual or lesbian or reported abuse by a current or former intimate female partner. In sum, none of the sample reported any female partners, abusive or otherwise, even though 43-year-old Tammy reported being stabbed several times while in a fight with a woman who was romantically interested in her. Tammy learned of the woman's interest only immediately prior to the physical altercation, and their friendship was discontinued after the stabbing.[30]

Although the existing literature on Blacks and family violence usually focuses on abuse in Black couples, intimate interracial relationships were also considered for the current study. Including non-Black perpetrators allowed for a comparative analysis to assist in determining the effect of Black culture on intimate partner abuse. Four women were abused by at least one non-Black batterer. Of the four men Naomi was abused by, two were Latino and one was White. Both of Keisha's abusers were non-Black: one White and one Latino. Last, Rebecca's and 43-year-old Grace's second (and last) batterers were White. Additionally, 24-year-old Phoebe's abuser was biracial (Pacific Islander and Black), as was the first of 26-year-old Erica's two batterers, who was White and Black, and the first of 51-year-old Wendy's two batterers, who was Latino and Black. However, according

TABLE 3. *Relationship Status at Time of Interviews*

	n	%
No intimate partner	23	57.5
Intimate partner	5	12.5
Living with intimate partner	1	2.5
Married	11	27.5

to these women, the biracial abusers primarily identified as Black or with Black culture. Regarding nationality, except in two cases, all batterers were identified as having been born in the United States; Lola's abusive partner was identified as a Black African, and Medea identified one of her abusive partners as African-Caribbean. The remaining batterers were identified by the women as Black Americans.

Table A.3 provides a breakdown of the women's relationship statuses. Eleven women in the sample were living with a male intimate partner at the time of the interviews, and 10 were legally married.[31] Not included in this count is 51-year-old Shahida, whose husband was incarcerated in a state prison at the time of her interview. Although Shahida had known her husband prior to his imprisonment, she never lived with her husband and married him after he was incarcerated. Twenty-three of the women were not in an intimate relationship at the time of the interviews. None of the women in relationships reported that they were being physically abused at the time of the interviews, but three women did report emotional abuse by their intimate partners at the time of the interviews.

Table A.4 displays the number of abusive relationships the women had been in. The number of abusive intimate relationships reported by the women ranged from one to five. Only a quarter of the women reported one abusive relationship. Two abusive relationships was the most common quantity, and this number was reported by 16 of the women; however, 14 women had been in three or more abusive relationships. Nine of the women reported three abusive relationships, four women reported four, and one woman reported five.

Table A.5 demonstrates the number of abusive relationships by socioeconomic class. Middle-class women were in the fewest abusive relationships. Women raised in middle-class settings had an average of 1.8 abusive relationships, and women classified as middle-class at the time of the interview had an average of 1.7. Women who were working-class at the time of the

TABLE 4. *Number of Abusive Intimate Relationships*

Number of Abusive Relationships	Number of Women	%
One	10	25.0
Two	16	40.0
Three	9	22.5
Four	4	10.0
Five	1	2.5

interview had an average of 2.2 abusive relationships, and those reared in this class status averaged 2.7 abusive relationships. Women raised in lower-class homes had an average of 2.3 abusive relationships, and women in this category at the time of the interview had 2.5 such relationships.

TABLE 5. *Number of Abusive Relationships by Class*

	During Childhood		During Abusive Relationships		At Time of Interview	
	No. of Women	Avg.	No. of Women	Avg.	No. of Women	Avg.
Low-income	15	2.3	10	2.7	15	2.5
Working-class	12	2.7	25	2.2	19	2.2
Middle-class	13	1.8	5	1.6	6	1.7

Parental Status

Thirty-six of the women had children. Table A.6 provides information on the number of children among the sample. All but one of the women with children were the birth mothers of their children. Lola and her former abusive husband adopted her husband's two nephews, who are now adults. Only one woman, 44-year-old Toni, who is the birth mother of two adult children, reported caring for and living with dependant-aged stepchildren at the time of the interview. Wendy was the only woman to care for minor children who were blood-related but not born to her; she had full custody of three of her grandchildren.

Slightly over half (21 women) of the interviewees had anywhere between one and four children age 17 and under at the time of the interviews.

TABLE 6. *Demographic Characteristics of the Sample:*
Number of Children at Time of Interviews

Number of Children	n	%
None	4	10.0
One	7	17.5
Two	10	25.0
Three	8	20.0
Four	9	22.5
Five	2	5.0

Four of the women (11% of those with children; 19% of those with minor children) had at least one of their minor children living away from them. Thirty-nine-year-old Angie's only child resided with Angie's mother but in the same city as Angie, and one of 36-year-old Gloria's two minor children lived with the child's biological father in another state. Naomi's two dependent children (she also had two adult children), the eldest of 35-year-old Cassandra's four minor children, and one of Zora's three dependent children (of four total) lived with their respective fathers, who were also these women's first batterers. Also, Grace's minor child (of two children total) resided with the child's father's current wife. The father was Grace's first abusive husband, who had recently lost custody of the child, temporarily, because of his brutal rape of Grace only a few months prior to my interview with her. Except for Angie, each of these women was in legal disputes to regain custody of these children. Sadly, two women had lost a child to neighborhood gun violence. Wendy and 51-year-old Bev each had suffered from the shooting deaths of an adult child.

The Interviews

The sole source of data collection for this study was the semistructured, open-ended, in-depth interviews. For this study, the data were gathered using a cross-sectional approach, rather than longitudinal design. The cross-sectional method provides a one-time measurement, within a narrow span of time, and is more exploratory and descriptive.[32] Because of the type of data that were gathered during my research (life histories), a cross-sectional design allowed sufficient analysis of the phenomenon.

Following Beth E. Richie's method of interviewing victims of intimate partner abuse, at the outset I asked "each woman to describe her family background and home environment, [and] the history, nature, and extent of violence in her intimate relationship(s)."[33] An interview guide was developed to direct the interviews and ensure consistency in data gathering while still allowing for rich data to emerge. This method of data collection, as opposed to a quantitative procedure, such as administering survey questionnaires, is also supported by other feminist researchers, who contend that the traditional form of interviewing (for example, a structured question-and-answer series) is paternalistic and hierarchical.[34]

Questions specific to my research goal were also administered during the interviews. For instance, I posed exhaustive queries regarding the women's religious beliefs, experiences, and practices, as religion has been deemed one of the central institutions for Black individuals and within Black communities. I also wanted to hear their views on the effectiveness of the criminal justice system in general and specifically with regard to intimate partner abuse issues. Another question specific to my research involved the women's views on why they believed their batterers were abusive. During the first approximately five interviews, I homed in on certain themes that arose as I gathered the data. For instance, the original interview guide did not include a question concerning women's perceptions of battered women of other races and ethnicities. It was during the first interview that this subject was introduced by Paula. Subsequently, I was sure to investigate this topic with the remaining informants, which became a major theme in this study.

Because of the highly sensitive subject matter of this study, the women were assured of their anonymity verbally and in writing by the use of an informed-consent form approved by the Human Research Committee of the University of Colorado at Boulder. A consent form was signed by each informant. As provided on the consent form, the women were told they could discontinue the interview at any time. Each woman completed the entire interview, although one interview was conducted during two sessions on consecutive days.

Each of the interviews was audio-recorded. I chose to record the interviews rather than take copious notes during the interviews, because it allowed me to be more attendant to each informant and not focused on making sure I was capturing the entire wording of the dialogue. Although the recording was optional, no woman refused to have her interview recorded.

The interviews were conducted in Denver-area public libraries, at my campus office in downtown Denver, or at the women's homes. The interviews were scheduled during times agreed upon by the women and me. I sought to have the interviews conducted where there was minimal interruption. This was not a concern for the interviews conducted in the libraries or at my office, but some of the interviews carried out in the women's homes involved some, but not major, interruption by children or others.

Because of the nature of the data collected, no time limits were set for the interviews. The average time of the interviews was one hour and 45 minutes. The shortest interview was 45 minutes, while the longest interview lasted four hours and 20 minutes. The longer interviews did not necessarily result in more substantive data; basically, some women were more verbose than the others.

The completed audiotaped interviews were transcribed verbatim by a professional transcriptionist. The women's contact and identifying information were maintained in a separate log for the purposes of conducting any follow-up interviews for clarification on subject matter (however, no follow-up was needed). Any identifying information relayed during the recorded interviews was entered into the transcriptions, but has been substituted with fictitious names and places throughout this publication.

At the conclusion of each interview, the women were provided with their $50 compensation fee (in cash), a thank-you note, and my business card with my contact information. None of the women refused the money. While I did not directly ask what they planned to do with the money upon receiving it, some women shared how they planned to spend it. One woman needed the money to keep her electricity from being turned off, while another woman stated she would use it to buy herself a new outfit. A few of the women contacted me after the conclusion of their interviews, mainly to determine the progress of the study and to express once more their interest in acquiring pieces I would write based on the research.

Addressing Limitations in the Method

Certain problems of reliability, validity, and generalizability are often raised when discussing the limitations of qualitative research methods. Reliability in research refers to the ability to obtain the same results any time the research is replicated.[35] Reliability may not be as achievable in qualitative research designs as in survey and experimental research because of the in-depth nature of the interviews, which tend to be especially personal. The duplication of previously conducted research is inherent in the natural sciences but rarely achieved in the social sciences, especially for qualitative research. Some qualitative research proponents assert that ethnographic studies should not be held to the same replication standards as statistics-oriented or quantified studies. Alex Stewart concludes that "[s]tability or consistency would be both a misguided and an impossible objective for ethnography." He suggests that the better test is to pose different questions. "The pivotal question is, . . . How well does this study *transcend* the perspectives of the researcher? A corollary question is, How well does this study transcend the perspectives of informants?"[36]

Internal validity in research "refers to the extent to which an empirical measure adequately reflects the *real meaning* of the concept under construction."[37] Earl Babbie insists that field research produces more valid measures than other methods because of the detailed illustration that is an obligatory part of qualitative method. It is in these in-depth descriptions that concepts and meanings can be discovered. Even so, the internal validity of in-depth interviews is challenged because of issues surrounding recollection of individuals' life histories and self-reports. Stewart provided an alternative criterion to consider when conducting ethnographic research, using the term "veracity." "The pivotal question raised by veracity is, How well, with what verisimilitude, does this study succeed in its *depiction*?"[38] I argue that because my analysis was deeply situated in the stories of the women and because I did not try to conceal what is typically referred to as the "dirty laundry" of the Black community, I have met Stewart's test of veracity.

External validity, or the ability to generalize the results of a study to the general population, is typically limited in qualitative studies because of the sampling plans and sample size.[39] Furthermore, the self-selection method by the women in my study may limit its generalizability to all battered Black women. For instance, since all of the women had succeeded in leaving at least one abusive relationship, there is the possibility that these women present a stronger front than those battered Black women who have not been able to terminate such relationships. In addition, because most of the respondents took it upon themselves to reply to the advertised solicitation for participants, they may be more active in their recovery from intimate abuse than battered Black women who are not ready to recognize and confront the significance of the abuse against them. Nonetheless, Emerson has proposed that "transferability" should be the preferred measure for evaluating qualitative research, rather than the ability to establish the general representation of the group studied.[40] Furthermore, Stewart proposes that one criterion geared to ethnographic research is "Does this research generate insights that are also applicable to other times, other places, in the human experience?"[41] In Chapter 3, I affirm this question when, using dynamic resistance as a foundation, I demonstrate that many of battered Black women's experiences are similar to those of Black women who have not been battered.

Regarding feminist research methods, critics have many arguments against this still-developing approach and its challenge to traditional methods. One such argument might be that the investigator cannot be "objective" if she or he strives to form a relationship with her or his participants and evaluates her- or himself in the research process. Regarding Black women researchers and informants specifically, Collins argues, "Black women [may] not [be] seen as credible witnesses for our own experiences. In this climate, Black women academics who choose to believe other Black women can become suspect."[42] However, it is important that studies of marginalized groups be conducted by members of the same groups. Group membership brings advantages to a study of individuals in that group. Additionally, it is preposterous to assume that a Black woman researcher will be more predisposed to inaccurate beliefs about battered Black women than a White woman or a White man.

The final potential limitation that may be raised by others regarding this method of research is in relation to the use of an all-Black sample. The argument may be that the study is lacking in a cross-cultural sampling of women, which might provide a comparative analysis based on race and ethnicity. Although cross-cultural or cross-racial inquiries are certainly useful, Mary P. Koss and her colleagues argue that the factors affecting Black women's entry into, escape from, and responses to intimate partner abuse are best examined among Black women, rather than comparing them to battered White women.[43] Robert M. Emerson's argument supports this, as he determined that in ethnographic research "the goal is to ground descriptions on distinctions consistently drawn from within the culture being described rather than from an outside culture."[44] This was the basis for the approach used in this study.

Despite these limitations, some of which are politically based (for example, stereotypes of feminist research and Black women researchers) and for which I have provided alternative explanations, I believe that the study design used and reported here was the best method for collecting data on battered Black women.

Appendix B

Pseudonyms and Demographic Information

Pseudonym	Age	SES During Youth	SES During Abuse	SES During Interview	Number of Abusive Relationships
Aaliyah	32	Middle	Low	Working	3
Angie	39	Low	Low	Low	3
Bev	51	Low	Low	Low	3
Billie	42	Low	Low	Low	4
Cassandra	35	Middle	Working	Working	2
Cicely	52	Low	Working	Working	3
Danielle	43	Low	Low	Low	3
Doreen	45	Low	Working	Working	2
Ebony	22	Working	Working	Low	2
Erica	26	Low	Working	Working	2
Felicia	59	Low	Working	Middle	1
Gloria	36	Working	Working	Low	4
Grace	43	Working	Working	Working	2
Harriet	47	Working	Middle	Low	1
Helene	45	Middle	Working	Low	2
Inez	43	Low	Low	Low	1
Isis	28	Low	Low	Low	3
Jade	35	Middle	Middle	Middle	1
Jacqueline	43	Middle	Working	Working	2
Keisha	18	Working	Working	Working	2
Kim	45	Working	Working	Low	4
Leah	38	Working	Working	Working	2
Lola	42	Middle	Middle	Working	1
Max	38	Working	Working	Working	5
Medea	54	Middle	Middle	Middle	3
Naomi	37	Working	Working	Working	4
Nicole	27	Low	Low	Low	2

Pseudonym	Age	SES During Youth	SES During Abuse	SES During Interview	Number of Abusive Relationships
Olivia	48	Middle	Low	Low	2
Paula	41	Middle	Working	Low	1
Phoebe	24	Working	Working	Working	1
Queen	50	Middle	Working	Working	1
Rebecca	39	Working	Working	Working	2
Renee	45	Middle	Working	Working	1
Shahida	51	Low	Middle	Middle	2
Tammy	43	Working	Working	Working	3
Toni	44	Low	Working	Middle	2
Victoria	33	Low	Low	Low	3
Wendy	51	Middle	Working	Working	2
Yolanda	44	Middle	Working	Working	2
Zora	39	Low	Working	Middle	1

Notes

1. Throughout this book I use "Black" to describe U.S. citizens or U.S. residents (those without legal citizenship) of Black African descent. "African Americans" is another term that is frequently used, but Black Americans remain divided as to which term is the most appropriate, particularly for Blacks whose ancestry is traced to U.S. slavery and who have little knowledge of and connection to the African continent and culture. Use of the term "Black" also can better encompass more recent immigrants of African descent who hail from Africa, the Caribbean, Europe, Canada, and so on but who do not typically identify themselves as "African American." Although there are instances where "Black" will not be capitalized, these involve direct quotations from others who do not capitalize the term. There is no set standard for whether or not the term is to be capitalized when referring to race.

2. Gandy, *Sacred Pampered Principles*, 8.

3. Many terms are used to describe abuse by a spouse, ex-spouse, girlfriend/boyfriend, ex-girlfriend/boyfriend, or dating partner. For example, domestic violence, intimate partner violence, intimate partner abuse, domestic abuse, woman battering, spouse abuse, wife abuse, and dating violence are often used to describe abuse by current or former intimate partners. In this book I use these terms interchangeably, though I most often use "intimate partner abuse" to convey violence and other forms of abuse directed toward women by their intimate companions. Using the word "abuse" instead of "violence" addresses acts that do not neatly fit within the strict definition of "violence," such as controlling and psychologically demeaning acts (Belknap and Potter, "Intimate Partner Abuse").

4. T. C. West, *Wounds of the Spirit*.

5. Wyatt et al., "Examining Patterns of Vulnerability."

6. Rennison and Welchans, *Intimate Partner Violence*. See also the Uniform Crime Reports of the Federal Bureau of Investigation.

7. See Collins, *Black Feminist Thought*; Davis, *Women, Race and Class*; hooks, *Ain't I a Woman*; hooks, *Feminist Theory*, 2nd ed.; hooks, *The Will to Change*; Morrison, *The Bluest Eye*; Morrison, *Song of Solomon*; Richie, *Compelled to Crime*; and A. Walker, *The Color Purple*.

8. Sanchez-Hucles and Dutton, "The Interaction Between Societal Violence and Domestic Violence."

9. M. Smith, "When Violence Strikes Homes," 23–24.

10. Crenshaw, "Mapping the Margins."

11. See, e.g., Garfield, *Knowing What We Know*; Richie, *Compelled to Crime*; T. C. West, *Wounds of the Spirit*.

12. Belknap, *The Invisible Woman*; Tierney, "The Battered Women Movement."

13. Schechter, *Women and Male Violence*.

14. Belknap and Potter, "Intimate Partner Abuse."

15. Tierney, "The Battered Women Movement."

16. Belknap, *The Invisible Woman*.

17. Tierney, "The Battered Women Movement."

18. Ibid.

19. Ibid.

20. Belknap, *The Invisible Woman*.

21. Johnson and Sigler, "Public Perceptions."

22. Brewster, "Domestic Violence Theories," 24.

23. hooks, *Talking Back*, 87.

24. Erez and Belknap, "In Their Own Words."

25. Belknap, *The Invisible Woman*; Rodriguez et al., "Screening and Intervention for Intimate Partner Abuse."

26. Fyfe, Klinger, and Flavin, "Differential Police Treatment."

27. Belknap, *The Invisible Woman*.

28. Center for the Advancement of Women, *Progress and Perils*.

29. Bograd, "Strengthening Domestic Violence Theories"; Richie, *Compelled to Crime*; Richie, "Reflection on the Antiviolence Movement."

30. Richie, "Reflection on the Antiviolence Movement"; C. M. West, *Violence in the Lives of Black Women*.

31. Crowell and Burgess, *Understanding Violence Against Women*; Rankin, Saunders, and Williams, "Predicting Woman Abuse by African American Men"; Sorenson, "Violence Against Women."

32. A. Smith et al., "The Color of Violence: Introduction."

33. hooks, *We Real Cool*, 57.

34. Chesney-Lind, "Doing Feminist Criminology"; Chesney-Lind, "Patriarchy, Crime, and Justice."

35. A. Smith et al., "The Color of Violence: Introduction."

36. Ibid., 4.

37. For an exception, see Tjaden and Thoennes, *Extent, Nature, and Consequences of Intimate Partner Violence*. The authors determined that "American Indians/Alaska Natives" have higher rates of intimate partner violence than members of other racial and ethnic groups.

38. Catalano, *Intimate Partner Violence in the United States*.

39. Tjaden and Thoennes, *Extent, Nature, and Consequences of Intimate Partner Violence.*

40. Rennison and Welchans, *Intimate Partner Violence.*

41. Including those conducted by Hampton and Gelles, "Violence Toward Black Women," and Straus, Gelles, and Steinmetz, *Behind Closed Doors.*

42. Benson et al., "Neighborhood Disadvantage, Individual Economic Distress."

43. Stark and Filtcraft, *Women at Risk.*

44. To protect the privacy of the women, each woman and the individuals mentioned by them were assigned pseudonyms.

CHAPTER 2

1. My 10 years of experience as a practitioner holding various positions in the criminal justice system and working with convicted offenders (e.g., as a counselor, a probation officer, and a halfway house administrator) gave me the ability and the confidence to address this situation with Billie.

2. Ammons, "Mules, Madonnas, Babies, Bath Water, Racial Imagery, and Stereotypes"; Bell and Mattis, "The Importance of Cultural Competence in Ministering to African American Victims of Domestic Violence"; Bennett, Goodman, and Dutton, "Systemic Obstacles to the Criminal Prosecution of a Battering Partner"; Oliver, "Preventing Domestic Violence in African American Community"; Richie, *Compelled to Crime*; Sharma, "Healing the Wounds of Domestic Violence"; Weis, "Race, Gender, and Critique"; O. J. Williams and Tubbs, *Community Insights on Domestic Violence Among African Americans.*

3. Nia wanted to contribute to the study, as well, but did not meet the criteria for participation.

4. While I initially believed that I coined the term "Black Feminist Criminology," after conducting an Internet search of the term I discovered a few mentions of it. However, I was unable to locate any complete account of what Black feminist criminology entailed and only found references stating that such a concept needs to be considered. Hence, the only known full treatment and development of Black feminist criminology is that which I applied in this (and my other) research and have previously published (see Potter, "An Argument for Black Feminist Criminology").

5. Britton, "Feminism in Criminology"; Daly and Chesney-Lind, "Feminism and Criminology"; Flavin, "Razing the Wall."

6. Britton, "Feminism in Criminology."

7. Daly, "Different Ways of Conceptualizing Sex/Gender for Criminology."

8. hooks, *Feminist Theory*, 2nd ed.; Lewis, "A Response to Inequality."

9. Belknap, *The Invisible Woman*; Britton, "Feminism in Criminology"; Chesney-Lind and Pasko, *The Female Offender*; Richie, *Compelled to Crime.*

10. hooks, *Feminist Theory*, 2nd ed.

11. Guy-Sheftall, *Words of Fire*; King, "Multiple Jeopardy, Multiple Consciousness."

12. Fishman, "Mule-Headed Slave Women"; Guy-Sheftall, *Words of Fire*.

13. Jones and Shorter-Gooden, *Shifting*.

14. hooks, *Feminist Theory*, 2nd ed.

15. Collins, *Black Feminist Thought*.

16. Crenshaw, "Mapping the Margins."

17. Collins, *Black Feminist Thought*, 25.

18. Wing, *Critical Race Feminism*, 2nd ed.

19. Wing, *Critical Race Feminism*, 1st ed. and 2nd ed.

20. Wing, *Critical Race Feminism*, 2nd ed.

21. Collins defined *essentialism* as the "belief that individuals or groups have inherent, unchanging characteristics rooted in biology or a self-contained culture that explain their status" (*Black Feminist Thought*, 2000, 299).

22. hooks, *Feminist Theory*, 2nd ed.

23. McKay, "Acknowledging Differences," 276.

24. Crenshaw, "Mapping the Margins," 94.

25. Collins, *Black Feminist Thought*.

26. Beale, "Double Jeopardy."

27. Gordon, *Black Women, Feminism and Black Liberation*.

28. King, "Multiple Jeopardy, Multiple Consciousness." See also Cleaver, "Racism, Civil Rights, and Feminism"; Collins, *Black Feminist Thought*; Gordon, *Black Women, Feminism and Black Liberation*; Guy-Sheftall, *Words of Fire*; Hull, Bell Scott, and Smith, *Black Women's Studies*; B. Smith, *Black Feminist Anthology*; Terrelonge, "Feminist Consciousness and Black Women"; Wing, *Critical Race Feminism*, 1st ed. and 2nd ed.

29. Wing, *Critical Race Feminism*, 2nd ed., 7.

30. See Collins, *Black Feminist Thought*; Cole and Guy-Sheftall, *Gender Talk*; hooks, *Ain't I a Woman*; hooks, *Feminist Theory*, 1st ed.; hooks, *Talking Back*; hooks, *Feminist Theory*, 2nd ed.; hooks, *The Will to Change*; Richie, *Compelled to Crime*; Richie, "A Black Feminist Reflection on the Antiviolence Movement."

31. See Allard, "Rethinking Battered Woman Syndrome"; Ammons, "Mules, Madonnas, Babies, Bath Water, Racial Imagery, and Stereotypes"; Coker, "Enhancing Autonomy for Battered Women"; Crenshaw, "Mapping the Margins"; Kupenda, "Law, Life, and Literature"; Rivera, "Domestic Violence Against Latinas by Latino Males"; Rivera, "Availability of Domestic Violence Services for Latina Survivors"; Valencia-Weber and Zuni, "Domestic Violence and Tribal Protection of Indigenous Women."

32. Richie, "Gender Entrapment and African-American Women," 203.

33. "Othermother" refers to a woman in the Black community who shares the responsibility of mothering children with biological mothers and who may or may not be related by blood or marriage (see Collins, *Black Feminist Thought*; Troester, "Turbulence and Tenderness").

34. Harding, *Feminism and Methodology*.

35. Ibid.

36. Reinharz, *Feminist Methods in Social Research*.

37. Ibid.

38. Ibid.

39. Pettiway, *Workin' It*, xvi

40. Mauthner and Doucet, "Reflexive Accounts and Accounts of Reflexivity in Qualitative Data Analysis."

41. Collins, *Black Feminist Thought*, 19. See also Baca Zinn, "Field Research in Minority Communities."

42. Collins, *Black Feminist Thought*, 260.

43. Ibid.

CHAPTER 3

1. hooks, *Feminist Theory*, 2nd ed.

2. Cleaver, "Racism, Civil Rights, and Feminism"; hooks, *Talking Back*.

3. In Richie's comparison of battered White women and battered Black women, she established that the *White* women left their abusive relationships sooner than the Black women and as a result were victims of less abuse (see Richie, *Compelled to Crime*).

4. M. Wallace, *Black Macho and the Myth of the Superwoman*.

5. hooks, *Talking Back*.

6. See, e.g., Collins, *Black Feminist Thought*; Gandy, *Sacred Pampering Principles*; T. Harris, *Saints, Sinners, Saviors*; hooks, *Salvation*; Mataka, *Being a Strong Black Woman*; Morgan, *When Chickenheads Come Home to Roost*; Neal-Barnett, *Soothe Your Nerves*; Sudarkasa, *Strength of Our Mothers*.

7. Bell and Mattis, "The Importance of Cultural Competence in Ministering to African American Victims of Domestic Violence"; Kupenda, "Law, Life, and Literature"; Ramos, Carlson, and McNutt, "Lifetime Abuse, Mental Health"; Richie, *Compelled to Crime*; Washington, "Disclosure Patterns of Black Female Sexual Assault Survivors."

8. Sudarkasa, *Strength of Our Mothers*, 296.

9. Ibid.; Neal-Barnett, *Soothe Your Nerves*; hooks, *Feminist Theory*.

10. Collins, *Black Feminist Thought*.

11. M. Wallace, *Myth of the Superwoman*, 106–107.

12. Lofland et al., *Analyzing Social Settings*.

13. All of the women reported that their mothers are Black (i.e., African American, Afro-Caribbean, or Latina of African descent).

14. Fishman, "The Black Bogeyman and White Self-Righteousness," 178.

15. A "debut" is a formal entrance of teenage girls into society that usually takes place during a formal debutante ball. Typically, the Black community

sponsors its own debutante balls separate from those promoted in the White community. These affairs are usually intended for upper-middle- to upper-class groups, though among African Americans the class variations are broader.

16. Although Olivia's actions helped her batterer to discontinue his abusive behavior, it is important that we remember that the onus remains on the batterer.

17. hooks, *Talking Back*; Sudarkasa, *Strength of Our Mothers*.

18. Belknap, *The Invisible Woman*.

19. Collins, *Black Feminist Thought*, 77.

20. See also Richie, *Compelled to Crime*.

21. See also hooks, *Talking Back*.

22. Hampton, Gelles, and Harrop, "Is Violence in Black Families Increasing?"; Joseph, "Woman Battering"; Stets, "Verbal and Physical Aggression in Marriage"; C. M. West and Rose, "Dating Aggression Among Low Income African American Youth."

23. Dunn, "'Victims' and 'Survivors'"; Gondolf and Fisher, *Battered Women as Survivors*; Hoff, *Battered Women as Survivors*.

24. Dunn, "Emerging Vocabularies," 21.

25. T. C. West, *Wounds of the Spirit*, 5.

26. Hoff, *Battered Women as Survivors*.

27. Gondolf and Fisher, *Battered Women as Survivors*.

28. Ibid., 20.

29. Sudarkasa, *Strength of Our Mothers*.

30. hooks, *Feminist Theory*.

31. K. T. Brown et al., "Skin Tone and Racial Identity Among African Americans"; Freeman et al., "Color Gradation and Attitudes"; Hall, "Bias Among African Americans"; Hill, "Skin Color and the Perception of Attractiveness Among African Americans"; Hughes and Hertel, "Skin Tone and Stratification"; Hunter, Allen, and Telles, "The Significance of Skin Color"; Keith and Herring, "Skin Tone and Stratification"; Russell, Wilson, and Hall, *The Color Complex*.

32. Collins, *Black Feminist Thought*; hooks, *Talking Back*; hooks, *Where We Stand*.

33. hooks, *Talking Back*.

34. Kleck and Gertz, "Armed Resistance to Crime," 151.

35. T. C. West, *Wounds of the Spirit*, 151.

36. Ibid., 161.

37. hooks, *Talking Back*, 87–88.

38. Belknap, *The Invisible Woman*; T. C. West, *Wounds of the Spirit*; C. M. West and Rose, "Dating Aggression Among Low Income African American Youth."

39. For instance, Black sports and entertainment figures such as Oprah Winfrey, Sean "Diddy" Combs, Kobe Bryant, and Tiger Woods receive notable press attention in relation to their economic gains.

40. E. B. Brown, "Womanist Consciousness"; Cleaver, "Racism, Civil Rights, and Feminism"; Gordon, *Black Women, Feminism and Black Liberation*; A. P. Harris, "Race and Essentialism in Feminist Legal Theory"; Lewis, "A Response to Inequality."

41. Baumgardner and Richards, *Manifesta*; MacKinnon, "Keeping It Real."

CHAPTER 4

1. In the National Violence Against Women Survey, Tjaden and Thoennes found that "[w]omen and men who were physically assaulted as children by adult caretakers were significantly more likely to report being victimized by their current partner." See *Extent, Nature, and Consequences of Intimate Partner Violence*, 34. See also Crowell and Burgess, *Understanding Violence Against Women*; Gelles and Straus, *Intimate Violence*; Huang and Gunn, "Domestic Violence in an African American Community"; Mihalic and Elliott, "Social Learning Theory Model of Marital Violence"; Ponce, Williams, and Allen, "Experience of Maltreatment as a Child"; Ramos, Carlson, and McNutt, "Lifetime Abuse, Mental Health"; Schafer, Caetano, and Cunradi, "Path Model of Risk Factors"; L. E. A. Walker, *The Battered Woman Syndrome*; Whitfield et al., "Violent Childhood Experiences."

2. Short et al., "Survivors' Identification of Protective Factors"; Wyatt et al., "Examining Patterns of Vulnerability."

3. Social learning theory stresses the importance of (a) observing and modeling the behaviors and emotional reactions of others, and (b) the level of consequences or reinforcement experienced as a result of exhibiting such behaviors (Bandura, *Social Learning Theory*). As it relates to batterers' abusive behaviors, social learning theory explains that when children witness the outcomes of aggressive and violent acts, particularly during childhood as they witness their parents' behaviors, it becomes more likely that they, too, will use such acts to achieve their desired outcomes (Foshee, Bauman, and Linder, "Family Violence and Adolescent Dating Violence"; O'Neill, "A Post-Structuralist Review of the Theoretical Literature Surrounding Wife Abuse"). "Many parents teach children that violence is the easiest way (if not the most acceptable way) to end conflict and assert power" when they use it to discipline (hooks, *Feminist Theory*, 2nd ed., 124).

The application of social learning theory to the victims' experiences may be appropriate for those victims who witnessed their mothers being abused by their fathers or other male intimates. That is, daughters of such situations may model themselves after their mothers by becoming involved in similar relationships when they reach adolescence and adulthood.

Social learning theory as applied to intimate partner abuse places emphasis on the family unit and other immediate and close influences on children, thus providing a micro-level analysis of woman battering. Social learning theory offers some explanation for Black women's entry into abusive relationships but does not consider other aspects in the traumatic childhood experiences of these women.

4. Tjaden and Thoennes, *Extent, Nature, and Consequences of Intimate Partner Violence*, 34.

5. Wyatt et al., "Examining Patterns of Vulnerability," 497–498.

6. I use "stepparent" not only to refer to the legally married spouse of a biological parent but also to represent a nonmarried, live-in intimate partner of a biological parent.

7. See, e.g., Dietz, "Disciplining Children"; Hernandez, Lodico, and DiClemente, "Effects of Child Abuse and Race"; Spearly and Lauderdale, "Prediction of Child Maltreatment Rates"; U.S. Department of Health and Human Services, *10 Years of Reporting Child Maltreatment*.

8. Malley-Morrison and Hines, *Family Violence in a Cultural Perspective*.

9. Ramos, Carlson, and McNutt, "Lifetime Abuse, Mental Health."

10. Gelles and Straus, *Intimate Violence*, 86.

11. A focus on materialistic, middle- and upper-class types of accomplishments is supported by Sanchez-Hucles and Dutton's argument that "[e]thnic minority cultures often have been described as 'face-oriented'; that is, appearance and status with respect to the outside world are important" (see Sanchez-Hucles and Dutton, "The Interaction Between Societal Violence and Domestic Violence," 192).

12. See Note 31, Chapter 3.

13. hooks, *Feminist Theory*, xii.

14. Hill, "Skin Color and African Americans"; Russell, Wilson, and Hall, *The Color Complex*.

15. However, Doreen was neglectful of her daughter Isis, which will be discussed shortly.

16. Jacobs related that "[i]t is an unfortunate truth that although women may be divided by wealth, by race, or by ethnicity, sexual violence and the trauma of incest are ties that bind women across generations" (see Jacobs, *Victimized Daughters*, 2).

17. Belknap, *The Invisible Woman*; Washington, "Disclosure Patterns of Black Female Sexual Assault Survivors."

18. Sexual abuses by an "intimate partner" are addressed in subsequent chapters.

19. These consequences of child sex abuse have been found in similar research, as well. See Cecil and Matson, "Psychological Functioning and Family Discord"; Jacobs, *Victimized Daughters*; Jasinski, Williams, and Siegel, "Childhood Physical and Sexual Abuse as Risk Factors"; Manetta, "Interpersonal Violence and Suicidal Behavior"; C. M. West, Williams, and Siegel, "Adult Sexual Revictimization Among Black Women."

20. Collins, *Black Feminist Thought*; Sudarkasa, *Strength of Our Mothers*.

21. Browne, *When Battered Women Kill*. Mihalic and Elliott determined that for women, witnessing violent behaviors within the family of origin was associated with adult marital dissatisfaction, as well as with abuse and victimization, leading to a greater likelihood of marital violence (see Mihalic and Elliot, "Social Learning Theory Model of Marital Violence"). In analyzing Black women specifically, Lockhart and White found that the Black women who witnessed their fathers' violence toward their mothers had a greater chance of being abused by an intimate partner (see Lockhart and White, "Understanding Marital Violence").

22. Many female victims of intimate partner violence "retaliate" at a time when they have a better chance of succeeding in their retaliation (Allard, "Rethinking Battered Woman Syndrome"), such as when they can catch the batterer off-guard or while he is sleeping.

23. Richie, *Compelled to Crime*, 32.

24. Ibid., 35, 39.

CHAPTER 5

1. "Section 8" is a federal government program that allows lower-income individuals to live in safe and clean private or government-subsidized housing at significantly reduced rates.

2. Collins, *Black Feminist Thought*, 161.

3. See Spurlock and Booth, "Stresses in Parenting," regarding the modeling of traditional White middle-class standards by middle-class African Americans.

4. Belknap, *The Invisible Woman*.

5. L. E. A. Walker, *The Battered Woman Syndrome*.

6. The findings on the shock of the first hit are consistent with other research (e.g., Browne, *When Battered Women Kill*; Richie, *Compelled to Crime*).

7. Belknap and Potter, "Intimate Partner Abuse."

8. Tong, *Women, Sex, and the Law*.

9. Belknap and Potter, "Intimate Partner Abuse."

10. Ibid.

11. Lambert and Firestone, "Economic Context and Multiple Abuse Techniques."

12. See Appendix A for my reasoning in placing military homes in the working class rather than the middle class or another category.

13. See, e.g., Follingstad et al., "The Role of Emotional Abuse in Physically Abusive Relationships"; Jones et al., "Partner Abuse and HIV Infection."

14. Belknap and Potter, "Intimate Partner Abuse."

15. See, e.g., Ferraro, "Battered Women"; Gondolf and Fisher, *Battered Women as Survivors*; Lambert and Firestone, "Economic Context and Multiple Abuse Techniques."

16. Ammons, "Mules, Madonnas, Babies, Bath Water, Racial Imagery, and Stereotypes"; C. M. West and Rose, "Dating Aggression Among Low Income African American Youth."

17. Beale, "Double Jeopardy," 146.

18. Ramos, Carlson, and McNutt, "Lifetime Abuse, Mental Health."

19. Lockhart, "Spousal Violence: A Cross-Racial Perspective."

20. Belknap, *The Invisible Woman*; Follingstad et al., "Justifiability, Sympathy Level, and Internal/External Locus of the Reasons Battered Women Remain in Abusive Relationships"; Nabi and Horner, "Victims With Voices"; Yoshioka, DiNoia, and Ullah, "Attitudes Toward Marital Violence."

21. hooks, *We Real Cool*, 66.

22. Collins, *Black Feminist Thought*.

23. Lawrence-Webb, Littlefield, and Okundaye, "African American Intergender Relationships."

24. C. M. West and Rose, "Dating Aggression Among Low Income African American Youth."

25. Lawrence-Webb, Littlefield, and Okundaye, "African American Intergender Relationships"; Lockhart, "Spousal Violence: A Cross-Racial Perspective"; Sudarkasa, *Strength of Our Mothers*.

26. Collins, *Black Feminist Thought*; Gillum, "Stereotypic Images and Intimate Partner Violence."

27. Asbury, "African-American Women in Violent Relationships"; Gillum, "Stereotypic Images and Intimate Partner Violence"; hooks, *Outlaw Culture* and *Feminist Theory*, 2nd ed.; Lawrence-Webb, Littlefield, and Okundaye, "African American Intergender Relationships."

28. hooks, *Feminist Theory*, 2nd ed.; Raj et al., "Prevalence and Correlates of Relationship Abuse Among a Community-Based Sample"; D. S. Williams, "African-American Women in Three Contexts."

29. Bell and Mattis, "The Importance of Cultural Competence in Ministering to African American Victims of Domestic Violence"; Richie, *Compelled to Crime*.

30. Richie, *Compelled to Crime*.

31. Ibid.

32. Taylor and McGee, *The New Couple*.

33. James, Ticker, and Mitchell-Kernan, "Marital Attitudes, Perceived Mate Availability."

34. Asbury, "African-American Women in Violent Relationships"; Hutchinson, "The Hip Hop Generation of African American Male-Female Relationships in a Nightclub Setting"; Plass, "African American Family Homicide."

35. Raj et al., "Prevalence and Correlates of Relationship Abuse Among a Community-Based Sample," 279.

36. Soler, Vinayak, and Quadagno, "Biosocial Aspects of Domestic Violence"; Straus, Gelles, and Steinmetz, *Behind Closed Doors*.

CHAPTER 6

1. Ferraro, "Battered Women"; Herbert, Silver, and Ellard, "Coping With an Abusive Relationship"; L. E. A. Walker, *The Battered Woman Syndrome*.

2. Abraham, *Speaking the Unspeakable*; Ferraro, "Battered Women"; Gelles and Straus, *Intimate Violence*; Gondolf and Fisher, *Battered Women as Survivors*.

3. Dutton, Goodman, and Bennett, "Battered Women's Responses to Violence." See also Abraham, *Speaking the Unspeakable*; Burke et al., "The Process of Ending Abuse"; J. C. Campbell et al., "Voices of Strength and Resistance"; Ferraro, "Battered Women"; Gelles and Straus, *Intimate Violence*; Gondolf and Fisher, *Battered Women as Survivors*; Richie, *Compelled to Crime*; Weitzman, *"Not to People Like Us"*; T. C. West, *Wounds of the Spirit*.

4. See, e.g., Abraham, *Speaking the Unspeakable*; Bachman and Carmody, "Fighting Fire With Fire"; Bachman et al., "'Disentangling the Effects of Self-Protective Behaviors on the Risk of Injury in Assaults Against Women"; Barnett, Lee, and Thelen, "Gender Differences in Attributions of Self-Defense and Control"; Browne, *When Battered Women Kill*; J. C. Campbell et al., "Voices of Strength and Resistance"; Ferraro, "Battered Women"; S. L. Miller, *Victims as Offenders*; Saunders, "When Battered Women Use Violence"; Swan et al., *Technical Report*.

5. See, e.g., Browne, *When Battered Women Kill*; Mann, *When Women Kill*; Walker, *The Battered Woman Syndrome.*

6. Hampton, Gelles, and Harrop, "Is Violence in Black Families Increasing?"; Joseph, "Woman Battering "; Stets, "Verbal and Physical Aggression in Marriage"; Straus, Gelles, and Steinmetz, *Behind Closed Doors*; C. M. West and Rose, "Dating Aggression Among Low Income African American Youth."

7. Rennison and Welchans, *Intimate Partner Violence*.

8. Mercy and Saltzman, "Fatal Violence Among Spouses."

9. Bureau of Justice Statistics, U.S. Department of Justice, "Homicide Trends in the U.S.: Intimate Homicide," http://www.ojp.usdoj.gov/bjs/homicide/intimates.htm.

10. However, Swan et al.'s National of Institute of Justice funded study incorporated a racially diverse sample to make a substantial inquiry into the effect of cultural and racial differences in battered women's responses to their abuse. The published outcomes of this portion of their study are awaited (see Swan et al., *Technical Report*).

11. Hamberger and Guse, "Men's and Women's Use of Intimate Partner Violence"; Shupe, Stacey, and Hazelwood, *Violent Men, Violent Couples*; Straus, "Victims and Aggressors in Marital Violence"; Swan and Snow, "Behavioral and Psychological Differences."

12. See Martin, "Double Your Trouble "; McMahon and Pence, "Making Social Change"; Melton and Belknap, "He Hits, She Hits."

13. Straus, "Measuring Intrafamily Violence and Conflict."

14. Straus, "Reflections."

15. For an overview of the debate see Dobash and Dobash, "Women's Violence Against an Intimate Male Partner"; Melton and Belknap, "He Hits, She Hits."

16. Belknap, *The Invisible Woman*; Dobash and Dobash, "Women's Violence against an Intimate Male Partner."

17. Dobash and Dobash, "Women's Violence Against an Intimate Male Partner," 343.

18. Straus, "Reflections," 196.

19. Archer, "Sex Differences in Aggression"; Dobash and Dobash, "Women's Violence Against an Intimate Male Partner"; Melton and Belknap, "He Hits, She Hits"; Rennison and Welchans, *Intimate Partner Violence*; Tjaden and Thoennes, *Extent, Nature, and Consequences of Intimate Partner Violence.*

20. Hamberger and Guse, "Men's and Women's Use of Intimate Partner Violence"; Henning and Feder, "A Comparison of Men and Women Arrested for Domestic Violence"; Melton and Belknap, "He Hits, She Hits."

21. Dobash and Dobash, "Women's Violence Against an Intimate Male Partner," 340.

22. Hamberger and Guse, "Men's and Women's Use of Intimate Partner Violence."

23. Henning and Feder, "A Comparison of Men and Women Arrested for Domestic Violence."

24. Abel, "Comparing the Social Service Utilization, Exposure to Violence, and Trauma Symptomology of Domestic Violence Female 'Victims' and Female 'Batterers.'"

25. Ibid.

26. Hamberger and Guse, "Men's and Women's Use of Intimate Partner Violence."

27. Dobash and Dobash, "Women's Violence Against an Intimate Male Partner."

28. Saunders, "When Battered Women Use Violence."

29. Abel, "Comparing the Social Service Utilization, Exposure to Violence, and Trauma Symptomology of Domestic Violence Female 'Victims' and Female 'Batterers'"; Barnett, Lee, and Thelen, "Gender Differences in Attributions of Self-Defense and Control"; Cascardi and Vivian, "Context for Specific Episodes of Marital Violence"; Coulter et al., "Police-Reporting Behavior"; Hamberger and Guse, "Men's and Women's Use of Intimate Partner Violence"; Melton and Belknap, "He Hits, She Hits"; Saunders, "When Battered Women Use Violence"; Swan and Snow, "Behavioral and Psychological Differences."

30. Swan and Snow, "Behavioral and Psychological Differences," 104.

31. Bachman and Carmody, "Fighting Fire With Fire"; Bowker, *Beating Wife Beating*; J. C. Campbell et al., "Voices of Strength and Resistance"; Dobash and

Dobash, "Women's Violence Against an Intimate Male Partner"; Ferraro, "Battered Women."

32. Dasgupta, "A Framework for Understanding Women's Use of Nonlethal Violence."

33. Bachman et al., ""Disentangling the Effects of Self-Protective Behaviors on the Risk of Injury in Assaults Against Women."

34. Dobash and Dobash, "Women's Violence Against an Intimate Male Partner." See also Perilla et al., "Women's Use of Violence."

35. Ferraro and Johnson, "How Women Experiencing Battering," 335.

36. Perilla et al., "A Working Analysis of Women's Use of Violence," 26.

37. T. C. West, *Wounds of the Spirit*, 166.

38. L. E. A. Walker, *The Battered Woman*; L. E. A. Walker, *The Battered Woman Syndrome*.

39. Seligman, *Helplessness*.

40. Allard, "Rethinking Battered Woman Syndrome."

41. Dutton, "Understanding Women's Responses to Domestic Violence."

42. Allard, "Rethinking Battered Woman Syndrome," 193–194.

43. Stark, "Race, Gender, and Woman Battering."

44. Follingstad et al., "Justifiability, Sympathy Level, and Internal/External Locus of Reasons Battered Women Remain in Abusive Relationships."

45. Wolfgang and Ferracuti, *The Subculture of Violence*.

46. Stets, "Verbal and Physical Aggression in Marriage"; Surrat et al., "Sex Work and Drug Use"; Wolfgang and Ferracuti, *The Subculture of Violence*.

47. Surrat et al., "Sex Work and Drug Use."

48. Wolfgang and Ferracuti, *The Subculture of Violence*, 140.

49. Also see descriptions of this theory as it is applied to Blacks in Bruce and Roscigno, "'Race Effects' and Conceptual Ambiguity"; Cao, Adams, and Jensen, "Test of the Black Subculture of Violence Thesis"; Covington, "The Violent Black Male"; Hampton, "Family Violence in the Black Community"; Hawkins, "Black and White Homicide Differentials"; Hawkins, "Devalued Lives and Racial Stereotypes."

50. Wolfgang and Ferracuti, *The Subculture of Violence*, 154.

51. Stets, "Verbal and Physical Aggression in Marriage."

52. See, e.g., Harer and Steffensmeier, "Race and Prison Violence"; Rice and Goldman, "Another Look at the Subculture of Violence Thesis"; Stets, "Verbal and Physical Aggression in Marriage"; Surrat et al., "Sex Work and Drug Use."

53. Mann, *When Women Kill*.

54. Ray and Smith, "Black Women and Homicide."

55. Gentry, *Six Models of Rape*.

56. See Cao, Adams, and Jensen, "Test of the Black Subculture of Violence Thesis"; Erlanger, "Empirical Status of the Subculture of Violence Thesis"; Shoemaker and Williams, "The Subculture of Violence and Ethnicity."

57. Hawkins, "Black and White Homicide Differentials."

58. Kposowa, Breault, and Harrison, "Reassessing the Structural Structural Covariates of Violent Crimes," 99.

59. Staples, "Race and Family Violence."

60. C. M. West and Rose, "Dating Aggression Among Low Income African American Youth," 488.

61. Collins, *Black Feminist Thought*, 159.

62. Richie, *Compelled to Crime*.

63. Rogers et al., "Substance Abuse and Domestic Violence."

64. According to an analysis of the National Crime Victimization Survey, of the offenders who victimized women (age 12 and older) between 1993 and 2004, 36.4 percent were described as friends/acquaintances, 22 percent as intimates, and 7.7 percent as some other relative. Strangers accounted for 33.9 percent of the violence against women and girls age 12 and older (Catalano, *Intimate Partner Violence in the United States*).

65. "Edith Bunker was a character in the popular 1970s television series, *All in the Family*, married to the main character, Archie, a bigot and a sexist. She is described as a devoted and dutiful wife [who] may in fact be a bit of a 'dingbat,' as Archie calls her, but she is also the glue that holds the Bunker home together. . . . [H]e is opinionated and short-tempered, she is patient and unbiased. She is completely devoted to her husband, and sees him as a good man. She is warm in her heart, and knows how to keep her hubby happy, even though she doesn't always quite have a grasp on what is happening around her" (www.TVLand.com, 2004).

66. "Fent" is a term that means "getting ready" or "preparing." A colloquial term similar to "fent to" is "fixing to."

67. One of the definitions of "lady" in the Merriam-Webster dictionary is "a woman of refinement and gentle manners." The dictionary provides a secondary definition of the term "ladylike" as "lacking in strength, force, or virility."

CHAPTER 7

1. Ferraro and Johnson, "How Women Experiencing Battering."

2. Short et al., "Survivors' Identification of Protective Factors."

3. Belknap, *The Invisible Woman*.

4. hooks, *Feminist Theory*, 2nd ed., 125–126.

5. J. Brown, "Working Toward Freedom From Violence"; Burke et al., "The Process of Ending Abuse"; Wuest and Merritt-Gray, "Not Going Back."

6. J. C. Campbell, "If I Can't Have You, No One Can"; Ellis, "Post-Separation Woman Abuse"; Ferraro, "Battered Women"; Mahoney, "Legal Images of Battered Women"; Pagelow, "Sex Roles, Power, and Woman Battering"; M. Wilson and Daly, "Spousal Homicide Risk and Estrangement."

7. Ferraro, "Battered Women."

8. Collins, *Black Feminist Thought.*

9. Conversely, a select few women had their abusers leave them, without prompting by the women.

10. Asbury, "African-American Women in Violent Relationships"; Belknap, *The Invisible Woman*; Browne, Salomon, and Bassuk, "Women's Capacity to Maintain Work."

11. England, Garcia-Beaulieu, and Ross, "Women's Employment."

12. J. Miller, "An Arresting Experiment."

13. Asbury, "African-American Women in Violent Relationships"; Plass, "African American Family Homicide."

14. Belknap, *The Invisible Woman.*

15. Stephens, "Battered Women's Views of Their Children."

16. Cazenave and Straus, "A Search for Potent Support Systems"; Collins, *Black Feminist Thought*; hooks, *Feminist Theory*, 2nd ed.; Sudarkasa, *Strength of Our Mothers.*

17. Asbury, "African-American Women in Violent Relationships"; Black and Weisz, "Dating Violence"; Fraser et al., "Social Support Choices"; Lockhart and White, "Understanding Marital Violence"; Short et al., "Survivors' Identification of Protective Factors."

18. Cazenave and Straus, "A Search for Potent Support Systems."

19. Black and Weisz, "Dating Violence."

20. Weis, "Race, Gender, and Critique."

21. Follingstad et al., "Justifiability, Sympathy Level, and Internal/External Locus of Reasons Battered Women Remain in Abusive Relationships"; Richie, *Compelled to Crime*. See also Asbury, "African-American Women in Violent Relationships"; M. N. Wilson, Cobb, and Dolan, "Raising the Awareness of Wife Battering in Rural Black Areas."

22. Mahlstedt and Keeny, "Female Survivors of Dating Violence."

23. Yoshioka et al., "Social Support and Disclosure of Abuse."

24. Mahlstedt and Keeny, "Female Survivors of Dating Violence."

25. Brashears and Roberts, "The Black Church as a Resource for Change"; Brice-Baker, "Domestic Violence in African-American and African-Caribbean Families"; Cole and Guy-Sheftall, *Gender Talk*; DuBois, *The Souls of Black Folk*; Ellison, "Religious Involvement Among African Americans"; Eugene, "Black Women and the Black Church"; hooks, *Rock My Soul*; Jackson, *Life in Black America*; Oliver, "Preventing Domestic Violence in the African American Community."

26. hooks, *Rock My Soul*; Taylor and Chatters, "Religious Life of Black Americans."

27. Short et al., "Survivors' Identification of Protective Factors."

28. hooks, *Rock My Soul*, 109.

29. Rennison and Welchans, *Intimate Partner Violence.*

30. Giesbrecht and Sevcik, "The Process of Recovery"; Horne and Levitt, "Religious Needs of Victims of Intimate Partner Violence"; Horton, Wilkins, and

Wright, "Women Who Ended Abuse"; Kaufman, *Sins of Omission*; Pagelow, "Sex Roles, Power, and Woman Battering."

31. Olivia viewed Catholic churches as those with mainly White congregations; therefore, they are "White churches."

32. Alkhateeb, "Ending Domestic Violence in Muslim Families."

33. Shahida stressed that no "foul play" was involved with her husband's removal from the home.

34. Richie, *Compelled to Crime*.

35. Crenshaw, "Mapping the Margins"; Short et al., "Survivors' Identification of Protective Factors."

36. Asbury, "African-American Women in Violent Relationships"; Sullivan and Rumptz, "Adjustment and Needs of African-American Women."

37. Ammons, "Mules, Madonnas, Babies, Bath Water, Racial Imagery, and Stereotypes African-American Woman and Battered Woman Syndrome"; Bell and Mattis, "The Importance of Cultural Competence in Ministering to African American Victims of Domestic Violence"; Oliver, "Preventing Domestic Violence in the African American Community"; Sharma, "Healing the Wounds of Domestic Violence"; O. J. Williams and Tubbs, *Community Insights on Domestic Violence Among African Americans*.

38. Rodriguez et al., "Screening and Intervention for Intimate Partner Abuse."

39. Short et al., "Survivors' Identification of Protective Factors."

40. T. C. West, *Wounds of the Spirit*, 176.

41. Bennett, Goodman, and Dutton, "Systemic Obstacles to the Criminal Prosecution of a Battering Partner"; Richie, *Compelled to Crime*; Weis, "Race, Gender, and Critique."

42. Brice-Baker, "Domestic Violence in African-American and African-Caribbean Families"; Fishman, "The Black Bogeyman and White Self-Righteousness."

43. Ammons, "Mules, Madonnas, Babies, Bath Water, Racial Imagery, and Stereotypes African-American Woman and Battered Woman Syndrome"; A. L. Robinson and Chandek, "Police Response to Black Battered Women."

44. Ammons, "Mules, Madonnas, Babies, Bath Water, Racial Imagery, and Stereotypes African-American Woman and Battered Woman Syndrome"; Kupenda, "Law, Life, and Literature"; T.C. West, *Wounds of the Spirit*.

45. Brice-Baker, "Domestic Violence in African-American and African-Caribbean Families"; Richie, *Compelled to Crime*; Sorenson, "Violence Against Women."

46. Brice-Baker, "Domestic Violence in African-American and African-Caribbean Families"; Fishman, "The Black Bogeyman and White Self-Righteousness"; Richie, *Compelled to Crime*; Sorenson, "Violence Against Women."

47. Busch and Rosenberg, "Women and Men Arrested for Domestic Violence."

48. Barnett, Lee, and Thelen, "Gender Differences in Attributions of Self-Defense and Control"; Cascardi and Vivian, "Gender and Severity of Violence Differences"; Coulter et al., "Police-Reporting Behavior"; Hamberger and Guse,

"Men's and Women's Use of Intimate Partner Violence"; Melton and Belknap, "He Hits, She Hits"; Saunders, "When Battered Women Use Violence"; Swan and Snow, "Behavioral and Psychological Differences."

49. Bourg and Stock, "Are Pro-Arrest Policies Enough?"

50. See, e.g., Jones and Belknap, "Police Responses to Battering"; Malloy et al., "Women's Use of Violence"; Martin, "Double Your Trouble"; McMahon and Pence, "Making Social Change "; S. L. Miller, *Victims as Offenders.*

51. Richie, *Compelled to Crime.*

52. S. L. Miller, *Victims as Offenders.*

53. Eigenberg et al., "Protective Order Legislation."

54. Fischer and Rose, "When 'Enough Is Enough.'"

55. Moe Wan, "Battered Women in the Restraining Order Process."

56. Bui, "Domestic Violence."

57. Weisz, "Prosecution of Batterers," 30.

CHAPTER 8

1. Smitherman, *Talkin and Testifyin*, 206.

2. Ibid., 112.

3. Ibid., 106.

4. Consider, for instance, the "call-and-response" tradition among the cult following of the film *The Rocky Horror Picture Show* during theater screenings of the film.

5. Sale, "Call and Response as Critical Method," 42.

6. Alkebulan, "Spiritual Essence of African American Rhetoric."

7. Reinharz, *Feminist Methods in Social Research.* See also Cook and Fonow, "Knowledge and Women's Interests."

8. For instance, San Francisco has a lengthy and successful history of engaging community members in addressing intimate partner abuse (Clark et al., *Coordinated Community Responses to Domestic Violence*). See also Loving, "Providing the Battered Victim With Choice."

9. See http://www.dvinstitute.org/.

10. See http://www.bcdvi.org/. See also Cole and Guy-Sheftall, *Gender Talk.*

11. As quoted in Cole and Guy-Sheftall, *Gender Talk*, 68.

12. Collins, *Black Feminist Thought.*

APPENDIX A

1. Harding, *The Science Question in Feminism*; Harding, *Feminism and Methodology*; Reinharz, *Feminist Methods in Social Research.*

2. Harding, *Feminism and Methodology.*

3. Keller, *Reflections on Gender and Science.*

4. Cancian, "Feminist Science."

5. Denzin, "The Art and Politics of Interpretation."

6. Keller, *Reflections on Gender and Science.*

7. Harding, *Feminism and Methodology.*

8. Reinharz, *Feminist Methods in Social Research*, 249.

9. R. A. Wallace, *Feminism and Social Theory.*

10. Reinharz, *Feminist Methods in Social Research.*

11. Collins, *Black Feminist Thought*, 266.

12. U.S. Census Bureau, 2002, available at http://www.census.gov.

13. See Lofland et al., *Analyzing Social Settings*, for a discussion on "starting where you are" regarding the choice to study individuals who are part of the investigator's current biography or remote biography and personal history.

14. Babbie, *The Practice of Social Research.*

15. Crenshaw, "Mapping the Margins"; Lee, "Asian Battered Women"; Roberts and Roberts, "A Comprehensive Model for Crisis Intervention with Battered Women."

16. Available at www.urbanspectrum.net. Information retrieved April 2003.

17. There is the possibility that others called the number listed on the solicitation but did not leave a message if they were not able to reach me directly. The 93 known inquiries do not include the two students who learned of the research project from the bulletin board flyer or one woman who called in mid-January 2004.

18. This study was unfunded, so all compensation (as well as advertisement and transcription fees) came from my personal funds.

19. The majority of the women (39) lived in the Denver metro area, which includes the city of Denver and the immediately surrounding cities and counties. Only one respondent lived outside the Denver metro area; she resided in Colorado Springs, a midsize city approximately 60 miles south of Denver.

20. Marable, *How Capitalism Underdeveloped Black America*; Oliver and Shapiro, *Black Wealth/White Wealth.*

21. DeNavas-Walt, Cleveland, and Webster, *Income in the United States: 2002.*

22. Ibid.

23. Oliver and Shapiro, *Black Wealth/White Wealth*, 2.

24. R. L. Harris, "The Rise of the Black Middle Class."

25. None of the women were enlisted in the military during the abusive relationships or at the time of the interviews.

26. Commissioned military officers typically hold college degrees and have higher salaries than enlisted personnel.

27. Taylor and Chatters, "Religious Life of Black Americans."

28. Wyche, "African American Muslim Women."

29. See Spurlock and Booth, "Stresses in Parenting."

30. Previous research, although limited, has addressed women battered by intimate female partners (see, e.g., Bernhard, "Physical and Sexual Violence Experienced by Lesbian and Heterosexual Women"; Giorgio, "Speaking Silence"; Renzetti and Miley, *Violence in Gay and Lesbian Domestic Partnerships*). The implications for Black women who identify as both lesbian and battered clearly require future research (A. Robinson, "There's a Stranger in This House").

31. Colorado is one of the few states with a common law marriage statute. For the parties to be considered married under common law, they must agree they are married, reside together, and present themselves as wife and husband. These marriages can be dissolved only through legal divorce or death. Nine of the women were married through the more typical means, by obtaining a marriage license and participating in a ceremony. Of the three women living with what others might consider a "boyfriend," two of these women asserted that they were "common-law."

32. Babbie, *The Practice of Social Research*.

33. Richie, *Compelled to Crime*, 24.

34. Collins, *Black Feminist Thought*; Reinharz, *Feminist Methods in Social Research*.

35. Babbie, *The Practice of Social Research*.

36. Stewart, *The Ethnographer's Method*, 15–16.

37. Babbie, *The Practice of Social Research*, 132.

38. Stewart, *The Ethnographer's Method*, 15.

39. Babbie, *The Practice of Social Research*.

40. Emerson, *Contemporary Field Research*.

41. Stewart, *The Ethnographer's Method*, 16.

42. Collins, *Black Feminist Thought*, 255.

43. Koss et al., *No Safe Haven*.

44. Emerson, *Contemporary Field Research*, 31.

Bibliography

Abel, Eileen Mazur. "Comparing the Social Service Utilization, Exposure to Violence, and Trauma Symptomology of Domestic Violence Female 'Victims' and Female 'Batterers.'" *Journal of Family Violence* 16 (2001): 401–420.

Abraham, Margaret. *Speaking the Unspeakable: Marital Violence Among South Asian Immigrants in the United States.* New Brunswick, NJ: Rutgers University Press, 2000.

Alkebulan, Adisa A. "The Spiritual Essence of African American Rhetoric." In *Understanding African American Rhetoric: Classical Origins to Contemporary Innovations,* ed. Ronald L. Jackson II and Elaine B. Richardson, 23–40. New York: Routledge, 2003.

Alkhateeb, Sharifa. "Ending Domestic Violence in Muslim Families." *Journal of Religion and Abuse* 1, 4 (1999): 49–59.

All in the Family: Edith Bunker. Retrieved September 9, 2004, from http://www. tvland.com/shows/aitf/character2.jhtml.

Allard, Sharon A. "Rethinking Battered Woman Syndrome: A Black Feminist Perspective." *UCLA Women's Law Journal* 1 (1991): 191–207.

Ammons, Linda L. "Mules, Madonnas, Babies, Bath Water, Racial Imagery, and Stereotypes: The African-American Woman and the Battered Woman Syndrome." *Wisconsin Law Review* 5 (1995): 1003–1080.

Archer, John. "Sex Differences in Aggression Between Heterosexual Partners: A Meta-Analytic Review." *Psychological Bulletin* 126 (2000): 651–680.

Asbury, Jo-Ellen. "African-American Women in Violent Relationships: An Exploration of Cultural Differences." In *Violence in the Black Family: Correlates and Consequences,* ed. Robert L. Hampton, 89–105. Lexington, MA: Lexington, 1987.

Babbie, Earl. *The Practice of Social Research.* 9th ed. Belmont, CA: Wadsworth, 2001.

Baca Zinn, Maxine. "Field Research in Minority Communities: Ethical, Methodological and Political Observations by an Insider." *Social Problems* 27 (1979): 209–219.

Bachman, Ronet, and Dianne C. Carmody. "Fighting Fire With Fire: The Effects of Victim Resistance in Intimate versus Stranger Perpetrated Assaults Against Females." *Journal of Family Violence* 9 (1994): 317–331.

Bachman, Ronet, Linda E. Saltzman, Martie P. Thompson, and Dianne C. Carmody. "Disentangling the Effects of Self-Protective Behaviors on the Risk of Injury in Assaults against Women." *Journal of Quantitative Criminology* 18 (2002): 135–157.

Bandura, Albert. *Social Learning Theory.* Englewood Cliffs, NJ: Prentice Hall, 1977.

Barnett, Ola W., Cheok Y. Lee, and Rose E. Thelen. "Gender Differences in Attributions of Self-Defense and Control in Interpartner Aggression." *Violence Against Women* 3 (1997): 462–481.

Baumgardner, Jennifer, and Amy Richards. *Manifesta: Young Women, Feminism, and the Future.* New York: Farrar, Straus, and Giroux, 2000.

Beale, Frances. "Double Jeopardy: To Be Black and Female." In *Words of Fire: An Anthology of African-American Feminist Thought,* ed. Beverly Guy-Sheftall, 146–155. New York: New Press, 1995(1970).

Belknap, Joanne. *The Invisible Woman: Gender, Crime, and Justice.* 3r ed. Belmont, CA: Wadsworth, 2007.

Belknap, Joanne, and Hillary Potter. "Intimate Partner Abuse." In *Rethinking Gender, Crime, and Justice: Feminist Readings,* ed. Claire M. Renzetti, Lynne Goodstein, and Susan L. Miller, 168–184. Los Angeles: Roxbury, 2006.

Bell, Carl C., and Jacqueline Mattis. "The Importance of Cultural Competence in Ministering to African American Victims of Domestic Violence." *Violence Against Women* 6 (2000): 515–532.

Bennett, Lauren, Lisa Goodman, and Mary Ann Dutton. "Systemic Obstacles to the Criminal Prosecution of a Battering Partner." *Journal of Interpersonal Violence* 14 (1999): 761–772.

Benson, Michael L., Greer L. Fox, Alfred DeMaris, and Judy Van Wyk. "Neighborhood Disadvantage, Individual Economic Distress and Violence Against Women in Intimate Relationships." *Journal of Quantitative Criminology* 19 (2003): 207–235.

Bernhard, Linda A. "Physical and Sexual Violence Experienced by Lesbian and Heterosexual Women." *Violence Against Women* 6 (2000): 68–79.

Black, Beverly M., and Arlene N. Weisz. "Dating Violence: Help-Seeking Behaviors of African American Middle Schoolers." *Violence Against Women* 9 (2003): 187–206.

Bograd, Michele. "Strengthening Domestic Violence Theories: Intersections of Race, Class, Sexual Orientation, and Gender." *Journal of Marital and Family Therapy* 25 (1999): 275–289.

Bourg, Sherrie, and Harley V. Stock. "A Review of Domestic Violence Arrest Statistics in a Police Department Using a Pro-Arrest Policy: Are Pro-Arrest Policies Enough?" *Journal of Family Violence* 9 (1994): 177–189.

Bowker, Lee H. *Beating Wife Beating.* Lexington, MA: Lexington, 1983.

Brashears, Freda, and Margaret Roberts. "The Black Church as a Resource for Change." In *The Black Family: Strengths, Self-Help, and Positive Change,* ed. Sadye L. Logan, 181–192. Boulder, CO: Westview Press, 1996.

Brewster, Mary P. "Domestic Violence Theories, Research, and Practice Implications." In *Handbook of Domestic Violence Intervention Strategies: Policies, Programs, and Legal Remedies,* ed. Albert R. Roberts, 23–48. New York: Oxford University Press, 2002.

Brice-Baker, Janet R. "Domestic Violence in African-American and African-Caribbean Families." *Journal of Social Distress and Homeless* 3 (1994): 23–38.

Britton, Dana M. "Feminism in Criminology: Engendering the Outlaw." *The Annals of the American Academy of Political and Social Science* 571, 1 (2000): 57–76.

Brown, Elsa Barkley. "Womanist Consciousness: Maggie Lena Walker and the Independent Order of Saint Luke." *Signs: Journal of Women in Culture and Society* 14 (1989): 610–633.

Brown, Jody. "Working Toward Freedom From Violence: The Process of Change in Battered Women." *Violence Against Women* 3 (1997): 5–26.

Brown, Kendrick T., Geoffrey K. Ward, Tiffany Lightbourn, and James S. Jackson. "Skin Tone and Racial Identity Among African Americans: A Theoretical and Research Framework." In *Advances in African American Psychology: Theory, Paradigms, and Research,* ed. Reginald L. Jones, 191–214. Hampton, VA: Cobb and Henry, 1998.

Browne, Angela. *When Battered Women Kill.* New York: Free Press, 1987.

Browne, Angela, Amy Salomon, and Shari S. Bassuk. "The Impact of Recent Partner Violence on Poor Women's Capacity to Maintain Work." *Violence Against Women* 5 (1999): 393–426.

Bruce, Marino A., and Vincent J. Roscigno. "'Race Effects' and Conceptual Ambiguity in Violence Research: Bringing Inequality Back In." In *Violent Crime: Assessing Race and Ethnic Differences,* ed. Darnell F. Hawkins, 238–253. New York: Cambridge University Press, 2003.

Bui, Hoan N. "Domestic Violence Victims' Behavior in Favor of Prosecution: Effects of Gender Relations." *Women and Criminal Justice* 12, 4 (2001): 51–75.

Burke, Jessica G., Andrea Carlson Gielen, Karen A. McDonnell, Patricia O'Campo, and Suzanne Maman. "The Process of Ending Abuse in Intimate Relationships: A Qualitative Exploration of the Transtheoretical Model." *Violence Against Women* 7 (2001): 1144–1163.

Busch, Amy L., and Mindy S. Rosenberg. "Comparing Women and Men Arrested for Domestic Violence: A Preliminary Report." *Journal of Family Violence* 19 (2004): 49–57.

Campbell, Jacquelyn C. "If I Can't Have You, No One Can: Power and Control in Homicide of Female Partners." In *Femicide: The Politics of Woman Killing,* ed. J. Radford and D. E. H. Russell, 99–113. New York: Twayne, 1992.

Campbell, Jacquelyn C., Linda Rose, Joan Kub, and Daphne Nedd. "Voices of Strength and Resistance: A Contextual and Longitudinal Analysis of Women's Responses to Battering." *Journal of Interpersonal Violence* 13 (1998): 743–762.

Cancian, Francesca M. "Feminist Science: Methodologies That Challenge Inequality." *Gender and Society* 6 (1992): 623–642.

Cao, Liqun, Anthony Adams, and Vickie J. Jensen. "A Test of the Black Subculture of Violence Thesis: A Research Note." *Criminology* 35 (1997): 367–379.

Cascardi, Michele, and Dina Vivian. "Context for Specific Episodes of Marital Violence: Gender and Severity of Violence Differences." *Journal of Family Violence* 10 (1995): 265–293.

Catalano, Shannan. *Intimate Partner Violence in the United States.* Washington, DC: Bureau of Justice Statistics, U.S. Department of Justice, 2006.

Cazenave, Noel A., and Murray A. Straus. "Race, Class, Network Embeddedness, and Family Violence: A Search for Potent Support Systems." *Journal of Comparative Family Studies* 10 (1979): 281–299.

Cecil, Heather, and Steven C. Matson. "Psychological Functioning and Family Discord Among African-American Adolescent Families With and Without a History of Childhood Sexual Abuse." *Child Abuse and Neglect* 25 (2001): 973–988.

Center for the Advancement of Women. *Progress and Perils: New Agenda for Women,* 2003. Retrieved March 21, 2004; available at http://www.advance-women.org/womens_research/progressandperils.pdf.

Chesney-Lind, Meda. "Doing Feminist Criminology." *The Criminologist* (1988, July–August): 1, 3, 16–17.

Chesney-Lind, Meda. "Patriarchy, Crime, and Justice: Feminist Criminology in an Era of Backlash." *Feminist Criminology* 1 (2006): 6–26.

Chesney-Lind, Meda, and Lisa Pasko. *The Female Offender: Girls, Women, and Crime.* 2nd ed. Thousand Oaks, CA: Sage, 2004.

Clark, Sandra J., Martha R. Burt, Margaret M. Schulte, and Karen E. Maguire. *Coordinated Community Responses to Domestic Violence in Six Communities: Beyond the Justice System.* Washington, DC: Urban Institute, 1996.

Cleaver, Kathleen Neal. "Racism, Civil Rights, and Feminism." *Critical Race Feminism: A Reader,* ed. Adrien K. Wing, 35–43. 2nd ed. New York: New York University Press, 1997.

Coker, Donna. "Enhancing Autonomy for Battered Women: Lessons from Navajo Peacemaking." In *Critical Race Feminism: A Reader,* ed. Adrien K. Wing, 287–297. 2nd ed. New York: New York University Press, 2003.

Cole, Johnnetta B., and Beverly Guy-Sheftall. *Gender Talk: The Struggle for Women's Equality in African American Communities.* New York: Ballantine, 2003.

Collins, Patricia Hill. *Black Feminist Thought: Knowledge, Consciousness, and the Politics of Empowerment.* 2nd ed. New York: Routledge, 2000.

Cook, Judith A., and Mary Margaret Fonow. "Knowledge and Women's Interests: Issues of Epistemology and Methodology in Feminist Sociological Research." *Sociological Inquiry* 56 (1986): 2–29.

Coulter, Martha L., Kathryn Kuehnle, Robert Byers, and Moya Alfonso. "Police-Reporting Behavior and Victim-Police Interactions as Described By Women in a Domestic Violence Shelter." *Journal of Interpersonal Violence* 14 (1999): 1290–1298.

Covington, Jeannette. "The Violent Black Male: Conceptions of Race in Criminological Theories." In *Violent Crime: Assessing Race and Ethnic Differences*, ed. Darnell F. Hawkins, 254–279. New York: Cambridge University Press, 2003.

Crenshaw, Kimberlé W. "Mapping the Margins: Intersectionality, Identity Politics, and Violence against Women of Color." In *The Public Nature of Private Violence: The Discovery of Domestic Abuse,* ed. Martha A. Fineman and Roxanne Mykitiuk, 93–118. New York: Routledge, 1994.

Crowell, Nancy A., and Ann Wolbert Burgess. *Understanding Violence Against Women.* Washington, DC: National Academy Press, 1996.

Daly, Kathleen. "Different Ways of Conceptualizing Sex/Gender in Feminist Theory and Their Implications for Criminology." *Theoretical Criminology* 1 (1997): 25–51.

Daly, Kathleen, and Meda Chesney-Lind. "Feminism and Criminology." *Justice Quarterly* 5 (1988): 497–538.

Davis, Angela Y. *Women, Race and Class.* New York: Vintage Books, 1983.

Dasgupta, Shamita Das. "A Framework for Understanding Women's Use of Nonlethal Violence in Intimate Heterosexual Relationships." *Violence Against Women* 8 (2002): 1364–1389.

Denavas-Walt, Carmen, Robert W. Cleveland, and Bruce H. Webster, Jr. *Income in the United States: 2002.* Washington, DC: U.S. Government Printing Office, 2003.

Denzin, Norman K. "The Art and Politics of Interpretation." In *Handbook of Qualitative Research,* ed. Norman K. Denzin and Yvonna S. Lincoln, 500–515. Thousand Oaks, CA: Sage, 1994.

Dietz, Tracy L. "Disciplining Children: Characteristics Associated With the Use of Corporal Punishment." *Child Abuse and Neglect* 24 (2000): 1529–1542.

Dobash, Russell P., and R. Emerson Dobash. "Women's Violence Against an Intimate Male Partner: Working on a Puzzle." *British Journal of Criminology* 44 (2004): 324–349.

DuBois, W. E. B. *The Souls of Black Folk.* New York: New American Library, 1903.

Dunn, Jennifer L. "'Victims' and 'Survivors': Emerging Vocabularies of Motive for 'Battered Women Who Stay.'" *Sociological Inquiry* 75 (2005): 1–30.

Dutton, Mary Ann. "Understanding Women's Responses to Domestic Violence: A Redefinition of Battered Woman Syndrome." *Hofstra Law Review* 21 (1993): 1191–1242.

Dutton, Mary Ann, Lisa A. Goodman, and Lauren Bennett. "Court-Involved Battered Women's Responses to Violence: The Role of Psychological, Physical, and Sexual Abuse." *Violence and Victims* 14 (1999): 89–104.

Eigenberg, Helen, Karen McGuffee, Phyllis Berry, and William H. Hall. "Protective Order Legislation: Trends in State Statutes." *Journal of Criminal Justice* 31 (2003): 411–422.

Ellis, Desmond. "Post-Separation Woman Abuse." *International Journal of Sociology and the Family* 19 (1987): 67–87.

Ellison, Christopher G. "Religious Involvement and the Subjective Quality of Family Life among African Americans." In *Family Life in Black America,* ed. Robert J. Taylor, James S. Jackson, and Linda M. Chatters, 117–131. Thousand Oaks, CA: Sage, 1997.

Emerson, Robert M., ed. *Contemporary Field Research: Perspectives and Formulations.* 2nd ed. Prospect Heights, IL: Waveland, 2001.

England, Paula, Carmen Garcia-Beaulieu, and Mary Ross. "Women's Employment Among Blacks, Whites, and Three Groups of Latinas: Do More Privileged Women Have Higher Employment?" *Gender and Society* 18 (2004): 494–509.

Erez, Edna, and Joanne Belknap. "In Their Own Words: Battered Women's Assessment of the Criminal Processing System's Responses." *Violence and Victims* 13 (1998): 251–268.

Erlanger, Howard S. "The Empirical Status of the Subculture of Violence Thesis." *Social Problems* 22 (1974): 280–291.

Eugene, Toinette M. "There Is a Balm in Gilead: Black Women and the Black Church as Agents of a Therapeutic Community." *Women and Therapy* 16 2/3 (1995): 55–71.

Ferraro, Kathleen J. "Battered Women: Strategies for Survival." In *Violence Between Intimate Partners: Patterns, Causes, and Effects,* ed. Albert P. Carderelli, 124–140. New York: Allyn and Bacon, 1997.

Ferraro, Kathleen J., and John M. Johnson. "How Women Experience Battering: The Process of Victimization." *Social Problems* 30 (1983): 325–339.

Fischer, Karla, and Mary Rose. "When 'Enough Is Enough': Battered Women's Decision Making Around Court Orders of Protection." *Crime and Delinquency* 41 (1995): 414–429.

Fishman, Laura T. "The Black Bogeyman and White Self-Righteousness." In *Images of Color, Images of Crime: Readings,* ed. Coramae Richey Mann and Marjorie S. Zatz, 177–191. 2nd ed. Los Angeles: Roxbury, 2002.

Fishman, Laura T. "'Mule-Headed Slave Women Refusing to Take Foolishness from Anybody': A Prelude to Future Accommodation, Resistance, and Criminality." In *It's a Crime: Woman and Justice,* ed. Roslyn Muraskin, 30–49. 3rd ed. Upper Saddle River, NJ: Prentice Hall, 2003.

Flavin, Jeanne. "Razing the Wall: A Feminist Critique of Sentencing Theory, Research, and Policy." In *Cutting the Edge: Current Perspectives in Radical/*

Critical Criminology and Criminal Justice, ed. Jeffrey Ian Ross, 145–164. West-port, CT: Praeger, 1998.

Flavin, Jeanne. "Feminism for the Mainstream Criminologist: An Invitation." *Journal of Criminal Justice* 29 (2001): 271–285.

Follingstad, Diane R., Larry L. Rutledge, Barbara J. Berg, Elizabeth S. Hause, and Darlene S. Polek. "The Role of Emotional Abuse in Physically Abusive Relationships." *Journal of Family Violence* 5 (1990): 107–120.

Follingstad, Diane R., Margaret M. Runge, April Ace, Robert Buzan, and Cindy Helff. "Justifiability, Sympathy Level, and Internal/External Locus of the Reasons Battered Women Remain in Abusive Relationships." *Violence and Victims* 16 (2001): 621–644.

Foshee, Vangie A., Karl E. Bauman, and G. Fletcher Linder. "Family Violence and the Perpetration of Adolescent Dating Violence: Examining Social Learning and Social Control Processes." *Journal of Marriage and Family* 61 (1999): 331–342.

Fraser, Idelle M., Louise-Anne McNutt, Carla Clark, Deborah Williams-Muhammed, and Robin Lee. "Social Support Choices for Help with Abusive Relationships: Perceptions of African American Women." *Journal of Family Violence* 17 (2002): 363–375.

Freeman, Howard E., David Armor, J. Michael Ross, and Thomas F. Pettigrew. "Color Gradation and Attitudes Among Middle-Income Negroes." *American Sociological Review* 31 (1966): 365–374.

Fyfe, James J., David A. Klinger, and Jeanne Flavin. "Differential Police Treatment of Male-on-Female Spousal Violence." *Criminology* 35 (1997): 455–473.

Gandy, Debrena Jackson. *Sacred Pampering Principles: An African-American Woman's Guide to Self-Care and Inner Renewal.* New York: Quill, 1997.

Garfield, Gail. *Knowing What We Know: African American Women's Experience With Violence and Violation.* Piscataway, NJ: Rutgers University Press, 2005.

Gelles, Richard J., and Murray A. Straus. *Intimate Violence.* New York: Simon and Schuster, 1988.

Gentry, Cynthia S. *Six Models of Rape: An Empirical Analysis.* Unpublished doctoral dissertation, 1989.

Giesbrecht, Norman, and Irene Sevcik. "The Process of Recovery and Rebuilding Among Abused Women in the Conservative Evangelical Subculture." *Journal of Family Violence,* 15, (2000): 229–248.

Gillum, Tameka L. "Exploring the Link Between Stereotypic Images and Intimate Partner Violence in the African American Community." *Violence Against Women* 8 (2002): 64–86.

Giorgio, Grace. "Speaking Silence: Definitional Dialogues in Abusive Lesbian Relationships." *Violence Against Women* 8 (2002): 1233–1259.

Gondolf, Edward W., and Ellen R. Fisher. *Battered Women as Survivors: An Alternative to Treating Learned Helplessness.* Boston: Lexington, 1988.

Gordon, Vivian V. *Black Women, Feminism and Black Liberation: Which Way?* Chicago: Third World Press, 1987.

Guy-Sheftall, Beverly, ed. *Words of Fire: An Anthology of African-American Feminist Thought.* New York: New Press, 1995.

Hall, Ronald E. "Bias Among African Americans Regarding Skin Color: Implications for Social Work Practice." *Research on Social Work Practice* 2 (1992): 479–486.

Hamberger, L. Kevin, and Clare E. Guse. "Men's and Women's Use of Intimate Partner Violence in Clinical Samples." *Violence Against Women* 8 (2002): 1301–1331.

Hampton, Robert L. "Family Violence and Homicides in the Black Community: Are They Linked?" In *Violence in the Black Family: Correlates and Consequences,* ed. Robert L. Hampton, 135–156. Lexington, MA: Lexington, 1987.

Hampton, Robert L., and Richard J. Gelles. "Violence Toward Black women in a Nationally Representative Sample of Black Families." *Journal of Comparative Family Studies* 25 (1994): 105–119.

Hampton, Robert L., Richard J. Gelles, and John W. Harrop. "Is Violence in Black Families Increasing? A Comparison of 1975 and 1985 National Survey Rates." *Journal of Marriage and Family* 51 (1989): 969–980.

Harding, Sandra. *The Science Question in Feminism.* Ithaca, NY: Cornell University Press, 1986.

Harding, Sandra. *Feminism and Methodology.* Bloomington: Indiana University Press, 1987.

Harer, Miles D., and Darrell J. Steffensmeier. "Race and Prison Violence." *Criminology* 34 (1996): 323–355.

Harris, Angela P. "Race and Essentialism in Feminist Legal Theory." *Stanford Law Review* 42 (1990): 581–686.

Harris, Robert L., Jr. "The Rise of the Black Middle Class." *The World and I Magazine* 14, 2 (1999): 40.

Harris, Trudier. *Saints, Sinners, Saviors: Strong Black Women in African American Literature.* New York: Palgrave, 2001.

Hawkins, Darnell F. "Black and White Homicide Differentials: Alternative to an Inadequate Theory." *Criminal Justice and Behavior* 10 (1983): 407–440.

Hawkins, Darnell F. "Devalued Lives and Racial Stereotypes: Ideological Barriers to the Prevention of Family Violence Among Blacks." In *Violence in the Black Family: Correlates and Consequences,* ed. Robert L. Hampton, 189–205. Lexington, MA: Lexington, 1987.

Henning, Kris, and Lynnette Feder. "A Comparison of Men and Women Arrested for Domestic Violence: Who Presents the Greater Threat?" *Journal of Family Violence* 19 (2004): 69–80.

Herbert, Tracy Bennett, Roxane Cohen Silver, and John H. Ellard. "Coping With an Abusive Relationship: How and Why Do Women Stay?" *Journal of Marriage and Family* 53 (1991): 311–325.

Hernandez, Jeanne T., Marc Lodico, and Ralph J. DiClemente. "The Effects of Child Abuse and Race on Risk-Taking in Male Adolescents." *Journal of the National Medical Association* 85 (1993): 593–597.

Hill, Mark E. "Skin Color and the Perception of Attractiveness Among African Americans: Does Gender Make a Difference?" *Social Psychology Quarterly* 65 (2002): 77–91.

Hoff, Lee Ann. *Battered Women as Survivors*. New York: Routledge, 1990.

hooks, bell. *Ain't I a Woman: Black Women and Feminism*. Boston: South End, 1981a.

hooks, bell. *Feminist Theory: From Margin to Center*. Cambridge, MA: South End, 1981b.

hooks, bell. *Talking Back: Thinking Feminist, Thinking Black*. Boston, MA: South End, 1989.

hooks, bell. *Outlaw Culture: Resisting Representations*. New York: Routledge, 1994.

hooks, bell. *Feminist Theory: From Margin to Center*. 2nd ed. Cambridge, MA: South End, 2000a.

hooks, bell. *Where We Stand: Class Matters*. New York: Routledge, 2000b.

hooks, bell. *Salvation: Black People and Love*. New York: Harper Collins, 2001.

hooks, bell. *Rock My Soul: Black People and Self-Esteem*. New York: Atria, 2003.

hooks, bell. *The Will to Change: Men, Masculinity, and Love*. New York: Atria, 2004a.

hooks, bell. *We Real Cool: Black Men and Masculinity*. New York: Routledge, 2004b.

Horne, Sharon G., and Heidi M. Levitt. "Shelter From the Raging Wind: Religious Needs of Victims of Intimate Partner Violence and Faith Leaders' Responses." *Journal of Religion and Abuse* 5, 2 (2003): 83–97.

Horton, Anne L., Meland M. Wilkins, and Wendy Wright. "Women Who Ended Abuse: What Religious Leaders and Religion Did for These Victims." In *Abuse and Religion: When Praying Isn't Enough*, ed. Anne L. Horton and Judith A. Williamson, 235–246. Lexington, MA: Lexington, 1988.

Huang, Chien Ju, and Tiffany Gunn. "An Examination of Domestic Violence in an African American Community in North Carolina: Causes and Consequences." *Journal of Black Studies* 31 (2001): 790–811.

Hughes, Michael, and Bradley R. Hertel. "Skin Tone and Stratification in the Black Community." *American Journal of Sociology* 97 (1991): 760–778.

Hull, Gloria T., Patricia Bell Scott, and Barbara Smith, eds. *All the Women Are White, All the Blacks Are Men, but Some of Us Are Brave: Black Women's Studies*. New York: Feminist Press, 1982.

Hunter, Margaret L., Walter R. Allen, and Edward E. Telles. "The Significance of Skin Color Among African Americans and Mexican Americans." *African American Research Perspectives* 7 (2001): 173–184.

Hutchinson, Janis Faye. "The Hip Hop Generation of African American Male-Female Relationships in a Nightclub Setting." *Journal of Black Studies* 30 (1999): 62–84.

Incite! Women of Color Against Violence. *Color of Violence: The INCITE! Anthology.* Cambridge, MA: Southend Press, 2006.

Jackson, James S., ed. *Life in Black America.* Newbury Park, CA: Sage, 1991.

Jacobs, Janet L. *Victimized Daughters: Incest and the Development of the Female Self.* New York: Routledge, 1994.

James, Angela D., M. Belinda Ticker, and Claudia Mitchell-Kernan. "Marital Attitudes, Perceived Mate Availability, and Subjective Well-Being Among Partnered African American Men and Women." *Journal of Black Psychology* 22 (1996): 20–36.

Jasinski, Jana L., Linda M. Williams, and Jane Siegel. "Childhood Physical and Sexual Abuse as Risk Factors for Heavy Drinking Among African-American Women: A Prospective Study." *Child Abuse and Neglect* 24 (2000): 1061–1071.

Johnson, Ida M., and Robert T. Sigler. "Public Perceptions: The Stability of the Public's Endorsements of the Definition and Criminalization of the Abuse of Women." *Journal of Criminal Justice* 28 (2000): 65–179.

Jones, Dana A., and Joanne Belknap. "Police Responses to Battering in a Progressive Pro-Arrest Jurisdiction." *Justice Quarterly* 16 (1999): 249–273.

Jones, Charisse, and Kumea Shorter-Gooden. *Shifting: The Double Lives of Black Women in America.* New York: HarperCollins, 2003.

Jones, Deborah J., Steven R. H. Beach, Rex Forehand, and Family Health Project Research Group. "Partner Abuse and HIV Infection: Implications for Psychosocial Adjustment in African American Women." *Journal of Family Violence* 18 (2003): 257–268.

Joseph, Janice. "Woman Battering: A Comparative Analysis of Black and White Women." In *Out of Darkness: Contemporary Perspectives on Family Violence,* ed. Glenda Kaufman Kantor and Jana L. Jasinski, 161–169. Thousand Oaks, CA: Sage, 1997.

Kaufman, Carol Goodman. *Sins of Omission: The Jewish Community's Reaction to Domestic Violence.* Boulder, CO: Westview Press, 2003.

Keith, Verna M., and Cedric Herring. "Skin Tone and Stratification in the Black Community." *American Journal of Sociology* 97 (1991): 760–768.

Keller, Evelyn Fox. *Reflections on Gender and Science.* New Haven, CT: Yale University Press, 1985.

King, Deborah K. "Multiple Jeopardy, Multiple Consciousness: The Context of Black Feminist Ideology." *Signs: Journal of Women in Culture and Society* 14 (1988): 42–72.

Kleck, Gary, and Marc Gertz. "Armed Resistance to Crime: The Prevalence and Nature of Self-Defense With a Gun." *Journal of Criminal Law and Criminology* 6 (1995): 150–187.

Koss, Mary P., Lisa A. Goodman, Angela Browne, Louise F. Fitzgerald, Gwendolyn Puryear Keita, and Nancy Felipe Russo. *No Safe Haven: Male Violence Against Women at Home, at Work, and in the Community.* Washington, DC: American Psychological Association, 1994.

Kposowa, Augustine J., Kevin D. Breault, and Beatrice M. Harrison. "Reassessing the Structural Covariates of Violent and Property Crimes in the USA: A County Level Analysis." *British Journal of Sociology* 46 (1995): 79–105.

Kupenda, Angela Mae. "Law, Life, and Literature: A Critical Reflection of Life and Literature to Illuminate How Laws of Domestic Violence, Race, and Class Bind Black Women." *Howard Law Journal* 42 (1998): 1–26.

Lambert, Linda C., and Juanita M. Firestone. "Economic Context and Multiple Abuse Techniques." *Violence Against Women* 6 (2000): 49–67.

Lawrence-Webb, Claudia, Melissa Littlefield, M., and Joshua N. Okundaye. "African American Intergender Relationships: A Theoretical Exploration of Roles, Patriarchy, and Love." *Journal of Black Studies* 34 (2004): 623–639.

Lee, Mo Yee. "Asian Battered Women: Assessment and Treatment." In *Handbook of Domestic Violence Intervention Strategies: Policies, Programs, and Legal Remedies*, ed. Albert R. Roberts, 472–482. New York: Oxford University Press, 2002.

Lewis, Diane K. "A Response to Inequality: Black Women, Racism, and Sexism." *Signs: Journal of Women in Culture and Society* 3 (1977): 339–361.

Lockhart, Lettie L. "Spousal Violence: A Cross-Racial Perspective." In *Black Family Violence: Current Research and Theory*, ed. Robert L. Hampton, 85–101. Lexington, MA: Lexington, 1991.

Lockhart, Lettie L., and Barbara W. White. "Understanding Marital Violence in the Black Community." *Journal of Interpersonal Violence* 49 (1989): 421–436.

Lofland, John, David A. Snow, Leon Anderson, and Lyn H. Lofland. *Analyzing Social Settings: A Guide to Qualitative Observation and Analysis.* 4th ed. Belmont, CA: Wadsworth, 2006.

Loving, Russell. "Providing the Battered Victim With the Choice Between Having the Batterer Arrested and Using Restorative Justice Intervention: One Size Does Not Fit All." Paper presented at the Western Society of Criminology Annual Conference, February 12,2007.

MacKinnon, Catharine A. "Keeping It Real: On Anti-'Essentialism.'" In *Crossroads, Directions, and a New Critical Race Theory*, ed. Francisco Valdes, Jerome McCristal Culp, and Angela P. Harris, 71–83. Philadelphia: Temple University Press, 2002.

Mahlstedt, Deborah, and Linda Keeny. "Female Survivors of Dating Violence and Their Social Networks." *Feminism and Psychology* 3 (1993): 319–333.

Mahoney, Martha R. "Legal Images of Battered Women: Redefining the Issue of Separation." *Michigan Law Review* 90 (1991): 2–94.

Malley-Morrison, Kathleen, and Denise A. Hines. *Family Violence in a Cultural Perspective: Defining, Understanding, and Combating Abuse.* Thousand Oaks, CA: Sage, 2004.

Malloy, Kathleen A., Kathy A. McCloskey, Nancy Grigsby, and Donna Gardner. "Women's Use of Violence Within Intimate Relationships." *Journal of Aggression, Maltreatment, and Trauma* 6, 2 (2003): 37–59.

Manetta, Ameda A. "Interpersonal Violence and Suicidal Behavior in Midlife African American Women." *Journal of Black Studies* 29 (1999): 510–522.

Mann, Coramae Richey. *When Women Kill*. Albany: State University of New York Press, 1996.

Marable, Manning. *How Capitalism Underdeveloped Black America: Problems in Race, Political Economy, and Society*. Updated ed. Cambridge, MA: South End, 2000.

Martin, Margaret E. "Double Your Trouble: Dual Arrest in Family Violence." *Journal of Family Violence* 12 (1997): 139–157.

Mataka, Laini. *Being a Strong Black Woman Can Get U Killed*. Baltimore: Black Classic Press, 2001.

Mauthner, Natasha S., and Andrea Doucet. "Reflexive Accounts and Accounts of Reflexivity in Qualitative Data Analysis." *Sociology* 37 (2001):413–431.

McKay, Nellie Y. "Acknowledging Differences: Can Women Find Unity Through Diversity?" In *Theorizing Black Feminisms: The Visionary Pragmatism of Black Women,* ed. Stanlie M. James and Abena P. A. Busia, 267–282. New York: Routledge, 1993.

McMahon, Martha, and Ellen Pence. "Making Social Change: Reflections on Individual and Institutional Advocacy With Women Arrested for Domestic Violence." *Violence Against Women* 9 (2003): 47–74.

Melton, Heather C., and Joanne Belknap. "He Hits, She Hits: Assessing Gender Differences and Similarities in Officially Reported Intimate Partner Violence." *Criminal Justice and Behavior* 30 (2003): 328–348.

Mercy, James A., and Linda E. Saltzman. "Fatal Violence Among Spouses in the United States, 1976–85." *American Journal of Public Health* 79 (1989): 595–599.

Mihalic, Sharon Wofford, and Delbert Elliott. "A Social Learning Theory Model of Marital Violence." *Journal of Family Violence* 12 (1997): 21–46.

Miller, JoAnn. "An Arresting Experiment: Domestic Violence Victim Experiences and Perceptions." *Journal of Interpersonal Violence* 18 (2003): 695–716.

Miller, Susan L. *Victims as Offenders: The Paradox of Women's Violence in Relationships*. New Brunswick, NJ: Rutgers University Press, 2005.

Moe Wan, Angela. "Battered Women in the Restraining Order Process: Observations on a Court Advocacy Program." *Violence Against Women* 6 (2000): 606–632.

Morgan, Joan. *When Chickenheads Come Home to Roost: My Life as a Hip Hop Feminist*. New York: Simon and Schuster, 1999.

Morrison, Toni. *The Bluest Eye*. New York: Holt, Rinehart, and Winston, 1970.

Morrison, Toni. *Song of Solomon*. New York: Knopf, 1977.

Nabi, Robin L., and Jennifer R. Horner. "Victims With Voices: How Abused Women Conceptualize the Problem of Spousal Abuse and Implications for Intervention and Prevention." *Journal of Family Violence* 16 (2001): 237–253.

Neal-Barnett, Angela M. *Soothe Your Nerves: The Black Woman's Guide to Understanding and Overcoming Anxiety, Panic, and Fear*. New York: Simon and Schuster, 2003.

Oliver, Melvin L., and Thomas M. Shapiro. *Black Wealth/White Wealth: A New Perspective on Racial Inequality.* New York: Routledge, 1995.

Oliver, William. "Preventing Domestic Violence in the African American Community: The Rational for Popular Culture Interventions." *Violence Against Women* 6 (2000): 533–549.

O'Neill, Damian. "A Post-Structuralist Review of the Theoretical Literature Surrounding Wife Abuse." *Violence Against Women* 4 (1998): 457–490.

Pagelow, Mildred D. "Sex Roles, Power, and Woman Battering." In *Women and Crime in America,* ed. Lee H. Bowker, 277–300. New York: Macmillan, 1981.

Perilla, Julia L., Kim Frndak, Debbie Lillard, and Cynthia East. "A Working Analysis of Women's Use of Violence in the Context of Learning, Opportunity, and Choice." *Violence Against Women* 9 (2003): 10–46.

Pettiway, Leon E. *Workin' It: Women Living Through Drugs and Crime.* Philadelphia: Temple University Press, 1997.

Plass, Peggy S. "African American Family Homicide: Patterns in Partner, Parent, and Child Victimization, 1985–1987." *Journal of Black Studies* 23 (1993): 515–538.

Ponce, Allison N., Michelle K. Williams, George J. Allen. "Experience of Maltreatment as a Child and Acceptance of Violence in Adult Intimate Relationships: Mediating Effects of Distortions in Cognitive Schemas." *Violence and Victims* 19 (2004): 97–108.

Potter, Hillary. "An Argument for Black Feminist Criminology: Understanding African American Women's Experiences With Intimate Partner Abuse Using an Integrated Approach." *Feminist Criminology* 1 (1996): 106–124.

Raj, Anita, Jay G. Silverman, Gina M. Wingood, and Ralph J. Diclemente. "Prevalence and Correlates of Relationship Abuse Among a Community-Based Sample of Low-Income African American Women." *Violence Against Women* 5 (1999): 272–291.

Ramos, Blanca M., Bonnie E. Carlson, and Louise-Anne McNutt. "Lifetime Abuse, Mental Health, and African American Women." *Journal of Family Violence* 19 (2004): 153–164.

Rankin, Larry B., Daniel G. Saunders, and Reg A. Williams. "Mediators of Attachment Style, Social Support, and Sense of Belonging in Predicting Woman Abuse by African American Men." *Journal of Interpersonal Violence* 15 (2000): 1060–1080.

Ray, Melvin C., and Earl Smith. "Black Women and Homicide: An Analysis of the Subculture of Violence Thesis." *Western Journal of Black Studies* 15 (1991): 144–153.

Reinharz, Shulamit. *Feminist Methods in Social Research.* New York: Oxford University Press, 1992.

Rennison, Callie Marie, and Michael R. Rand. *Criminal Victimization, 2002.* Washington, DC: Bureau of Justice Statistics, U.S. Department of Justice, 2003.

Rennison, Callie Marie, and Sarah Welchans. *Intimate Partner Violence*. Washington, DC: Bureau of Justice Statistics, Office of Justice Programs, U.S. Department of Justice, 2000.

Renzetti, Claire M., and Charles Harvey Miley, eds. *Violence in Gay and Lesbian Domestic Partnerships*. New York: Harrington Park, 1996.

Rice, Tom W., and Carolyn R. Goldman. "Another Look at the Subculture of Violence Thesis: Who Murders Whom and Under What Circumstances?" *Sociological Spectrum* 14 (1994): 371–384.

Richie, Beth E. *Compelled to Crime: The Gender Entrapment of Battered Black Women*. New York: Routledge, 1996.

Richie, Beth E. "A Black Feminist Reflection on the Antiviolence Movement." *Signs: Journal of Women in Culture and Society* 25 (2000): 1133–1137.

Richie, Beth E. "Gender Entrapment and African-American Women: An Analysis of Race, Ethnicity, Gender, and Intimate Violence." In *Violent Crime: Assessing Race and Ethnic Differences,* ed. Darnell F. Hawkins, 198–210. New York: Cambridge University Press, 2003.

Rivera, Jenny. "Domestic Violence Against Latinas by Latino Males: An Analysis of Race, National Origin, and Gender Differentials." In *Critical Race Feminism: A Reader,* ed. Adrien K. Wing, 259–266. New York: New York University Press, 1997.

Rivera, Jenny. "Availability of Domestic Violence Services for Latina Survivors in New York State: Preliminary Report." In *Critical Race Feminism: A Reader,* ed. Adrien K. Wing, 270–277. 2nd ed. New York: New York University Press, 2003.

Roberts, Albert R., and Beverly Schenkman Roberts. "A Comprehensive Model for Crisis Intervention With Battered Women and Their Children." In *Handbook of Domestic Violence Intervention Strategies: Policies, Programs, and Legal Remedies,* ed. Albert R. Roberts, 365–395. New York: Oxford University Press, 2002.

Robinson, Amorie. "There's a Stranger in This House: African American Lesbians and Domestic Violence." In *Violence in the Lives of Black Women: Battered, Black, and Blue,* ed. Carolyn M. West, 125–136. Binghamton, NY: Haworth, 2003.

Robinson, Amanda L., and Meghan S. Chandek. "Differential Police Response to Black Battered Women." *Women and Criminal Justice* 12, 2/3 (2000): 29–61.

Rodriguez, Michael A., Heidi M. Bauer, Elizabeth McLoughlin, and Kevin Grumbach. "Screening and Intervention for Intimate Partner Abuse: Practices and Attitudes of Primary Care Physicians." *Journal of the American Medical Association* 28 (1999): 468–474.

Rogers, Barbara, Gloria McGee, Antonia Vann, Naceema Thompson, and Oliver J. Williams. "Substance Abuse and Domestic Violence: Stories of Practitioners That Address the Co-Occurrence Among Battered Women." *Violence Against Women* 9 (2003): 590–598.

Russell, Kathy, Midge Wilson, and Ronald Hall. *The Color Complex: The Politics of Skin Color Among African Americans.* New York: Anchor/Doubleday, 1992.

Sale, Maggie. "Call and Response as Critical Method: African-American Oral Traditions and *Beloved.*" *African American Review,* 26 (1992): 41–50.

Sanchez-Hucles, Janis, and Mary Ann Dutton. "The Interaction Between Societal Violence and Domestic Violence: Racial and Cultural Factors." In *What Causes Men's Violence against Women?,* ed. Michele Harway and James M. O'Neil, 183–203. Thousand Oaks, CA: Sage, 1999.

Saunders, Daniel G. "When Battered Women Use Violence: Husband-Abuse or Self-Defense?" *Violence and Victims* 1 (1986): 47–58.

Schafer, John, Raul Caetano, and Carol B. Cunradi. "A Path Model of Risk Factors for Intimate Partner Violence Among Couples in the United States." *Journal of Interpersonal Violence* 19 (2004): 127–142.

Schechter, Susan. *Women and Male Violence: The Visions and Struggles of the Battered Women's Movement.* Boston: South End Press, 1982.

Seligman, Martin E.P. *Helplessness: On Depression, Development, and Death.* San Francisco: W. H. Freeman, 1975.

Sharma, Anita. "Healing the Wounds of Domestic Violence: Improving the Effectiveness of Feminist Therapeutic Interventions With Immigrant and Racially Visible Women Who Have Been Abused." *Violence Against Women* 7 (2001): 1405–1428.

Shoemaker, Donald J., and J. Sherwood Williams. "The Subculture of Violence and Ethnicity." *Journal of Criminal Justice* 15 (1987): 461–472.

Short, Lynn M., Pamela M. McMahon, Doryn Davis Chervin, Gene A. Shelley, Nicole Lezin, N., Kira Sue Sloop, and Nicola Dawkins. "Survivors' Identification of Protective Factors and Early Warning Signs for Intimate Partner Violence." *Violence Against Women* 6 (2000): 272–285.

Shupe, Anson, William A. Stacey, and Lonnie R. Hazelwood. *Violent Men, Violent Couples.* Lexington, MA: Lexington, 1978.

Smith, Andrea, Beth E. Richie, Julia Sudbury, and Janelle White (with the assistance of Incite! Women of Color Against Violence collective members). "The Color of Violence: Introduction." In *Color of Violence: The Incite! Anthology,* ed. Incite! Women of Color Against Violence, 1–10. Cambridge, MA: South End Press, 2006.

Smith, Barbara, ed. *Home Girls: A Black Feminist Anthology.* New York: Kitchen Table: Women of Color Press, 1983.

Smith, Marcia. "When Violence Strikes Home." *The Nation* 264, 25 (1997): 23–24.

Smitherman, Geneva. *Talkin and Testifyin: The Language of Black America.* Detroit: Wayne State University Press, 1986.

Soler, Hosanna, Preeti Vinayak, and David Quadagno. "Biosocial Aspects of Domestic Violence." *Psychoneuroendocrinology* 25 (2000): 721–739.

Sorenson, Susan B. "Violence Against Women: Examining Ethnic Differences and Commonalities." *Evaluation Review* 20 (1996): 123–145.

Spearly, James L., and Michael Lauderdale. "Community Characteristics and Ethnicity in the Prediction of Child Maltreatment Rates." *Child Abuse and Neglect* 7 (1983): 91–105.

Spurlock, Jeanne, and Martin B. Booth. "Stresses in Parenting." In *Black Families in Crisis: The Middle Class,* ed. Alice F. Coner-Edwards and Jeanne Spurlock, 79–89. New York: Brunner/Mazel, 1988.

Staples, Robert. "Race and Family Violence: The Internal Colonialism Perspective." In *Crime and Its Impact on the Black Community,* ed. Lawrence E. Gary and Lee P. Brown, 85–96. Washington, DC: Institute for Urban Development Center, Howard University, 1976.

Stark, Evan. "Race, Gender, and Woman Battering." In *Violent Crime: Assessing Race and Ethnic Differences,* ed. Darnell F. Hawkins, 171–197. New York: Cambridge University Press, 2003.

Stark, Evan, and Anne Filtcraft. *Women at Risk: Domestic Violence and Women's Health.* Thousand Oaks, CA: Sage, 1996.

Stephens, Debra Lynn. "Battered Women's Views of Their Children." *Journal of Interpersonal Violence* 14 (1999): 731–746.

Stets, Jan E. "Verbal and Physical Aggression in Marriage." *Journal of Marriage and Family* 52 (1990): 501–514.

Stewart, Alex. *The Ethnographer's Method.* Thousand Oaks, CA: Sage, 1998.

Straus, Murray A. "Measuring Intrafamily Violence and Conflict: The Conflict Tactics Scales." *Journal of Marriage and Family* 41 (1979): 75–88.

Straus, Murray A. "Victims and Aggressors in Marital Violence." *American Behavioral Scientist* 23 (1980): 681–704.

Straus, Murray A. "Reflections on 'Measuring Intrafamily Violence and Conflict.'" In *Violence Against Women: Classic Papers,* eds. Raquel L. Kennedy Bergen, Jeffrey L. Edelson, and Claire M. Renzetti, 195–197. Boston: Allyn and Bacon, 2005.

Straus, Murray A., Richard J. Gelles, and Suzanne K. Steinmetz. *Behind Closed Doors: Violence in the American Family.* Garden City, NY: Doubleday, 1980.

Sudarkasa, Niara. *The Strength of Our Mothers: African and African American Women and Families: Essays and Speeches.* Trenton, NJ: Africa World Press, 1996.

Sullivan, Cris M., and Maureen H. Rumptz. "Adjustment and Needs of African-American Women Who Utilized a Domestic Violence Shelter." *Violence and Victims* 9 (1994): 275–286.

Surratt, Hilary L., James A. Inciardi, Steven P. Kurtz, and Marion C. Kiley. "Sex Work and Drug Use in a Subculture of Violence." *Crime and Delinquency* 50 (2004): 43–59.

Swan, Suzanne C., and David L. Snow. "Behavioral and Psychological Differences Among Abused Women Who Use Violence in Intimate Relationships." *Violence Against Women* 9 (2003): 75–109.

Swan, Suzanne C., David L. Snow, Tami P. Sullivan, Laura Gambone, and Alice Fields. *Technical Report for "An Empirical Examination of a Theory of Women's Use of Violence in Intimate Relationships."* Washington, DC: National Institute of Justice, U.S. Department of Justice, 2005.

Taylor, Maurice, and Seana McGee. *The New Couple: Why the Old Rules Don't Work and What Does.* San Francisco: Harper, 2000.

Taylor, Robert J., and Linda M. Chatters. "Religious Life of Black Americans." In *Life in Black America*, ed. James S. Jackson, 105–123. Newbury Park, CA: Sage, 1991.

Terrelonge, Pauline. "Feminist Consciousness and Black Women." In *Women: A Feminist Perspective*, ed. Jo Freeman, 557–567. 3rd ed. Palo Alto, CA: Mayfield, 1984.

Tierney, Kathleen J. "The Battered Women Movement and the Creation of the Wife Beating Problem." *Social Problems* 29 (1982): 207–220.

Tjaden, Patricia, and Nancy Thoennes. *Extent, Nature, and Consequences of Intimate Partner Violence.* Washington, DC: U.S. Department of Justice, 2000.

Tong, Rosemarie. *Women, Sex, and the Law.* Totowa, NJ: Rowman and Allanheld, 1984.

Troester, Rosalie Riegle. "Turbulence and Tenderness: Mothers, Daughters, and 'Othermothers' in Paule Marshall's *Brown Girl, Brownstones.*" *Sage: A Scholarly Journal on Black Women* 1, 2 (1984): 13–16.

U.S. Department of Health and Human Services. *10 Years of Reporting Child Maltreatment.* Washington, DC: Administration for Children and Families, Administration on Children, Youth, and Families Children Bureau, 1999.

Valencia-Weber, Gloria, and Christine P. Zuni. "Domestic Violence and Tribal Protection of Indigenous Women in the United States." In *Critical Race Feminism: A Reader*, ed. Adrien K. Wing, 278–286. 2nd ed. New York: New York University Press, 2003.

Walker, Alice. *The Color Purple.* New York: Harcourt Brace Jovanovich, 1982.

Walker, Lenore E. A. *The Battered Woman.* New York: Harper and Row, 1979.

Walker, Lenore E. A. *The Battered Woman Syndrome.* 2nd ed. New York: Springer, 2000.

Wallace, Michele. *Black Macho and the Myth of the Superwoman.* New York: Dial Press, 1979.

Wallace, Ruth A., ed. *Feminism and Social Theory.* Newbury Park, CA: Sage, 1989.

Washington, Patricia A. "Disclosure Patterns of Black Female Sexual Assault Survivors." *Violence Against Women* 7 (2001): 1254–1283.

Weis, Lois. "Race, Gender, and Critique: African-American Women, White Women, and Domestic Violence in the 1980s and 1990s." *Signs: Journal of Women in Culture and Society* 27 (2001): 139–169.

Weisz, Arlene N. "Prosecution of Batterers: Views of African American Battered Women." *Violence and Victims* 17 (2002): 19–34.

Weitzman, Susan. *"Not to People Like Us": Hidden Abuse in Upscale Marriages.* New York: Basic, 2000.

West, Carolyn M., ed. *Violence in the Lives of Black Women: Battered, Black, and Blue.* Binghamton, NY: Haworth Press, 2003.

West, Carolyn M., and Suzanna Rose. "Dating Aggression Among Low Income African American Youth: An Examination of Gender Differences and Antagonistic Beliefs." *Violence Against Women* 6 (2000): 470–494.

West, Carolyn M., Linda M. Williams, and Jane A. Siegel. "Adult Sexual Revictimization Among Black Women Sexually Abused in Childhood: A Prospective Examination of Serious Consequences of Abuse." *Child Maltreatment* 5 (2000): 49–57.

West, Traci C. *Wounds of the Spirit: Black Women, Violence, and Resistance Ethics.* New York: New York University Press, 1999.

Whitfield, Charles L., Robert F. Anda, Shanta R. Dube, and Vincent J. Felitti. "Violent Childhood Experiences and the Risk of Intimate Partner Violence in Adults: Assessment in a Large Health Maintenance Organization." *Journal of Interpersonal Violence* 18 (2003): 166–185.

Williams, Delores S. "African-American Women in Three Contexts of Domestic Violence." In *Violence Against Women,* ed. Elisabeth Schussler Fiorenza and Mary Shawn Copeland, 34–43. Maryknoll, NY: Orbis, 1994.

Williams, Oliver J., and Carolyn Y. Tubbs. *Community Insights on Domestic Violence Among African Americans: Conversations About Domestic Violence and Other Issues Affecting Their Community.* St. Paul, MN: Institute on Domestic Violence in the African American Community, 2002.

Wilson, Melvin N., Debra D. Cobb, and Regina T. Dolan. "Raising the Awareness of Wife Battering in Rural Black Areas of Central Virginia: A Community Outreach Approach." In *Violence in the Black Family: Correlates and Consequences,* ed. Robert L. Hampton, 121–131. Lexington, MA: Lexington, 1987.

Wilson, Margo, and Martin Daly. "Spousal Homicide Risk and Estrangement." *Violence and Victims* 8 (1993): 3–15.

Wing, Adrien K., ed. *Critical Race Feminism: A Reader.* New York: New York University Press, 1997.

Wing, Adrien K., ed. *Critical Race Feminism: A Reader.* 2nd ed. New York: New York University Press, 2003.

Wolfgang, Marvin E., and Franco Ferracuti. *The Subculture of Violence: Towards an Integrated Theory in Criminology.* London: Tavistock, 1967.

Wuest, Judith, and Marilyn Merritt-Gray. "Not Going Back: Sustaining the Separation in the Process of Leaving Abusive Relationships." *Violence Against Women* 5 (1999): 110–133.

Wyatt, Gail E., Julie C. Axelrod, Dorothy Chin, Jennifer Vargas Carmona, and Tamra Burns Loeb. "Examining Patterns of Vulnerability to Domestic Violence Among African American Women." *Violence Against Women* 6 (2000): 495–514.

Wyche, Karen Fraser. "African American Muslim Women: An Invisible Group." *Sex Roles* 51 (2004): 319–328.

Yoshioka, Marianne R., Jennifer Dinoia, and Komal Ullah. "Attitudes Toward Marital Violence: An Examination of Four Asian Communities." *Violence Against Women* 7 (2001): 900–926.

Yoshioka, Marianne R., Louisa Gilbert, Nabila El-Bassel, and Malahat Baig-Amin. "Social Support and Disclosure of Abuse: Comparing South Asian, African American, and Hispanic Battered Women." *Journal of Family Violence* 18 (2003): 171–180.

Index

About the Author

HILLARY POTTER is Assistant Professor of Sociology at the University of Colorado at Boulder.